D0982658

INDIANA-
PURDUE
LIBRARY

FORT WAYNE

Patronage in British Government

By the same author

DELEGATION IN LOCAL GOVERNMENT
HONOURABLE MEMBERS

PATRONAGE
in British Government

BY
PETER G. RICHARDS

Senior Lecturer in Politics
University of Southampton

UNIVERSITY OF TORONTO PRESS

FIRST PUBLISHED IN 1963

Published in Canada by University of Toronto Press.

This book is copyright under the Berne Convention.
Apart from any fair dealing for the purposes of private
study, research, criticism or review, as permitted under
the Copyright Act, 1956, no portion may be reproduced
by any process without written permission. Inquiries
should be addressed to the publisher.

© George Allen & Unwin Ltd, 1963

JN 428
R 5

INDIANA-
PURDUE
LIBRARY

FORT WAYNE

WITHDRAWN

PRINTED IN GREAT BRITAIN
in 11 on 12 point Janson type
BY SIMSON SHAND LTD
LONDON, HERTFORD AND HARLOW

PREFACE

This book provides a critical survey of patronage exercised by Ministers of the Crown in Great Britain. The collection of material on this subject has presented substantial difficulties. There are three categories of information about British government—that which is published, that which is confidential and that which falls into the no-man's-land between. Much information about patronage, especially in relation to individual cases, is necessarily confidential. But a great deal comes within the intermediate group and I am most grateful to the civil servants and Members of Parliament who have talked with me and answered my letters on many aspects of the subject. It is heartening that busy men, deeply immersed in public affairs, are able to find time to deal with academic inquiries.

Acknowledgment is due to Messrs Stevens for permission to reproduce material about the selection of Justices of the Peace which appeared originally in *Public Law*, Summer, 1961. The material in the Appendix, the lists of offices which disqualify their holders from the House of Commons, is reproduced from the House of Commons Disqualification Act, 1957, with the permission of the Director of Publications of Her Majesty's Stationery Office.

I have also had much assistance from colleagues at the University of Southampton. Professor A. H. Phillips provided valuable comment on the section dealing with judicial appointments and Professor W. I. Lucas did the same for the chapter on the Church. Mr. I. D. Shelley, M.Sc.(Econ.), formerly a research student at Southampton, collected some of the historical material on Honours. Mrs P. E. Dunn and her assistants in the office of the Economics Department have helped with the typing. Miss D. Marshallsay, B.A., A.L.A., Librarian of the Ford Collection of Parliamentary Papers, has checked many references and is responsible for the index.

The greatest aid has come from my wife: as before she has combined the tasks of critic and secretary with constant devotion.

PETER G. RICHARDS
University of Southampton
October 1962

CONTENTS

CONTENTS

CHAPTER ONE

Introduction:
Selection for Public Office

◉

The choice of individuals to hold positions of authority in society is a central interest of students of politics. In recent years many detailed studies have appeared which illustrate the working of electoral systems. Yet the seats of power are filled not only by elections. In this country the great majority of important posts are filled by a simple process of appointment. This book is born of a conviction that there is inadequate realization of the extent and the consequences of patronage powers held by Ministers of the Crown.

There are four basic methods of choosing people to occupy positions of public responsibility—chance, heredity, competition and patronage. The category of competition is capable of almost infinite sub-division, but the major distinction is between a contest to assess popularity, i.e. some form of election, and a contest to assess ability, normally conducted through interview or an academic type of examination. The suitability of these four techniques, even if the case for democratic government be assumed, must depend on the type of post to be filled. Our legislators, judges and civil servants perform distinct tasks, their terms of employment vary and different desiderata govern their selection. In consequence, no common method can be used in the systems of appointment.

Chance, the first of the techniques noted above, is little used in modern times. It can be democratic, as Aristotle argued, if it gives all men an equal opportunity of office. But it is essentially an irrational method unless each candidate for a post is thought to be equally suitable, or suitability is not regarded as a major criterion to govern choice. These conditions, of course, are rarely fulfilled. The drawing of lots now occurs only in the unique case where a popularity contest results in a tie with two candidates having an equal number of votes.

Heredity offers notable advantages as a system of selection. It provides continuity and certainty—so long as the principle is accepted. Hereditary office-holders also acquire exceptional experience of their duties. But the shortcomings of this arrangement are obvious. It is essentially undemocratic since no account is taken of popular will. Where an hereditary ruler or functionary suffers no restraint of public accountability, there can be no guarantee that duties will be performed conscientiously or that powers will not be used arbitrarily or even tyrannically. Finally, the high qualities which suit a man for an important office are not necessarily possessed by successive generations of his family, or by the senior member of each generation. Thus hereditary systems have little part to play in a democratic state or, indeed, in modern autocracies based on one-party government. The British Constitution still retains an hereditary element with its Monarchy and House of Lords. But the hereditary office-holders survive on the conditions that their powers are limited and—in the case of the Crown—are used in a non-controversial manner. Even so, with a regal family, it may become necessary to pass over a natural successor who is either unwilling or unsuitable to carry out monarchical functions.

Some type of popular election is used in democratic states to choose members of the legislature in order to ensure that the legal rules which govern the community are broadly in accord with public feeling. Elections are held at intervals so that legislators can be kept in touch with movements of opinion. It is inevitable that most individuals in a mass electorate have no knowledge of the personal qualities of candidates, but everyone can be informed of the views of candidates. Thus voting tends to take place on the basis of a choice of opinions—or a party basis. The personal suitability of potential candidates is judged by the influential members of political organizations which sponsor contestants at the polls. As personal shortcomings may damage the chance of success at an election, political groups normally aim to choose standard-bearers of reasonable quality; but where a constituency is effectively dominated by one party the capability of its candidate is irrelevant to the prospect of electoral victory. Members of a representative legislature, therefore, will have not only widely differing opinions and interests but will also be of varying calibre. Not all will be suited for the tasks of high office. A great merit of a Cabinet system of government is that it enables the elected legislators to choose national leaders from among themselves. Parliament serves as a training-ground and testing-ground for future ministers, and its members will have close personal knowledge of those chosen to be party leaders. It is arguable that a system of direct election to the highest positions of authority in the state increases the possibility of mistaken and dangerous choices being made because the voters or candidate-selectors may not have such an intimate understanding of the personal characteristics of those they support. Further, a leader personally elected may feel a sense of personal power deriving from the popular mandate and, therefore, be less willing to listen to words of advice and caution from subordinates.

Elections can, of course, be used to distort public opinion and to produce a spurious cachet of popular agreement for the actions of an authoritarian government. In a one-party state officially approved candidates only will be allowed to stand for office. Alternatively, if the authoritarian rulers are a little less ruthless or efficient, opposition parties may exist on sufferance but the electoral system is manipulated to ensure their defeat. Even where the forms of democracy are more fully respected its operation may be affected by patronage and corruption—as in eighteenth-century Britain. Restrictions on the franchise have an important effect, and did on our elections until the last half-century. Constituencies may be 'gerrymandered' to the advantage of the ruling political party. Finally, the electoral system, even if devoid of obvious blemishes, may produce results which cannot be said to reflect fairly the popular will; this is especially probable where the representatives of a single-member constituency can succeed, as in this country, with a simple plurality of votes. To minimize this possibility various schemes of proportional representation have been advocated.

Popular election is not a suitable method through which to choose those who interpret, apply or administer the law. We require judges to impose the law equitably and impartially, without regard to contemporary passions of either ministers or the general public. Thus judges are not normally subject to the restraints of public accountability, nor is any term set on their tenure of office other than a retiring age. In Britain the idea that local councils should elect local magistrates has failed to gain significant support, except for a brief period after 1835 when the municipal boroughs were reformed on a basis of ratepayer democracy. Clearly it would be impractical to choose the multitude of civil servants and local government officials through elections, but in many states the more important local officials are chosen in this way. However, if an elected council or legislature is required to work in co-operation with administrators who also have been directly elected, the influence of the former is necessarily diminished. British local authorities have lost power through the growth of central control by Government departments, but they are not held in check by the wide personal popularity of Town or County Clerks. In our system of Government the influence of public officials is exercised *in camera* and arises out of respect for advice based on expert knowledge.

The optimum method of selecting public employees is through some kind of test that will establish their competence and suitability. But the distribution of jobs can provide natural opportunities for corruption and the use of undercover influence. The following two chapters describe the consequences of patronage in the British Civil Service and its replacement in stages by examinations conducted by an independent body, the Civil Service Commission. As the traditional type of academic examination cannot test personal qualities of temperament and character it is not used for highly responsible positions. The most brilliant intellectual may not be the best administrator. The most able lawyer is not necessarily the best judge. Even for more routine jobs there is proper reluctance to accept the principle that those who earn the highest examination marks shall have first claim on vacant posts, and final appointment depends upon interview. Examination success, therefore, becomes a necessary but not a sufficient qualification for promotion or appointment. Examinations provide a guarantee that public servants have a minimum standard of competence and this standard can be raised when the number and quality of applicants permit. For senior positions high personal qualities are required in addition to basic qualifications. In a unified Civil Service such posts can be filled by promotion within the organization, and internal records will furnish the evidence on which such decisions are based. Where internal promotions cannot normally be made, as in local government or with some specialized Civil Service posts, recourse must be had to the method of competitive interview. Whether this system gives satisfactory results must depend wholly on the wisdom of the interviewers, or the nature of their prejudices.

From time to time suggestions are heard, albeit humorous ones, that election candidates should be required to submit to some type of examination which would test their competence to occupy the position to which they aspire. This idea ignores not only the difficulty of framing an acceptable test but also the basic concept of a democratic election. An election is a popularity contest: if voters choose between candidates on the basis of opinions and not personal qualities—as they do—they are acting in conformity with the concept of representative government. Voters select the policy they support; they are not choosing community leaders or professional administrators. There is another fatal obstacle to the proposal. Many people would object to the indignity of submitting themselves to examination, especially if there were any significant chance of failure and of the failure becoming public knowledge. Thus in the case of unpaid (or ill-paid) elected positions any prior tests of suitability would do grave damage to the supply of candidates. Similarly, and this is a far more important matter, where unpaid offices are filled through patronage it is not practicable to insist that nominees of the patron should undergo preliminary examinations. For this reason the patron should obtain reliable information about the people he nominates.

The fourth main technique is patronage. Here the power to

select is in the hands of an individual or, possibly, a group of people; the power may stem from law, tradition, political or social influence. Patronage is not wholly dissimilar from selection by competitive interview, for the interviewing body is exercising a patronage power. Yet there are a number of reasons for insisting on the distinction between the two methods. A post filled by patronage is not subject to public advertisement, which is the common pre-condition of competitive interview. A patronage appointment may be preceded by preliminary discussions with or about one or more candidates and such talks are informal and probably *sub rosa*: where a job is open to competition, a preliminary discussion with any candidate is often thought improper. When competition is used no unnecessary secrecy is imposed on the proceedings: patronage is surrounded by a veil of confidence that makes its operation extremely obscure. A board conducting a competitive interview is chosen for its professional experience or it has a representative basis; in either case it is less likely to be swayed by personal preference or prejudice than is an individual patron. Finally, the right to make an appointment is an overt demonstration of a patron's authority and frequently he will be responsible to no one for his actions.

Patronage is of greatest importance in an authoritarian system of government. It can well be the major force helping to keep a régime in power. Those who enjoy the favour of the mighty enjoy place and prosperity: those who offend them are jobless or worse. Democratic governments depend on public support for their security and they may be publicly answerable for their patronage decisions. Thus in the United States appointments made by the President are subject to approval by the Senate. Great Britain has no parallel tradition of extensive separation of powers. Also party discipline in the Commons is too strong for the British Cabinet to suffer the type of rebuff a President must endure when one of his nominations is rejected. Indeed, some appointments in this country are shielded altogether from Parliamentary questioning because of the tradition of the royal prerogative.

The operation of patronage may be restricted by law or convention. In Britain judicial office-holders are required by statute to have certain qualifications and experience. Members of the Government, with rare or minor exceptions, are drawn from members of the Lords or the Commons. In the Civil Service, ministerial patronage extends to but a few very senior appointments, and the choice is limited to men in the Service who have already obtained promotion to the grade immediately below that of the post to be filled. (The double-jump promotion of Mr W. Armstrong from Third Secretary to Joint Permanent Secretary of the Treasury is the exception to prove the rule.) The choice of bishops is restricted to ordained members of the Anglican Church. Elsewhere, notably with administrative appointments and the bestowal of honours, there are no firm barriers on the patron's choice.

Patronage is, of course, an emotive word. It is associated in the public mind with a variety of abuses, for it provides obvious opportunities for corruption, peculation, undercover influence and power-seeking of various kinds. All these are not of the essence of patronage; they are merely probable consequences unless measures are taken to avoid such evil effects. A large part of the following chapters will be devoted to showing how steps have been taken to try to ensure that the patronage of Ministers of the Crown in Britain shall be operated in the public interest. In many fields this has now been achieved, e.g. the Civil Service and the judiciary. Yet, inevitably, patronage cannot always be controlled and it may be used to create or maintain a power relationship. The sharp distinction between appointments made for the good of a service and those made for political reasons is clear in theory but can be obscure in practice. It will not be accepted by those who make appointments. A Prime Minister, reshuffling his Cabinet, is probably convinced that he is choosing the best men for the various jobs, but he may also be selecting men who are unlikely to obstruct his will on a major issue close to his heart. A minister seeking members for a departmental committee will look for those well able to make a constructive contribution to the problem under examination, and this could lead automatically to the exclusion of those whose ideas do not fall within his definition of constructive. It follows that a study of patronage will embrace a search for administrative efficiency, a quest for justice and a critical analysis of political considerations and social implications.

The concept of patronage does, of course, extend beyond the distribution of jobs. It covers also the allocation of other types of benefit and financia aid—honours, pensions and support for the arts. What follows does not pretend to be an exhaustive treatment of the subject; nothing is said, for example, about military or diplomatic appointments or about State aid for cultural activities. The topic is vast, for the nineteenth-century decline in patronage has been decisively reversed as a consequence of the increasing scope of public administration. And for the *active* members of the House of Lords it has almost replaced heredity as the means of selection. In preparing this book a main limitation has been the curtain of silence surrounding patronage. This secrecy is not enforced —at least for the most part—because those who operate patronage have anything to hide. To have to choose a man for a responsible post is a delicate and sometimes invidious task. The collection of information about individuals is necessarily a confidential process. However, no covers should be drawn over criteria of selection or the channels through which information is gathered; where these are hidden, as in the case of honours, suspicion of motive is inevitable.

CHAPTER TWO

Government by Patronage

⊙

I

Here rests all that was mortal of Mrs Elizabeth Bate
A woman of unaffected piety
And exemplary virtue.

She was honourably descended
And by means of her Alliance to
The illustrious family of Stanhope
She had merit to obtain
For her husband and Children
Twelve several employments
In Church and State.
She died June 7, 1751, in the 75th year of her age.

This epitaph, quoted by G. M. Trevelyan,[1] portrays the
eighteenth-century attitude in this country towards patronage. Public offices and positions in the Established Church were
obtained by favour. The leaders of society, the most powerful
men, had the right to confer favours; those of second rank
competed to obtain these advantages. No moral stain was
associated with supplication for the favour of the mighty.
Indeed, success in obtaining employments would confirm or
enhance the social status of the supplicant.

The widespread acceptance of patronage as the national
method for arranging the distribution of desirable posts could
not fail to have profound political implications. The powerful
would not dispense favours to those who opposed their will.

[1] *English Social History* (Longmans, 1944), p. 359.

On each rung of the social ladder men concerned with public affairs would tend to hesitate before offending their superiors. They might also have to consider with care whether an associate was a superior or an equal, or how far his influence extended. Thus a society accustomed to this type of patronage is a highly class-conscious society. If social mobility is limited and no profound conflicts exist to raise political tempers, patronage can be used as a sort of social cement that helps to give stability. It was commonly argued in eighteenth-century England that patronage was essential to the maintenance of the Constitution. If the King, or the King's Ministers, did not possess this means of persuading men to accept their authority, would not the conflict between Crown and Parliament break out once more?

Between 1742 and 1830 ministers were not once defeated at a General Election. Cabinet changes—and there were many —were caused not by the actions of the electorate but by disputes between the King and his ministers, between ministers themselves, or between ministers and their supporters. The impotence of the voters was the result of the limited franchise, and their general inclination to carry out the wishes of the local magnates who dominated the nomination of candidates. The common phrase 'pocket borough' well describes this technique of political control. Ministers who could command the allegiance of sufficient 'patrons' of Parliamentary seats had little to fear from the electorate. Indeed, the majority of seats were normally uncontested.

The degree of control exercised by patrons of constituencies varied from place to place and from time to time. Essentially a *de facto* relationship, it fluctuated with changing circumstances; the death of the head of a family, the sale of property, family quarrels or the advent into the district of a wealthy and ambitious man could upset previous 'arrangements'. Double-member constituencies were often shared between two patrons, often of opposed political views. The control in some areas was absolute and unchallenged; elsewhere 'influence' was not always successful. From his extensive researches into the election of 1761, Sir Lewis Namier has shown that 51 peers could control or influence the election of 101 borough M.P.s and 55 commoners had sway over a further 91 borough seats.[1] Namier estimates that in 81 of these 192 seats the authority of the patron was absolute. The Duke of Newcastle, who spent a fortune on electioneering, was the most powerful patron and could expect to command seven seats; by 1768 his tally may have been as high as twelve, ten in the boroughs and two county seats.[2]

Ministers could also exercise direct influence over elections in a considerable number of constituencies where large sums of public money were spent, notably by the Admiralty and the Treasury, and where many voters were on the public pay-roll. Government influence was especially strong in seaports, south-west England and the Isle of Wight where the five seats were managed for the Government by Lord Holmes. The extent of the 'Government interest' cannot be precisely defined but in 1761 it covered a minimum of thirty-two seats, including about a dozen Admiralty boroughs.

Government by patronage demands a flow of favours to keep going. Men who controlled pocket boroughs and M.P.s themselves would ask Ministers for jobs to suit relatives and friends. At least some of the requests from the most influential applicants had to be satisfied. M.P.s, especially from county seats, were fond of describing themselves as 'independent', meaning that they were free from control by a patron or the Government and that their political judgments were their own; but these 'independents' would commonly ask favours. Unless an 'independent' was constantly hostile to the administration his requests had to command some attention. Fortunately for Ministers, the amount of patronage available to them increased during the eighteenth century. Wars added to public expenditure so more public contracts were available and more tax-collectors were needed. Successful wars produced colonies and more men were required for colonial administration. Also during this period State control over the patronage of the Established Church was developed largely so that politicians could satisfy demands from the more influential place-

---

[1] *The Structure of Politics at the Accession of George III* (Macmillan, 1929), pp. 175-82.
[2] *Ibid.*, p. 13.

seekers. Control over the Church could also serve political ends more directly as clerical dignitaries could aid the election of ministerial supporters in cathedral towns. In 1781 Archbishop Markham reminded his clergy that membership of associations for Parliamentary reform was 'foreign to their functions, and not the road to preferment'.[1] After 1782 when the beginning of the economical reform movement restricted the range of patronage available, Prime Minister Pitt fell back on honours. Peerages were eagerly sought by commoners who controlled boroughs and also M.P.s.[2] Between 1784 and 1830 the peerage increased in size from 208 to 314 and the total of barons from 79 to 160. In *Sybil*, Disraeli said of Pitt's peers: 'He created a plebian aristocracy and blended it with the patrician oligarchy. He made peers of second-vote squires and fat graziers. He caught them in the alleys of Lombard Street and clutched them from the counting-houses of Cornhill.'

M.P.s were able to use their position to advance their personal or professional interests. Out of fifty merchants returned to the Commons in 1760, thirty-seven had had business dealings with the Government.[3] A seat in Parliament improved the chance of securing a lucrative contract and merchants were encouraged to contest seats not easily controlled by a patron and which, therefore, were expensive to win. Army and naval officers combined Service careers with Parliamentary life, and promotion became a consequence of political loyalty to Ministers. It is true that there was much resistance to political interference with Service appointments, especially in the Navy, the efficiency of which was recognized to be vital to national security. Even so, nine out of the eleven admirals in 1761 were, or had been, M.P.s: the corresponding proportion for vice-admirals was a little above 50 per cent, that for rear-admirals a little below 50 per cent.[4] Lawyers also found the Commons a useful avenue for advancement. In addition, the Commons contained a few civil servants, and their presence

[1] R. Pares, *King George III and the Politicians* (Oxford, 1953), p. 24.
[2] A. S. Turberville, *The House of Lords in the Age of Reform* (Faber, 1958), Ch. III.
[3] Namier, p. 61.
[4] *Ibid.*, pp. 38-9. On political interference with naval appointments, see also M. Lewis, *A Social History of the Navy* (Allen & Unwin, 1959).

was naturally convenient for Ministers.

Sinecures provided patronage of the most unprincipled kind. They varied in character. Some consisted of offices the duties of which had lapsed or had been transferred elsewhere—but the office remained, and with it the salary. Others retained very limited duties which were negligible in comparison with the salary received. A third group involved the performance of a significant amount of work—but work that could be left to a deputy appointed by the office-holder. The pay of the deputy was normally considerably less than the official salary and the office-holder pocketed the difference. Endless descriptions of sinecures can be found in the literature of the period; a striking example is the discovery in 1784 that one of the two solicitors on the staff of the Treasury had not been required to attend since the date of his appointment in 1744.[1] A large number of functionless officers existed in the establishments of the Royal Household, the Duchies of Lancaster and Cornwall, the Earldom of Chester, the Exchequer, and in the offices of the pipe, the pells and the fruits. In the Customs there were 200 sinecures.[2]

A remarkable feature of this method of making appointments through the personal favour of Ministers is the amount of time that the highest men in the land must have devoted to patronage problems. Even the award of a small contract might have political implications. Letters would flow in from borough patrons, M.P.s and many others who had—or who pretended to have—a claim on the attention of Ministers. Here is one example, a letter written in 1765 to the Prime Minister, the Duke of Newcastle, by one of the more 'independent' Whig Members.[3]

'Serjeant Hewitt who has nothing to ask of the Government for himself and who has never received any beneficial mark of public favour, begs leave to recommend his brother, Mr William Hewitt, for something at home or abroad which may

[1] J. E. D. Binney, *British Public Finance and Administration 1744-1792* (Oxford, 1958), p. 170.
[2] A. S. Foord, 'The Waning of "The Influence of the Crown"', *English Historical Review*, Vol. LXII, p. 499.
[3] Quoted by Namier, p. 28.

carry some publick mark of respect to the serjeant and therein do him credit.'

Faced with such pressing demands, Ministers were commonly at odds with each other over the right to nominate to the posts available. Appointments were secured by the most influential claimants—not the most able. Necessarily the administration of Government business was incompetent, uneconomic and sometimes corrupt. Too often the prizes went to the toadies, the hangers-on: virtue had to be its own reward. A pattern of social and political relationships flourished which satisfied the select circle of important personages; to continue, this system needed to absorb steadily a proportion of the *nouveau riche*. It had scant moral authority with which to defend itself against reform: its defences were tradition, the authority of wealth and—on occasion—the coercive power of the State.

II

The fifty years before 1832 were a period of hesitant, spasmodic reform. As the power of the King declined, that of his Ministers grew. The influence of the Commons increased as Ministers depended increasingly on parliamentary support. Public opinion became more virile with the spread of democratic ideas. Many of the changes that came were not directly related to the reduction of patronage; the control of political action in the eighteenth century manner became a little more difficult with each adjustment in the cause of greater administrative efficiency and each minor success of the radicals. But the decay of the old political pattern was slow. The excesses of the French Revolution made opinion hostile to constitutional reform; some of the Whig measures that reached the statute book failed to produce the intended results; with a restricted electorate it remained possible for patronage and corruption to retain a major hold in public affairs. Yet the shift in economic power caused by the Industrial Revolution steadily undermined the foundations of the English *ancien régime*: the first Reform Bill was the spectacular collapse which marked the culmination of the preceding erosion.

The attacks on patronage may be divided into political and administrative measures. In 1782 two reforms directly challenged corrupt influence at elections. Crewe's Act disenfranchised revenue officers and Clarke's Act disqualified government contractors from membership of the Commons. These minor changes did nothing to diminish public acceptance of bribery at elections—an attitude well illustrated by Pitt's limited proposal for electoral reform in 1785. He suggested the elimination of 36 pocket boroughs, subject to the consent of the electors and subject to the payment of compensation for the lost of their 'property'.[1] In the following year a Bill to prevent bribery at county elections passed the Commons, only to be wrecked by the Lords. Elections were still 'managed' in the interests of Ministers, notably that of 1784. Ashley's *Life of Palmerston* shows how the Whigs bought seats in 1806 at below market prices and made good the difference by the distribution of honours and appointments.[2] An Act of 1809, however, imposed penalties for making corrupt agreements relating to the return of M.P.s. This had but partial effect, although it did mark an advance in public sentiment. Electoral manipulation by Ministers and public officials was inhibited, yet little impact was made on bargaining by private individuals.

Throughout the reign of George III the number of placemen in the Commons declined steadily. If placemen are defined as those holding government posts, court appointments and other sinecures and those in receipt of official pensions, the total was about 150 in 1760 and 115 in 1780, so the drop in the numbers of court appointees and sinecurists during this period was very marked.[3] By 1809 the corresponding total was 84, including 28 who held pensions or sinecures.[4] It is important, however, not to exaggerate the effect of these

[1] C. Davis, *The Age of Grey and Peel* (Oxford, 1929), p. 69.
[2] Vol. I, p. 31 (Bentley, 1879).
[3] Ian R. Christie, 'Economical Reform and "The Influence of the Crown"' *Cambridge Historical Journal*, Vol. XII, p. 146. Christie's figures have been adjusted since he includes army and naval officers and government contractors within the definition of 'placemen'.
[4] *Public Expenditure of the United Kingdom*. Select Committee. Supplementary Report to the Third Report. P. 347; 1809 (200) iii.

figures. Because an M.P. received an official income of some kind—or had been nominated in his constituency through Treasury influence—it was not always certain that he would support the policy of Ministers. The Commons was a more unpredictable body at the end of the eighteenth century than it is in our own day. A technique of control that depends on personal relationships is more susceptible to individual changes of temper than one which relies on the impersonal authority of a modern party organization.

Administrative reforms are more complicated to describe. Parliamentary demands for action in this sphere sprang from the repeated over-spending of the Civil List. The Civil List was the money granted by Parliament to each King with which to defray the civil expenses of government. When the Civil List revenue proved inadequate to meet the demands made upon it, arrears mounted up until Parliament was asked to provide additional funds to clear off the deficit. Naturally, such requests were unpopular and gave reformers their opportunity. A Bill for 'economical reform' was moved by Edmund Burke in a famous speech to the Commons on February 11, 1780. As an Opposition member, Burke was unsuccessful on this occasion, but in 1782 a change of ministry gave Burke the fairly minor post of Paymaster-General. In office, Burke introduced and carried a modified version of his proposals. The details of his Civil Establishments Bill need not concern us here; nor does the fact that parts of his reforms were ill-considered and had to be amended subsequently. Yet the Civil Establishments Bill sumceeded in restricting Civil List expenditure by the abolition of some 134 sinecure offices and by limiting the payment of pensions from Civil List funds. In addition, the annual contri- to the Secret Service Fund was set at £10,000, which was a considerable reduction. The Secret Service money had been used, in the main, for political purposes, election expenses and the granting of pensions: Namier, after much research, concluded that in the whole system of patronage the Secret Service money was a mere supplement to places and other open favours and that 'there was more jobbery, stupidity and human charity about it than bribery'.[1]

[1] *The Structure of Politics at the Accession of George III*, Vol. I, p. 290.

Of major importance for the probity of the nation's finances was the series of official investigations into administration in public offices. The first of such inquiries, a Commission on Public Accounts, was established by the Prime Minister, Lord North, in 1780. It had statutory powers which were renewed annually until the Commission decided its work was complete in 1787. The reports of this body[1] gave Parliament much fuller information about the organization of public business and helped to stimulate Pitt to introduce administrative reforms. Thus in 1785 a new system of audit was instituted. Other inquiries were started, one of which examined the payment of fees in public offices. The system of paying public servants by a salary supplemented by fees, or by fees alone, was very ancient. As the volume of public business grew the size of the fee payments mounted, often to unreasonable heights. Where the work could be performed by deputy, the fee system increased the value of the patronage available to the King and his Ministers. The Commission on Fees produced ten reports between 1786-1788, but as these were made to the King-in-Council, not to Parliament, they received less publicity. The last report on the Post Office was so embarrassing that Prime Minister Pitt locked it in his desk for four years and the joint Postmasters-General were unable to obtain a copy.[2] Another notable body was the Select Committee created in 1797 which produced thirty-six reports that gave Parliament the first comprehensive statement on the condition of the nation's finance.

It was noted above that Burke's Act of 1782 opened the attack on sinecures by the abolition of 134 offices. Shortly afterwards Shelburne at the Treasury ended another 144 useless posts in the Customs. Pitt terminated 765 offices in 1789, and a further 196 in 1798. The Reports of the Committee on Sinecure Offices issued in the period 1810-12 showed the need for further reform. The First Report of the Committee gave the following examples of 'perfect' sinecures, i.e. offices without any duties, Chief Justice in Eyre, Law Clerk in the Secretary of State's office, Collector and Transmitter of State

[1] The reports are analysed briefly by D. L. Keir, 'Economical Reform', in *Law Quarterly Review*, Vol. L, pp. 368-85.
[2] Binney, p. 17.

Papers, Housekeeper in Excise, Warehouse-Keeper to the Stamp Office and the Constable of the Castle of Limerick. The Report also showed that a very large number of official posts in the colonies were carried out wholly or partly by deputy. Thus the Hon. C. Wyndham, M.P., held the office of Secretary and Clerk of the Enrolments of Jamaica for fifty years; the duties of the office were performed by deputy but Wyndham made an annual net profit of at least £2,500 out of this arrangement.[1] Confronted with such evidence the Select Committee recommended the abolition of a large number of sinecures or semi-sinecures after the 'expiration of existing interests'. Sinecures were regarded as a form of property which could not be arbitrarily discontinued: even after the abolition of a post was agreed, it tended to remain until the existing office-holder died or resigned. But the pace of reform, if slow, was steady. The Select Committee on Finance of 1817 condemned another 313 offices[2] but in 1833 a further Committee could discover a mere 55 useless posts. The law courts are notably resistant to change but an Act of 1832 abolished the following sinecure offices in the Court of Chancery as from the death or resignation of their holders: Keeper of His Majesty's Hanaper, Patentee of the Subpoena Office, Registrar of Affidavits, Clerk of the Crown in Chancery, Clerk of the Patents, Clerk of the Custodies of Lunatics and Idiots, the Prothonotary of the Court of Chancery, the Chaff Wax, the Sealer, Clerk of the Presentations, Clerk of the Inrolments in Bankruptcy, Clerk of the Dispensations and Faculties and the Patentee for the Execution of the Laws and Statutes concerning Bankrupts. These posts had been in the gift of the Lord Chancellor and, as compensation for the loss of this patronage, future Lord Chancellors were compensated with a retirement pension of £5,000 p.a.

The limitation of pensions had started also with the Civil Establishments Act of 1782 which restricted the total annual sum paid in pensions from the English Civil List to a maximum of £95,000: in addition, the secrecy that had previously surrounded these payments was ended. Thus a check was placed

---

[1] P. 33; 1810 (362) iii.
[2] Pp. 14-19; 1817 (159) iv.

on a possible method of secret corruption. But the English
Civil List was not the only source of state pensions. There were
pensions charged to the Scottish and Irish Civil Lists, diplomatic and military pensions, colonial pensions and pensions
met out of special exchequer revenues. The diplomatic, military and colonial pensions were often paid to men who had
retired after holding official positions and had no possible political import. Other pensions were compensation for loss of
office. The Irish pensions were large in number but small in
amount. A few large pensions were in recognition of outstanding service in war. Some were granted during pleasure, i.e.
were in theory terminable at any time; some were granted for
life; a few passed on to a wife or an heir, e.g. the Nelson
annuity of £5,000 was granted in perpetuity to the Admiral's
heirs male.[1] The sum paid out in Civil List pensions was steadily
reduced. Scottish pensions, which amounted to £38,588 in
1807, were restricted to £25,000 p.a. in 1810. Irish pensions
were limited to £80,000 in 1793, and this figure was cut to
£50,000 in 1820. The amounts paid to recipients were subject
to certain deductions so that the net cost of Civil List pensions
in 1831 was about £145,000. The Select Committee on the
Civil List 1830-31 reported that this figure should be cut to
£75,000.[2] At the start of Victoria's reign the question of pensions was again reviewed and criteria with statutory authority
were established to govern future awards. Thus pensions were
restricted to those who had given personal service to the
Crown, performed important public duties, made scientific
discoveries or had attainments in literature and the arts; in
recent years the pensioners have all had scientific, literary or
artistic claims to beneficence.[3]

[1] These payments ceased in 1951 under the terms of the Trafalgar Estates
Act, 1947, which provided that the pension should end on the deaths of the
present Earl Nelson and his brother.
[2] See p. 4; 1830-31 (269) iii.
[3] The annual amount now paid out to Civil List pensioners is a little over
£30,000. The largest pension is £500 p.a., and the total of pensioners is about
180. Up to the session 1939-40 an annual return was published which listed the
recipients of new and supplementary pensions and the sums awarded. Publication ceased presumably for war-time economy reasons. The annual return
is still presented to Parliament as required by the Civil List Act, 1837. In
1952, the Prime Minister, Sir Winston Churchill, refused to resume the

Associated with the limitation of sinecures and pensions was the reform of the Civil List. In 1802 some branches of civil expenditure became subject to annual supply and, therefore, to annual parliamentary review: thus the deficit on the Civil List was made good each year. By 1816 some expenditure was removed from the Civil List altogether and separate Civil Estimates were instituted. On the accession of William IV in 1830 the Civil List was restricted to 'such Expenses as affect the Dignity and State of the Crown, and the proper maintenance of Their Majesties' Household'.[1]

The combined effects of these changes were such that ten years before the First Reform Bill Charles Arbuthnot argued in a Treasury note that 'if the just and necessary influence of the Crown be further reduced it would be quite impossible for any set of men to conduct the government of this country'.[2] This restatement of the idea that patronage is a necesssary cement to hold together the Constitution shows that the concept of government by patronage was still neither dead nor unrespectable. In 1820 Castlereagh had summoned a meeting of M.P.s who were placeholders and warned them that the fate of the government might depend on their votes on the following day.[3] But the tradition of dismissing army and naval officers and Lords Lieutenant hostile to the government had ended. Church appointments also became less political and the Duke of Wellington was obliged to appoint bishops 'who had distinguished themselves by their professional merits'.[2] The development of professional standards also restricted patronage available in the Customs after 1829.

The steady reduction of patronage increased the difficulty of controlling Parliament. To compensate for this loss the

printed publication of the list; his comment was, 'This is a matter in which there is no secrecy, but on the other hand undue publicity is not encouraged by convention and custom followed by both parties' (H. C. Deb., Vol. 504, col. 275). These lists, however, are available to the public at the House of Lords Record Office. Parliamentary disqualification of Civil List pensioners ended in 1957.

[1] Civil List. Select Committee. Report p. 1; 1830-31 (269) iii.
[2] Foord, p. 488.
[3] A. Aspinall, 'English Party Organisation in the early nineteenth century', *English Historical Review*, Vol XLI (1926), p. 395.

King and his Ministers introduced a new weapon against the Commons—dissolution.[1] After the Septennial Act of 1715 a convention had developed that a Parliament should last the whole, or nearly the whole, of its seven year period. Thus, if during the lifetime of a parliament the Ministers could no longer co-operate smoothly with the Commons, the Ministers were changed but the Commons remained. Often these changes of government involved little more than a shuffle of some Ministers. But the use of the dissolution in 1784, three years before the end of the Parliament's 'natural' term, altered the pattern. An election could be used to appeal to the electorate against the Commons. To the extent that the power of the Commons was reduced that of the electorate grew. The premature election of 1784 was a brilliant success for Pitt, but this degree of success was not repeated after subsequent 'early' dissolutions. As the loss of patronage made the Commons less manageable, so also did it increase the difficulty of managing elections. Yet the use of the dissolution weapon was symptomatic of the creaking of government by patronage. Its end came when the 1830 Election returned a House of Commons with a strong majority dedicated to parliamentary reform. After the 1832 Reform Act middle-class opinion was the ultimate determinant of election results and the political colour of the Government.[2]

III

Why was the calm acceptance of the techniques of political patronage challenged towards the end of the eighteenth century? What motives inspired the men who promoted reform?

[1] Cf. Betty Kemp, *King and Commons 1660-1832* (Macmillan, 1957), pp. 133-7.
[2] Powerful landowners were still often able to control individual seats. Hanham suggests that in 1868 possibly as many as eighty-four seats (fifty-three Conservative, thirty-one Liberal) were under the thumb of a patron. The Ballot Act, 1872, and the franchise and constituency reforms of 1884-85 reduced the number to a maximum of fifteen, and the patron's hold was commonly precarious. H. J. Hanham, *Elections and Party Management* (Longmans, 1959), Appendix III.
  Even in our own day the Guinness connection continues to occupy Southend West and the Heathcote Amory link with Tiverton was severed only in 1960.

Such inquiries must start with Edmund Burke, who both played a leading rôle in the 'economical reform' movement of 1780-82 and wrote voluminously to relate his political philosophy to the events of the age.

Burke had no moral objections to the dispensation of patronage by men in official positions. A political system had to accept that self-interest was a potent factor in human behaviour. In a letter written shortly after leaving the Government, Burke commented that when in office he had done little to advance his own interests, but he added, 'though I have certainly a natural desire and a natural right, and duty too, to take care of my own interest whenever I can do it consistently with my superior duty to the public'.[1] The effect of the last clause is open to interpretation. However, it provided in theory for the distinction between patronage and corruption. And if the motive of self-interest in public life be squarely accepted it becomes easier to recognize undercover and corrupt practices. For this reason Burke was unenthusiastic about a Place Bill, i.e. a Bill to restrict the ability of office-holders to sit in the Commons. 'It were better, undoubtedly, that no influence at all could affect the mind of a member of Parliament. But of all modes of influence, in my opinion, a place under the Government is the least disgraceful to the man who holds it, and by far the most safe to the country. I would not shut out that sort of influence which is open and visible, which is connected with the dignity and the service of the state, when it is not in my power to prevent the influence of contracts, of subscriptions, of direct bribery, and those innumerable methods of clandestine corruption, which are abundantly in the hands of the court, and which will be applied as long as these means of corruption, and the disposition to be corrupted, have existence amongst us.'[2]

Burke's argument was that patronage provided a means for the satisfaction of legitimate ambition; properly used it should provide a barrier against corruption.[3] The prospect that

[1] *Correspondence of Edmund Burke*, ed. by Earl Fitzwilliam and Sir Richard Bourke (Rivington, 1844), Vol. III, p. 13.
[2] From *Thoughts on the Cause of the Present Discontents* (1770).
[3] Cf. C. Parkin, *The Moral Basis of Burke's Political Thought* (Cambridge, 1956), pp. 76-8.

patronage could lead to waste and inefficiency did not seem to concern him. He was content that the state should make provision, generous provision, for those who had served it well. In later years his literary crusade against the French Revolution made him a favourite of the Court and he received a Civil List pension. Burke reacted strongly against criticism of this award. Writing in self-defence his *A Letter to a Noble Lord* (1796) specifically denied that desire for economy in public spending had been a dominant motive for his Civil Establishments Bill. This appears to be inconsistent. Can we accept that 'economical reform' was not activated mainly by interest in economy? As far as Burke is concerned, the answer is 'Yes'. No doubt his emphasis changed a little over the years, but the main target in 1780-82 had been the influence of the Crown.

His point, then, was essentially political. Burke believed in a balanced constitution—the settlement of 1689 and 1701. A balance had been struck between the Crown on the one hand and the public opinion of the mighty and the wealthy on the other. Parliament, consisting of the peerage, the country gentlemen and their nominees, should keep a check on the policies of the King and his Ministers. This equipoise in the Constitution was the secret of British freedom. The whole pattern of our institutions was endangered when Parliament ceased to exercise vigilance against the Crown. But the influence of the Crown had been used to give favours to its supporters and to undermine the independence of the Commons. In *Thoughts on the Cause of the Present Discontents*, Burke showed that the results of this tendency would be disastrous.

'On the side of the court will be, all honours, offices, emoluments; every sort of personal gratification to avarice or vanity; and, what is of more moment to most gentlemen, the means of growing, by innumerable petty services to individuals, into a spreading interest in their country. On the other hand, let us suppose a person unconnected with the court, and in opposition to its system. For his own person, no office, or emolument, or title; no promotion, ecclesiastical, or civil, or military, or naval, for children, or brothers, or kindred.' In electioneering, Burke argued, a supporter of the Court had many advantages. 'He can do an infinite number of acts of generosity and kindness, and even of public spirit. He can procure indemnity from quarters. He can obtain a thousand favours, and avert a thousand evils. He may, while he betrays every valuable interest of the kingdom, be a benefactor, a patron, a father, a guardian angel to his borough. The unfortunate independent member has nothing to offer, but harsh refusal, or pitiful excuse, or despondent representation of a hopeless interest.'

Thus the Civil Establishments Bill and allied measures were needed to restrict the political influence that could be exercised by patronage. Viewed in this way, these reforms are conservative—with a small 'c'. They were necessary, Burke argued, to spike demands for more radical reforms—i.e. of parliamentary representation, demands which had been stimulated by the abuses associated with the intervention of the Crown in politics. The essence of his attitude to patronage was embodied in Dunning's famous resolution of 1780—'the influence of the Crown is increasing, has increased, and ought to be diminished'.

Other reasons for administrative reform gained in importance as the political position of the Whigs declined. Tory Pitt, who depended on royal support, had different motives. His view was that the existing system of parliamentary representation had become indefensible and needed at least minor amendments. His attitude towards sinecures was also one of cautious reform based on the belief that national revenues could not afford so many useless offices. While the French Revolution set back the cause of political reform, the war against France increased the levies made on the taxpayer. Higher taxation produces greater concern for how taxes are spent and this resulted, as noted above, in a long series of Parliamentary inquiries into the national finances. The publicity attracted by these reports focused more attention on the existence of functionless and lucrative sinecures. Middle-class, industrial, commercial and nonconformist opinion became more hostile. The growing middle-class did not overlap socially with Court circles, the politicians and the fox-hunting gentry, but its opinions could no longer be entirely ignored. The holders of pensions and sinecures were pushed on to the defensive; for some the nature of their incomes caused a little discomfort. In

1812 a political storm broke over the 'tellers of the Exchequer'. The fees attaching to one of these offices appear to have risen to about £26,000 per annum. No immediate reform occurred because the powerful Grenville family was involved; subsequently one of the tellers, the Marquis of Camden, voluntarily resigned the fees of the office and accepted only the regular annual salary of £2,500.[1] A contemporary letter from Lord Holland to the young Lord John Russell gave an unconvincing defence of sinecures to the future Prime Minister. Sinecures, Lord Holland admitted, were an evil but an evil that was grossly over-rated: a sinecure was simply a bad, uneconomical and uncertain method of rewarding public services. They might be awarded with more discrimination but, he concluded, the positive harm they did was very small indeed.[2]

By the 1820s objections to the political power of patronage were submerged in the broader agitation for parliamentary reform. Detailed information about pensions and sinecures were provided for radical orators in successive editions of *The Black Book*; but by this time the worst abuses had been ended. The Utilitarians had Bentham's attack on 'sinister interests' to form an important part of their doctrine. Classical scholars were reminded of Aristotle's dictum that public office should be divorced from opportunities of personal gain. Periodical literature, especially the *Westminster Review*, the *Edinburgh Review* and the *Quarterly Review* stimulated critical interest in public affairs. The rise in the circulation of *The Times* at this period, at the price of 7d a copy, under the left-wing editorship of Barnes, shows the trend of influential middle-class opinion.

But perhaps the greatest challenge to the established system of government came from the rising tide of puritanism, the onward march of the nonconformist conscience, and the scale of values they supported. The pace of the Industrial Revolution depended on toil, thrift, sobriety and piety among the entrepreneurs who provided the driving force of initiative. They observed strict codes of commercial ethics: respectable businessmen would not get into debt with the impunity of the

[1] Leslie Stephen, *The English Utilitarians* (Duckworth, 1900), Vol. II, pp. 65-6.
[2] C. Davis, *The Age of Grey and Peel* (Oxford, 1929), p. 267.

nobility. A great gap developed between such attitudes and the laxity, financial and otherwise, of the older generation of politicians. The phrase 'economical reform' has a sound more appropriate to 1830 than 1780: certainly Burke, with his personal extravagance and money troubles, had nothing in common with the Philosophical Radicals. The conflict between patrician and puritan was symbolized in public opinion on the private life of George IV. Black bands of mourning announced the King's death in *The Times*, but they surrounded obituary notices of great severity. *The Times* explained its policy quite simply, 'Flattery cannot reach him now and Truth may be of advantage to his successors'.

As the climate of opinion moved towards the values that are now regarded as the quintessence of the Victorian period, public men found it convenient to pay lip-service to ideals for which, in private, they had little enthusiasm. The extension of the franchise both accentuated this tendency and increased its significance. It became essential to match public utterance by performance when the flame of democracy grew stronger. In the new atmosphere the problem of patronage changed as it turned into the task of choosing men *to work*, to work in the public service at rates of pay that were not always attractive.

CHAPTER THREE

Civil Service Reform

⊙

I

The impact of the Reform Bill forced many changes in the habits and attitudes of politicians. Taper and Tadpole adjusted themselves quickly. They realized at once that the passport to office had become a good cry and a good registration. ' "I am all for a religious cry," said Taper. "It means nothing, and if successful, does not interfere with business when we are in".' Tadpole sought aid from the Wesleyans, 'of which pious body he had suddenly become a fervent admirer'. County magnates lost sole control of admission to Parliament as the efforts to ensure that potential supporters claimed their new right to be on the electoral register widened the base of political life. Power did not stem from patronage: limited patronage was derived from power.

A volume entitled *The Statesman* was published in 1832 by Henry Taylor, a civil servant in the Colonial Office. His comments on patronage are of special interest as he had no sympathy with the radical thought of the period. *The Statesman* owes something to the manner of Bacon and Machiavelli as may be seen from its sub-title, *An ironical treatise on the art of succeeding*. Taylor's view was that patronage should be concentrated in a few hands and not widely dispersed. In this way, after 'private interests' had been satisfied, the remainder of the patronage could be used according to the public interests. If, however, there were more patrons each with fewer places to award, then private interests would secure all the positions available. By 'private interests' Taylor clearly meant relations and friends: he did not believe that patronage could do much to strengthen the political position of the patron. Thus he wrote '. . . the minister who has been long in office will be the

37

most likely to dispense his patronage properly; for the circle of his private friends is saturated'.[1] When considering how civil servants should be chosen, Taylor makes a division between those whose work was routine copying and those who had more intellectual and responsible duties. On the recruitment of the former group, *The Statesman* is silent, but for higher grade clerkships it recommends selection by a combination of examination and probation.[2] It was assumed that the candidates would all be nominees of influential men and thus this double check against the appointment of incompetents was desirable. By 1832 there was fairly widespread agreement that the efficiency of the public service should not suffer through the unfettered use of patronage.

As previously noted, successive waves of reform had steadily reduced the amount of patronage available to Ministers. Soon after becoming Prime Minister in 1841, Peel wrote to Charles Arbuthnot who had been Patronage Secretary[3] for nearly twenty years under Tory Governments of the pre-Reform Bill era:

'So far as I can judge, I have nothing to dispose of except Household offices, Parliamentary offices and chance seats occasionally falling vacant at a Board of Revenue. Every other appointment within the range of my patronage either requires previous service in subordinate situations, as in the Revenue, or professional knowledge and habits if it be connected with the law. . . . Some civil employment is what every lady asks for, but the patronage of the executive government is in truth professional patronage.'[4]

Tadpole, Taper and their like were hoping for parliamentary and Household jobs, but for the young kinsmen of country gentry in reduced circumstances the cupboard was

[1] *The Statesman*, p. 156 of the 1927 edition published by Heffer and Sons.
[2] P. 125.
[3] The Patronage Secretary is the Government's Chief Whip. Although his patronage powers have declined, he remains responsible for the maintenance of the Cabinet's majority in the Commons. His official title is Parliamentary Secretary to the Treasury.
[4] Quoted by E. Hughes in 'Civil Service Reform 1853-55'. *Public Administration*, Vol. XXXII, p. 19.

bare of lucrative posts. In 1843 Lady Fremantle, wife of Peel's Patronage Secretary, wrote to the Prime Minister on behalf of a nephew of her old governess: the Prime Minister had no suitable post in his own gift to offer but recommended the young man to the Commissioners of Customs for the relatively humble position of tide-waiter—a post, moreover, subject to a probationary period of satisfactory service.[1] The dearth of patronage among Ministers was general. By the 1840s it had affected even the Colonial Office largely because—contrary to Taylor's advice—patronage had been shared out among the Governors of colonies.

Naturally, political influence continued to affect the allocation of posts, especially those that were most attractive. Yet public opinion was more alive to charges of jobbery and corruption, and Ministers were more sensitive to public opinion. In 1843 the Patronage Secretary suggested to the Prime Minister that the M.P. for Evesham be given a post in the Diplomatic Service as he was likely to desert the ministerialist lobby. Peel refused unless he could be satisfied about the good character of the M.P. in question. Peel's sense of honour is again illustrated by the negotiations relating to filling a new post, the Registrar-General in Ireland. Captain Boyd, M.P. for Coleraine, wished his son to get this appointment; accordingly as a *quid pro quo* he offered to resign his seat in favour of Peel's nephew. Peel would have nothing to do with the proposition; his comment to Fremantle, the Patronage Secretary, was 'a regular Irish job . . . pray discourage it in every way you can'.[2] But tradition dies hard. The Patronage Secretary was flooded with requests for jobs and felt that it was his duty to satisfy only the most influential claimants. Fremantle's attitude was clearly set out in the following letter to Gladstone dated December 27, 1843:

'I hear that your application in favour of young Mr Walker is not founded on strong political claims. It is more a case of kindness and charity—such as I should more readily consider than any others if I were at liberty to do so—but at the

[1] *Ibid.*
[2] *Ibid.,* p. 22.

Treasury we must look first to the claims of our political supporters and our patronage is, as you know, quite inadequate to
meet the applications of members of the H. of C. in favour of
their constituents who naturally consider all our patronage as
theirs . . . pray excuse me for my frankness in explaining to
you how these things are viewed within the corrupt walls of
a Sec[retary of the] Treasury's room."[1]

Similarly in 1832 the Whig Patronage Secretary had crossed
swords with Sir James Graham at the Admiralty over the
distribution of posts. 'I have undoubted authority,' he wrote,
'that the Tories are at a loss to divine any other motive in your
recent dispensation of the patronage at the Admiralty than
a desire to conciliate and cultivate the Conservative Party.'[2]
Graham, however, was not to be moved, and asserted that he
was concerned only with the efficiency of naval officers and
not with their politics.[3]

But to assert the need to give priority to the demands of your
strongest political friends was still not to claim that patronage
was a major asset. If, as often occurred, only one of a dozen
requests could be satisfied, the amount of disappointment
caused might well outweigh—in political terms—the effect of
gratitude. Further, patronage was a nuisance because of the
inordinate time consumed in dealing with the correspondence
it caused. Peel spent several hours a day for the first weeks after
becoming Prime Minister in dealing with the flood of letters
from job-seekers. An appointment even to a minor post could
lead to very considerable correspondence: in 1845, eight or
nine letters were written by two Ministers concerning the

---

[1] Quoted by E. W. Hughes from the Gladstone MSS. in *English Historical
Review*, 1949, Vol. LXIV, p. 67.
[2] Quoted by E. Cohen, *The Growth of the British Civil Service* (Allen &
Unwin, 1941), p. 76.
[3] In spite of Sir James Graham, the hold of patronage in the Admiralty was
particularly strong. The Admiralty was not one of the departments which
introduced an entrance examination prior to 1854. Political influence in the
dockyard appointments was notorious, but measures taken in 1847 and 1849
to check it appear to have been successful. An attempt by Stafford, Tory
Secretary to the Admiralty in 1852, to revive political patronage resulted in
Parliamentary inquiry and condemnation. Cf. Report from Select Committee on Dockyard Appointments, 1852-53, (511).

post of letter-carrier in Lasswade, Midlothian, a post worth about £25 a year.[1] Not only Ministers felt this pressure; to a lesser extent M.P.s were plagued by their local electors. There was a tradition that purely local positions, e.g. in the Post Office, should be filled only after consultation with the local M.P. In county areas this practice was even followed when the M.P. was politically opposed to the government of the day. Thus patronage was commonly looked upon as a burdensome and sometimes unpleasant duty with little more than marginal benefit attaching to it.

Patronage was politically insignificant basically because British politicians had never turned it into a 'spoils system'.[2] A party coming into office did not automatically eject the nominees of their predecessors: patronage was limited to vacancies and new positions and even there the conventions about promotion for those already in the public service were respected. The one example of a purge was the dismissal of some supporters of the Duke of Newcastle in 1763, but when the political pendulum swung back in 1765 the new Ministry did not carry out a counter-purge—it merely reinstated those who had been dismissed previously. Why did the spoils system fail to develop as it had done in the United States? Changes of government in the eighteenth century were not usually the result of a clear defeat of one well organized party by another. Governments were based rather on coalitions of personal and political interests and often there would be some continuity between an outgoing Ministry and its successor. The security of public servants was further strengthened by the idea that an office, including a sinecure office, was a piece of personal property that could not be arbitrarily expropriated in the life-time of the holder. This principle is well illustrated by the concluding sentence of the introductory section of the Report of the Select Committee on Miscellaneous Expenditure, 1847-48. '[The Committee] are also especially desirous not to affect in any recommendations the interests of those who have embarked their fortunes on the faith of the public in any employ-

---

[1] N. Gash, *Politics in the Age of Peel* (Longmans, 1953), pp. 354-5.
[2] Cf. S. E. Finer, 'Patronage and the Public Service', *Public Administration*, Vol. XXX, pp. 355-7.

ment of reputed permanency, being well aware that nothing more tends to preserve abuses than the notion that their correction may involve the infliction of serious individual injury."[1] Thus after 1832 when party allegiance became more closely defined, the general assumption that civil servants should have a guarantee of security prevented any possibility of the growth of an American-style spoils system.

II

The Northcote-Trevelyan Report, which urged the introduction of competitive entry into the Civil Service, was published in February 1854. Sir Charles Trevelyan, Assistant Secretary to the Treasury, then played the major part in securing the acceptance of this reform. His career is of particular interest since it symbolizes much of the nineteenth-century rejection of earlier habits in the world of public administration.

Trevelyan was born in 1807 and spent four terms at Haileybury as a prelude to service in India. Haileybury had been established in 1806 to provide training for young men nominated to join the staff of the East India Company. The foundation of the college was an important step in restricting the patronage of the Directors of the Company and in improving the quality of their staff. When the Company's charter was renewed in 1813 a new provision made residence at Haileybury a pre-condition of appointment as a writer in India. Against much opposition the staff of the college had introduced internal examinations to raise the standard of attainment of students. In 1833, Macaulay, Trevelyan's brother-in-law, then Secretary of the Board of Control, persuaded Parliament that writerships in India should be awarded as a result of limited competition with four candidates to be nominated for each vacancy, the best being chosen by means of examination.[2] In his fourteen years in India, Trevelyan

---

[1] P. x; 1847-48 (543) xviii, Pt I.
[2] The Directors managed to secure the postponement of the application of this reform, but the Charter Act of 1853 deprived the Directors of patronage altogether. It enacted that the I.C.S. should, in future, be recruited by open competitive examination.

achieved a reputation as a fearless opponent of corruption. Two years after going to India he had accused a senior and popular member of the Indian Service, Sir Edward Colebrook, of taking bribes from natives. After an inquiry Sir Edward was sent home in disgrace.[1] Such was Trevelyan's background when he was appointed Assistant Secretary to the Treasury in 1840.

In 1848 Trevelyan gave evidence before the Select Committee on Miscellaneous Expenditure on the need for administrative reorganization at the Treasury.[2] He argued that a division should be recognized between intellectual work and routine copying; that the concept of promotion throughout the grades of the Service should be abandoned; that young men for the superior work should be recruited from those who had completed a university education and that such entrants should not be expected to start at the bottom with many frustrating years of unintelligent duties. The Committee expressed no views on these suggestions: it was essentially concerned with attempting to reduce public expenditure. In the following years Trevelyan sat on a number of small committees which investigated the organization of public departments. These inquiries yielded a mass of detailed information about the working of individual departments—the Treasury, Colonial Office, the group of Irish offices, Board of Trade, Department of Practical Science and Art, Poor Law Board, Privy Council Office, Copyhold, Enclosure and Tithe Commission, Colonial Land and Emigration Office, the Board of Ordnance and the Office of Works. The paper by Stafford Northcote and Charles Trevelyan, *The Organization of the Permanent Civil Service*, is the concluding document in this series of reports.[3] It provided a summary of conclusions drawn from four years of detailed work and suggested general principles on which the future of the Service should be based.

To enter into a detailed discussion of the problems of the Civil Service in the mid-nineteenth century would be beyond

[1] E. Cohen, *op. cit.*, p. 84.
[2] Minutes of evidence, especially Q. 1664 *et seq;* 1847-48 (543) xviii, Pt I.
[3] 1854 (1713) xxvii. Northcote, born 1818, educated at Balliol, had been Gladstone's private secretary and a civil servant. He had not at this stage commenced his Parliamentary career.

the present purpose.[1] But, in brief, the proposals of the Report were to base entry to the Service on a scheme of competitive examination, to promote officers on account of merit rather than seniority, to make separate arrangements for the recruitment of young men of university education who would subsequently undertake the more responsible duties and generally to urge that the Civil Service be treated as a unified whole, not as a number of separate departmental units. The Report was highly critical of civil servants as a whole in relation to their intellectual quality and sense of industry, although it admitted there were many honourable exceptions that did not merit the general strictures. It noted the evil effect of patronage on initial appointments: the ability of a young clerk employed on routine duties was not regarded as of great moment. However, the Report noted that entrance examinations of varying severity had been established in the Treasury, the Colonial Office, the Board of Trade, the Privy Council Office, the Poor Law Board, the War Office, the Ordnance Office, the Audit Office, the Paymaster General's Office, the Inland Revenue Office, the Emigration Office and some other offices. It proposed that a unified examination system be established to test the suitability of candidates for Civil Service positions. These examinations should not be held in relation to specific appointments and should be conducted regularly. Examiners would concern themselves solely with the quality of candidates, the right of appointment would remain with individual departments. A period of probation would be retained. Examinations would be open to all; the system of nomination by Ministers and senior officials would thus be ended. The Report recommended a wide range of optional subjects in the examination for senior posts, and that for the lower class of appointments, examinations be held in provincial centres. The Report also noted that an entrance examination would not be applicable to positions for which recognized professional qualifications were an essential.

Trevelyan devoted great efforts to obtaining support for

[1] On this topic see *inter alia* E. Cohen, *The Growth of the British Civil Service*. The Northcote-Trevelyan Report was reprinted in *Public Administration*, 1954, Vol. XXXII, p. 1.

these proposals. He circulated copies of the Report before its official publication among educationalists, the conclusions of the Report were leaked to *The Times*,[1] and he literally bombarded his ministerial chief, Gladstone, with memoranda on the subject. One of these documents, headed *Thoughts on Patronage* and dated January 17, 1854, merits quotation in full.[2]

'Whatever difficulty there may be in dealing with the subject of Parliamentary Reform taken as a whole, one evil which is keenly felt is in a great degree susceptible to an early remedy. We mean electoral corruption, the constitutional malady of popular forms of government. The Executive Government depends upon its Party in Parliament: each member of that Party depends upon his Constituents; hence a tacit agreement to share the public Patronage and a perverted state of public feeling which prevents the matter from being seen in its true light. We do not appear to be aware of the portentous significance of the fact that a Functionary of high standing is attached to the central Department of the Government with the recognized official duty of *corrupting* Members of Parliament and Constituencies. We use the word advisedly. We are aware that in the conventional language of this false system, the transaction is called "gaining", or "securing" or "influencing" a Representative or an Electoral Body; but if the avowed substitution of interested motives for a simple sense of duty be not corruption, what can deserve that name? The bearing of Patronage upon the public service also demands serious attention. From the broken down spendthrift who is

---

[1] *The Times* published a leader on Civil Service reform a month before the Report was issued. It commented: 'The truth is, the Service is not open; it requires interest and connection. The educated but friendless youth cannot carry his talents to a ready market, sure that, as far as possible the true value will be given for them. Whenever a field of exertion is hemmed in by a system of nomination, there the standard of ability at once falls; while if it be thrown open to the ambition of all, it is at once brought before that great body of men who are in search of occupation, and a class of persons is obtained superior to what might be expected from the pecuniary rewards offered.'

[2] Reproduced by E. Hughes from the Gladstone MSS. in the *English Historical Review*, Vol. LXIV, pp. 69-70.

sent to repair his fortune in a Colonial Government, or the
infirm, incompetent General who covers our name with disgrace and increases the horror of war a hundred-fold, or the
Admiral of notoriously impracticable temper who goads our
sailors into mutiny, to the idle, useless young man who is provided for in a Public Office because he is unfit to earn a liveli-
hood in any of the open professions the efficiency of the Public
Establishments is habitually sacrificed to this system.

'Patronage in all its varied forms is the great abuse and
scandal of the present age but we see reason to hope that its
days are numbered. Public opinion has made some progress
since Sir Robert Walpole's time. Last session a Government
which relied for support upon the excellence of its measures
began in a minority, and ended in a strong majority; and the
time is probably arrived when a Government will gain more
by a direct single-minded attention to the public interests than
by having any amount of Patronage at its disposal. Many
Members of Parliament never cross the threshold of the
Patronage Room and many others would gladly be released
from the importunities of their Constituents and the necessity
of asking for places for them and their Dependents. The public
morality of our Statesmen has outgrown the system they have
to administer which is itself a proof that the time has come for
discontinuing that system. So long, however, as the Loaves
and Fishes are distributed according to the old practice, the
majority of those who vote for the Government will expect
the accustomed dole; but if the temptation were removed, the
difficulty would cease. It has been proposed that the first
appointments made by Her Majesty's Government to the Civil
Establishments at home and abroad should, according to the
precedent of last session in regard to the Indian Writerships,
be employed in stimulating the education of our youth, instead
of corrupting our Constituencies; and considerable progress
has been made in working out the practical details of the plan.
If this could be satisfactorily accomplished every object would
be attained. The Public Establishments would be recruited by
the best of the rising generation. The tone of Parliament itself
would be raised. Interested motives would have less to do
both with obtaining a seat in Parliament, and with the use made

of it when obtained. Above all, the Government and the Governing class would cease to be on the side of corruption. The essence of the evil consists in the sanction which is given to the system by their example

> *Hôc fonte derivata clades*
> *In patriam populumque fluxit.*

'We are apparently on the threshold of a new era pregnant with great events, and England has to maintain in concert with her allies the cause of right and liberty and truth in every quarter of the world. Our people are few compared with the Multitudes likely to arrayed against us; and we must prepare for the trial by cultivating to the utmost the superior morality and intelligence which constitute our real strength. It is proposed to invite the flower of our youth to the aid of the public-service; to encourage the rising generation to diligence and good conduct by a more extensive system of rewards than has ever been brought to bear upon popular education, and to make a nearer approach to disinterested political action by removing one prevailing temptation from Electors and Representatives. These are genuine elements of national power and if they are cordially adopted, their invigorating influence will be felt through every vein of the body politic.'

This document is indicative of the intellectual vigour and spirit of challenge that dominated the Northcote-Trevelyan Report. Equally it shows Trevelyan to be out of step with the political climate of the day. Early in 1854 public opinion was lethargic. Proposals for changes were unwelcome unless they involved a promise of reductions in public expenditure. Thus suggestions to reform the Civil Service fell on ears that, if not hostile, were deaf. Trevelyan had the support of Gladstone, but general acceptance of his ideas was insufficient to secure immediate action.

Resistance to the Report can be classified conveniently under three headings. First, since the Report constituted an attack on an established institution of the State, a counter-attack was inevitable. The views of a number of senior civil servants and educationalists on the Report were published in another official document.[1] With some exceptions, the civil servants defended the existing arrangements and claimed that criticisms were exaggerated. Sir Thomas Fremantle, Peel's Patronage Secretary, now Chairman of the Board of Customs, declared that civil servants were faithful and diligent; many of them performed their duties 'with exemplary zeal'. Others who asserted the competence of their staffs were George Arbuthnot, Auditor of the Civil List; James Booth, Secretary of the Board of Trade; Edwin Chadwick, of the Poor Law Board; H. U. Addington, ex-Under-Secretary at the Foreign Office; H. Waddington, Under-Secretary to the India Board; and Sir Alexander Spearman, Trevelyan's predecessor at the Treasury.

Second, widespread doubt was expressed as to the desirability of a method of recruitment which depended on success in an examination. Oxford and Cambridge had welcomed the idea heartily. A long letter of support from the Rev. B. Jowett, Fellow and Tutor at Balliol, had been published as an appendix to the Report. But worldly men of affairs were unconvinced of the value of academic attainments. In modern language, there was a reaction against the claims of the education lobby. The cynical argued that the universities were concerned largely with the need to find posts for their pupils, that the scheme of examinations would be costly to operate and would provide lucrative jobs for academics. More seriously, it was urged that the Civil Service demanded qualities of character and discretion that could not be judged by an examination. This is obviously true. It also happened to ignore what had been proposed. The Report had advocated that success in an examination should be a necessary—but not a sufficient—qualification for appointment. Thus it would still be for the departments to fill their vacancies having made their own assessment of the merits of any candidates who had satisfied the examiners. Further, the Report had insisted on the need to retain a system of probation which would enable newcomers to be weeded out.

Third, there was the effect of the Report on possibilities of

[1] 1854-55 [1870] xx.

48

patronage. This worked in converse ways. The concept that promotion be based on merit rather than seniority was resisted by civil servants of middle and lower rank because it was feared that this principle opened the way for unfettered favouritism. Seniority can be valued objectively: merit is a matter of subjective assessment. If political patronage could get a young man into an office, at least promotion by seniority restricted his rate of advance. It followed, as Trevelyan realized, that suspicion of promotion by merit could not be dispelled so long as political influence was important in initial appointments. On the other hand, Ministers and senior civil servants were loath to lose their control over admission to the Service. This was the cause of much opposition to the idea of open competition. Something of a tradition had been established that a civil servant of long service and good standing might expect to arrange for his son(s) to follow the same career. That a son might be rejected if unsuitable or incompetent was acceptable doctrine: that he be placed on an equal footing with an outsider was not. It should be noted that the idea of open competition was not put foward as a reform inspired by the democratic ideal of 'careers open to talent'. On the contrary, it was admitted that advanced education was expensive, so that if academic training became a prerequisite of a Civil Service post, the probability was that the tendency for the Civil Service to become a preserve of the well-to-do would be intensified.

Faced with much opposition the Government took no immediate action on the Report. The whole situation was then transformed by the events of the Crimea War. Military disaster caused by incompetent organization evoked widespread public criticism. The Aberdeen Cabinet was defeated in the Commons through resisting Roebuck's demand for an inquiry into the conduct of the war. An Administrative Reform Association was founded and held meetings in many provincial centres: the Association received some support from *The Times*. The new Palmerston Cabinet took action although the new Chancellor of the Exchequer, Sir G. Cornewall Lewis, was less progressive in his views than Gladstone. It decided to establish a Civil Service Commission, with very limited powers, by the procedure of an Order-in-Council. In spite of the Administrative Reform Association there seems to have been little Parliamentary interest in the matter, and the lack of a Bill to empower the change limited opportunity for discussing it in the Commons.

The task of the Commissioners was to ensure that candidates nominated for jobs in the Civil Service were of suitable age, health, character and knowledge to carry out their duties. Nomination of candidates and their final appointment remained with the departments—essentially in the gift of politicians and senior officials. The departments consulted with the Commissioners on the nature and extent of the knowledge that might be required for various types of appointment. The retention of the practice of nominating candidates meant that the reform amounted to little more than unifying the entrance examinations that many departments already conducted. It remained for the department to decide whether one or more candidates should be nominated for examination for a particular vacancy. Even limited competition might not be genuine because of the possibility of using the 'Treasury idiots' technique, i.e. the patron would nominate for examination the man intended for the post together with (say) a couple of others chosen because of their limited intellectual powers. Indeed, the 1860 Committee on Civil Service Appointments described the system of competition between nominees as a 'delusion on the public, a fertile source of abuse. For it is clear that while such a system prevails, any Minister who may be disposed, has it in his power to retain, virtually, the right of nomination as before, while diminishing his responsibility for the appointments he makes by a semblance of partially open competition."[1]

The Order-in-Council of 1855 was strengthened by the Superannuation Act, 1859, which limited superannuation rights to those who had been admitted to the Civil Service with the certificate of the Civil Service Commissioners, or who held their appointments directly from the Crown. Patronage was now controlled by a central agency: it was not eliminated. The work of the Commission and their series of extensive annual reports greatly increased public and Parliamentary

[1] Report, p. xiii; 1860 (440) ix.

attention to recruitment problems of the Civil Service. Their First Report in 1856 recorded that 309 out of 1,078 candidates nominated by the departments had had to be rejected for gross ignorance; the next year 880 were rejected out of 2,686 examined. This rate of failure caused much surprise in influential quarters. Sponsors were irritated when their protégés did not get jobs. In their Second Report[1] the Commissioners noted that they had refused to allow a department to see the papers of a rejected candidate. It was widely urged that the Commission set standards that were unreasonably high. To justify their position, the Commissioners used their reports to illustrate the extent of the ignorance of candidates and also to print specimen examination questions for the benefit of future candidates and their instructors.

Meanwhile a steady agitation developed for the adoption of the principle of open competition. Debates in the Commons in 1855, 1856 and 1857 showed that a substantial minority of Members were in favour of further reform. Evidence given by Sir Charles Trevelyan to the Select Committee on Civil Service Superannuation (1856) argued that patronage interests and the unco-ordinated arrangements of the Civil Service made it difficult to move officials when pressure of work eased in a particular department. This led to waste and unnecessarily large pension charges.[2] Sir William Hayter, the Patronage Secretary, opposed these views somewhat unconvincingly.[3] In 1858 the Act for the Better Government of India led to open competition for some appointments in India and the first such competition was held by the Civil Service Commission in 1859. The next year saw the establishment of a Select Committee of the Commons to inquire into Civil Service appointments —in spite of resistance from Sir William Hayter, now supported by Sir Stafford Northcote.

Inevitably the 1860 Report retraces much of the ground

---

[1] P. 1; 1857 Sess. 1 [2171] iii.
[2] Cf. Report, pp. 63-6, 152-9; 1856 (337) ix.
[3] There is evidence in this Report of personal antipathy between Trevelyan and Hayter. Trevelyan returned to India in 1859 as Governor of Madras. Hayter, Patronage Secretary from 1850 to 1858 (except for a few months in 1852) subsequently explained to his electors in Wells that as their representative he had secured 300 jobs for constituents.

already surveyed by Northcote and Trevelyan seven years
before. It provided more documentation to uphold charges
of the incompetence of the Service pre-1854. Major Graham,
the Registrar-General, told the Select Committee of the
arrangements made when his office was established in 1836:
these were extremely unsatisfactory because of the age, bad
health, bad character and lack of proper qualifications amongst
the persons appointed.[1] Mr Romilly, Chairman of the Board of
Audit, said that before 1854 a man appointed to his office was
'almost an idiot' and could not really read or write.[2] But, more
important, the Report is the first general view of the experience gained by the Civil Service Commission. The nomination
of a single candidate for a vacancy caused delay whenever he
failed to reach the required standard, since it became necessary
to find and examine an alternative. Rejected candidates and
their patrons were aggrieved. The Committee recognized that
with open competition these difficulties would tend to disappear. No one failed; the unsuccessful were defeated by those
who had proved themselves superior. There was no pressure
to lower the pass standard of the examination, as the competition itself in most cases determined the minimum standard.
As already noted, the Committee showed that a limited competition might be a fraud: to prevent this possibility it urged
that competitions should be held only between nominees
who had passed an initial proficiency test. Lastly—this is the
most significant passage in the Report—the Committee decided
that it could not recommend the immediate introduction of
open competition. The weight of argument was clearly in its
favour and the Report suggested that the experiment at India
House could usefully be extended to other departments. But
the Committee felt that it was impossible politically to go any
further. 'But your Committee [because they] desire the ultimate success of the competitive method are anxious to avoid
such precipitancy in its adoption as might lead to a temporary
reaction of public feeling. They do not conceal from themselves that, in proportion as the practice of simple nomination
is departed from, private interests are disturbed, the prescrip-

[1] P. ix; 1860 (440) ix.
[2] *Ibid.,* p. x.

tive custom of political patronage is broken in upon, and many persons exercising local influence find themselves no longer able to obtain for relatives and friends that ready admission into public offices which was formerly within their reach.'[1]

Such political considerations postponed further change for ten more years. Successive governments took refuge in the pretence that the compromise of 1855 worked well enough. But the facts were otherwise: the thirteenth report of the Civil Service Commission noted that the technique of nomination did not provide a sufficiency of able candidates while the few open competitions that had been held produced entries that were entirely satisfactory.[2] The case for open competition was proved abundantly, and after the Second Reform Bill and the Liberal victory of 1868 the time was ripe to harvest the seed sown by Northcote and Trevelyan in 1854. The Prime Minister, Gladstone, and the Chancellor of the Exchequer were agreed on the need for reform. Some of their ministerial colleagues offered resistance but ultimately all departments except the Foreign Office came into line. The Order-in-Council of 1870 directed that all vacancies in a list of offices should be subject to open competition: the Foreign Office was excluded from the list. Thus 1870 is the watershed. Henceforward the opportunities for patronage in public service appointments were the exception and not the rule. The next section will attempt to show how these boltholes were stopped.

When G. G. Glyn, Gladstone's Patronage Secretary, heard of the proposed reform he sent a letter of protest to the Prime Minister. 'Your patronage at the Treasury which has been left to me as "Secretary" is *entirely* swept away. . . . My position in the Treasury as "Patronage Secretary" is gone. . . . Without entering into the very debatable ground of the advantage or otherwise to the party of political patronage, I will only say that I lose, without notice, and at once, the great advantage of the daily correspondence and communication with members of the party . . . to say nothing of the power

[1] *Ibid.*, p. xiv.
[2] P. 8; 1867-68 [4080] xxii.

53

which it placed in my hands.''[1] Glyn exaggerated. Treasury patronage did not disappear overnight. Certainly it was much reduced and had lost the seal of official approval. In future, patronage had to be justified and perhaps excused; it could not be assumed.

III

The Order in Council of 1870[2] was followed by Treasury regulations which revised the examination system of the Civil Service Commission. Under Regulation I, the examination was devised to select young men with a university training for the higher grades of the Service: Regulation II covered more modest examinations for lesser posts. This distinction accepted the Northcote-Trevelyan idea of a clear division in the Civil Service between routine work and more responsible duties. To the rule of recruitment by examination there were three types of exception—certain officers appointed directly by the Crown; in the case of professional officers the Civil Service Commission had discretion to dispense with an examination; in individual cases the Commission could dispense with an examination at the request of the Head of a Department and the Treasury. The writ of the Commission covered only permanent civil servants, so the large number of unestablished clerks without superannuation rights fell outside their orbit. Any prospect that departmental patronage might survive in the choice of unestablished clerks was killed by a further Order-in-Council in 1871. This decreed that such officials, renamed writers, were to be examined by the Commission and be liable to serve in any department.

Initially, the Commission were not concerned with promotion. In 1874 the Chancellor of the Exchequer stated that in his experience political and social connections could still influence promotion.[3] A general discussion of the merits and demerits of patronage by the Playfair Commission in 1875

[1] The full text of this letter will be found in *Public Administration*, Vol. XXXIII, pp. 305-6. On p. 303 of the same volume is a list of offices which had, and had not, instituted competitions for clerkships between nominated candidates prior to 1870.

[2] The text of this Order-in-Council can be found in the 15th Report of the Civil Service Commissioners; 1870, C. 197, xix.

[3] Playfair Commission. Minutes of evidence, Q. 3129; 1875 C. 1113-1, xxiii.

noted that the nominee of a Minister entering through a lower grade examination might be promoted without further test.[1] The following year another Order-in-Council stopped this loophole: in future promotion from the Lower Division to the Higher Division depended on the recommendation from the Head of the Department, Treasury sanction, at least ten years' service and a certificate from the Civil Service Commission. This did not touch promotion within a Division and, no doubt, political influence on promotion did not disappear until at least the last generation of officers recruited by nomination had retired.

The Foreign Office steadfastly resisted attempts to tamper with its exclusive character. The system of nomination to enter a qualifying examination was retained, although the standard of this test was improved in 1871, and it was normal practice to have three candidates examined for each vacancy.[2] Entrance to the Diplomatic Service was not put on a similar basis of limited competition until 1883 and the need to have a private income of £400 p.a. remained until 1919. The Foreign Secretary took a diminishing personal interest in recruitment and in 1907 a Selection Committee of permanent officials was established to decide on the suitability of candidates prior to admission to the Civil Service entrance examination. Permission from the Secretary of State to appear before the Selection Board was needed; this may be regarded as an opportunity to weed out the obviously unsuitable rather than a remnant of patronage.[3] An upper class background appeared to be one criterion of suitability and the Foreign Office continued as a preserve of a social *élite*. It was also sometimes convenient to award senior posts overseas to politicians rather than career officials: A. M. Brookfield, M.P., became consul at Danzig in 1903 after he had lost his fortune in an American financial crash.

[1] *Ibid.*, p. 7. The Playfair Commission also noted that clerks appointed by favour were less discontented than those recruited by competition. It is true that discontent among civil servants grew after 1870.
[2] *Diplomatic Service.* Sel. Cttee. Minutes of evidence, Q. 220; 1861 (459) vi.
[3] The MacDonnell Commission was critical of these arrangements. See its Fifth Report; 1914-16 Cd. 7748, xi; also the Minority Report, *ibid.* For another view see Sir John Tilley, *The Foreign Office* (Putnam, 1933), Ch. IV.

Patronage was difficult to eliminate from public services of a decentralized character, e.g. the Post Office and the Customs. Especially for the humbler jobs there might be very real administrative obstacles in the way of the normal safeguards of public advertisement and open competition. Before 1895 Post Office patronage was divided between the Patronage Secretary and the Postmaster General. The former had the gift of the minor posts, sub-postmasters earning less than £120 p.a. in England and Wales and less than £100 in Scotland and Ireland; the latter was responsible for appointments above these income levels. M.P.s were often asked to make nominations to fill vacancies, and this practice sometimes extended to Opposition M.P.s.[1] In 1887 the Postmaster General took over Irish appointments and all other appointments in 1895 after a general attack on the existing system in the Commons.[2] The Postmaster, however, still continued to receive suggestions from M.P.s until 1907 when Sidney Buxton ended the tradition because requests for jobs by Liberal Members became as 'thick as leaves in Vallombrosa'.[3] Henceforward, appointments were arranged through permanent officials. The right to nominate Distributors and Sub-distributors of Stamps was surrendered by the Patronage Secretary in 1911. In the following year the Committee on the Customs Waterguard Service recommended that the recruitment of preventive men by the direct nomination of the Patronage Secretary be stopped. These nominations had originated mostly from M.P.s.[4] The Liberal Government accepted the recommendation and the Patronage Secretary, the Master of Elibank, announced that he would give up his remaining patronage rights. *The Times* suggested that he had done this in order *inter alia* to devote more time to Liberal

---

[1] H. J. Hanham, 'Political Patronage at the Treasury, 1870-1912', *The Historical Journal*, Vol. 3, p. 81.
[2] Parl. Deb. (4th Series), Vol. 30, cols 1118-34.
[3] *Ibid.*, Vol. 159, col. 397.
[4] Cf. Report; 1912-13, Cd. 6290, xvii. When the Committee heard evidence that the men nominated were often of poor physical physique, one of its members asked, 'May we infer that the man who has recourse to patronage is by nature disposed to be a weakling?' (Minutes of evidence, Q. 4284; 1912-13 Cd. 6299, xvii.)

Party organization in view of recent adverse by-election results.[1]

Also in 1912 another Royal Commission—the MacDonnell Commission—was appointed to undertake a new general inquiry into the Civil Service. The Commission devoted considerable energy to tracking down remnants of patronage which it consistently condemned. It discovered a few cases at the Board of Agriculture in which temporary posts had been offered to relatives of civil servants, and the posts had tended to become permanent.[2] A custom had developed at the Admiralty of nominating temporary 'extra clerks' who had a prospect of promotion to the permanent establishment.[3] The Commission listed about forty types of posts covering some 250 persons where the appointment was held directly from the Crown and thereby excluded from the surveillance of the Civil Service Commission.[4] The MacDonnell Commission also reviewed the method of filling professional posts, for which specialized training and qualifications were required: this was still done by Heads of Departments, commonly without any public notification of vacancies. It criticized the method of making such appointments at the Road Board, the Charity Commission and the Board of Agriculture. It proposed that all professional posts should be publicly advertised, and that the preliminary selection of candidates submitted to the Minister should be made not by any individual but by a committee including a representative of the Civil Service Commission. These proposals formed the basis of the reforms made at the end of the 1914-18 war: vacancies were advertised and selection was made by competitive interview.

[1] *The Times*, June 27, 1912, gave a list of the offices surrendered. These included County Court examiners, Irish Collectors of Income Tax (for both of which suggestions had been collected from M.P.s), female typists in the Treasury and Inland Revenue, various positions for charwomen, messengers and public auditors and valuers (usually nominated by the Registrar of Friendly Societies). Cf. also the First Report of the MacDonnell Commission. Minutes of evidence, App. IVc, 1912-13 Cd. 6210, xv.
[2] Second Report. Minutes of evidence, Qq. 8948-99; 1912-13 Cd. 6535, xv.
[3] Fourth Report, p. 70; 1914 Cd. 7338, xvi.
[4] Fourth Report, App. I; 1914 Cd. 7339, xvi. The list included members of various Boards and Commissions, diplomatic and consular posts, inspectors of schools and positions in the Scottish courts.

The most remarkable survival of patronage in the Civil Service in 1912 concerned the senior officials at the Board of Education. These men, known as Examiners, were appointed under Section 4 of the Superannuation Act, 1859, which permitted the exemption of professional posts from the examinations of the Civil Service Commission. Originally their duties had consisted mainly in operating the 'payment by results' scheme which governed the distribution of state grants to schools provided by voluntary bodies. As time passed their duties widened and became analogous to those of senior civil servants in other departments—but their title and method of recruitment remained unchanged. Thus the Vice-President of the Council (after 1899 the President of the Board of Education) had possessed an eighteenth-century style of patronage restricted only by the need to obtain Treasury sanction for additional appointments. Giving evidence before the McDonnell Commission the Permanent Secretary to the Board, Mr Selby-Bigge, vigorously defended the existing system.[1] He argued that the business of the Board, especially its negotiations with local authorities and voluntary bodies, required men of exceptional ability and tact. The right to nominate Examiners had enabled the Board to obtain the services of men with special distinction and experience. But the Commission found his defence unconvincing and recommended that in future vacancies in this grade be filled from those who had competed successfully in the Class I examination of the Civil Service Commission. This was done after 1918. No one outside the Board was likely to be sympathetic to the claim that its work entailed unique difficulties. The Commission showed that the Examiners had not obtained academic distinctions superior to those of men recruited for other departments by the Class I examination. It also noted two appointments that smacked of favouritism, the son of a Permanent Secretary to the Treasury and the stepson of a 'Parliamentary Education Minister'.[2]

The experience of the Board of Education at the turn of the century does, in fact, amount to a striking condemnation of the system of political nomination. It became notorious that its

[1] Second Report. Minutes of evidence, Q. 8731 *et. seq.*; 1912-13 Cd. 6535, xv.
[2] First Report. Minutes of evidence, Q. 1075 *et. seq.*; 1912-13 Cd. 6210, xv.

senior officials were prone to allow personal views to influence their official actions. Sadler had been nominated to the staff by Acland; he had to be warned against discussing the business of the Board with Acland after the latter had ceased to be the responsible Minister. The internal discord in the Board was acute.[1] A few examples are Sadler's anonymous letter to *The Times* criticizing the administration of the department; the famous feud between Sadler and Morant; Morant's methods of negotiation—often described as intrigue; the antipathy between the President of the Board, Sir John Gorst, and the Permanent Secretary, Sir George Kekewich. Ultimately Sir George was requested to resign in favour of Morant because Conservative Ministers were doubtful of his loyalty in the difficult task of bringing the controversial Education Act of 1902 into force. This mistrust appears justified. Ten days after his resignation Sir George was chosen as the Liberal candidate for Exeter and he also joined the Reform Club with two Liberal ex-Ministers, Asquith and Acland, as his sponsors. The lesson is clear. Men appointed through patronage are less likely to accept easily the conventions which ensure the political neutrality of the Civil Service.

Civil Service promotion is now almost wholly controlled by civil servants themselves. The last major step in the process of freeing the Civil Service from political influence came in 1920 when 'the Government of the day affirmed the principle of requiring the consent of the Prime Minister to the appointment of permanent heads of departments, their deputies, principal financial officers and principal establishment officers. It is now the duty of the Permanent Secretary of the Treasury . . . to submit advice for the consideration of the Prime Minister and the Minister of the department in which the vacancy occurs.'[2] Thus the voice of the Civil Service was to be heard whenever a major appointment became due. And the voice has been highly powerful. A Cabinet Minister, however, can still secure the transfer of his chief officials should he feel they obstruct

[1] Cf. B. M. Allen, *Sir Robert Morant* (Macmillan, 1934), M. Sadleir, *Michael Ernest Sadler* (Constable, 1949), Miss L. Grier, *Achievement in Education* (Constable, 1952), and two articles by D. N. Chester in *Public Administration* at Vol. XXVIII, p. 109 and Vol. XXXI, p. 49.

[2] Civil Service. Royal Commission. Report, p. 7; 1930-31 Cmd. 3909, x.

his policy, e.g. the move of Sir Evelyn Murray from the Post Office in 1934 was arranged by the Postmaster-General, Sir Kingsley Wood.[1] Other posts in the administrative class down to the rank of Assistant Secretary, or its equivalent, are filled by the Minister of the department on the advice of his own Permanent Secretary. At all lower levels Ministers are not concerned at all: promotions are determined by boards composed of civil servants who work through a system of internal staffing records and reports.

IV

1854-55, 1870, 1912—these are the dates that dominate the story of how patronage was eliminated from the Civil Service. The Tomlin Commission on the Civil Service (1929) paid no attention to possibilities of patronage. It had ceased to be a problem.

Reform came always from Liberal Governments. Job filling troubled the Liberal conscience in a way unknown to the Tory mind. It is instructive to contrast the attitudes of Gladstone and Disraeli on this question. To Gladstone belongs the honour of carrying through the major changes of 1870 and of having given full support to Trevelyan in 1854. Disraeli seemed to regard any public office for which there was no established means of recruitment or ladder of promotion as a legitimate political prize. He was alert to assert his own rights to make nominations. The Disraeli papers reveal an acid dispute in February 1877 between the Prime Minister and the President of the Board of Trade over the right to choose a member of the Railway Commission. Also in 1877 Disraeli filled the Assistant Directorship of Kew Gardens personally and instructed Treasury officials that he was to be consulted about all appointments in his gift. He instructed Sir William Stephenson, Chairman of the Board of Inland Revenue, that vacancies on the Board would be political appointments—not opportunities to promote civil servants: this decision was reversed by the Liberal Government of 1880.[2]

[1] Cf. H. J. Laski, *Reflections on the Constitution* (Manchester University Press, 1951), p. 172.
[2] H. J. Hanham, *op. cit.*, The Historical Journal, Vol. 3, pp. 76-7.

Civil Service Reform

Yet the reforms made cannot be explained wholly in terms of Liberal dislike of favouritism or a Liberal belief in equality of opportunity. Another important influence was the growth of public business, which meant not only an increase in the number of public servants, but also that those in senior positions had to bear increased responsibilities. In the interests of economy and efficiency it became steadily more essential to obtain men of high quality: at least it was recognized that this aim was achieved better by competition than by nomination. There were also more negative reasons for change. Busy men found patronage a nuisance; the correspondence it provoked was very time-consuming. Finally, as noted above, the political gain from it had steadily disintegrated. The absence of a spoils system reduced the number and quality of jobs available. And the acceptance of the democratic assumption that political parties tend to alternate in office meant that no one believed that patronage could give a long-term advantage to Whig or Tory, Liberal or Conservative.

CHAPTER FOUR

Political Appointments

◉

Membership of Her Majesty's Government does, of course, constitute the most important class of political appointments. Within this group are a number of sub-divisions, conferring superior, intermediate and inferior status, and which form a well defined ladder of promotion for Ministers to climb. At the top are members of the Cabinet, many of whom are in charge of the more important Government departments. Below them come Ministers of the lesser departments who are outside the Cabinet. Next come the Ministers of State, a title sometimes given to the second-in-command of a large department. Next come the four Law Officers. Next are the Junior Ministers, i.e. the Under-Secretaries of State and the Parliamentary Secretaries. Last come the whips.

All these positions are filled in accordance with the wishes of the Prime Minister. The initial question in an analysis of political patronage is, therefore, how is a Prime Minister chosen? His appointment is in the hands of the Monarch who selects the man best able to command the confidence of the House of Commons. It is now an accepted convention of the constitution that the Prime Minister must belong to the Commons and not the Lords. Thus, in normal circumstances, the Prime Minister is the leader of the majority party in the House of Commons. Should no party have a majority in the Commons or if a coalition Government is formed in a time of emergency, then, as in 1916 and 1931, intricate negotiations may be needed to settle who shall head the Government. But with a two-party system firmly established the Prime Minister is likely to be the Conservative leader or the Labour leader.

The Conservative leader is elected for an unlimited term, which ends either in death or resignation. The formal election takes place at a meeting to which are invited all Peers and Members who receive the Conservative whip, all prospective candidates adopted by constituency associations and members of the Executive Committee of the National Union of Conservative and Unionist Associations. This is, indeed, a large body to assemble to elect a Leader, but the election is always pre-arranged and unanimous. The meeting is a demonstration rather than electoral college. Only once in modern times has the succession to the leadership been in doubt when the Party was in opposition, and then (1911) the two strongest contenders, Austen Chamberlain and Walter Long, both stood down to avoid a contest and Bonar Law was unanimously elected. When the Conservatives are in office the electoral college has no problem. The choice falls on the politician already nominated to be Prime Minister by the Monarch, it being understood that in cases of difficulty the Monarch will first consult with elder Conservative statesmen and, if possible, the outgoing Prime Minister. This system was demonstrated fully by the appointment in 1957 of Mr Macmillan as Prime Minister and subsequently as Leader. Do Conservative backbenchers, therefore, play no part in this process? The answer is not clear because the relative standing of the most prominent Conservatives must owe something to their reputation among parliamentarians; when it was rumoured that Sir Anthony Eden might resign many Conservative Members wrote to their Chief Whip to express a preference for Mr Macmillan rather than Mr Butler. Also, according to J. P. Mackintosh,[1] a straw poll of the Cabinet was conducted by Lords Salisbury and Kilmuir, who were excluded from consideration themselves through membership of the Lords: this poll produced only one voice in favour of Mr Butler. No doubt, this had a powerful effect on the ultimate advice given to the Queen by Lord Salisbury and Sir Winston Churchill.

The average Labour Member has more obvious influence. An annual election is held for the posts of Leader and Deputy Leader when the Party is not in office. The initial election of a Leader produces a keen contest but between 1922 and 1960 his re-election was always unopposed. Then, in 1960, Mr

[1] *The British Cabinet* (Stevens, 1962), p. 523.

Gaitskell decisively defeated Left-wing opposition. The first Chairman—the term Leader was not used until 1922—was Keir Hardie who obtained the position in 1906 by a majority of one: in 1922 MacDonald's majority over Clynes was five: in 1935 Attlee won a triangular fight against Morrison and Greenwood on the second ballot. When Labour is called upon to form the Government, the Monarch invites the Leader to become Prime Minister and the annual elections cease. In 1945 some important Labour politicians felt that the Parliamentary Labour Party should meet to choose a Leader *before* anyone accepted the post of Prime Minister,[1] but the fact that Mr Attlee did take office without re-election and without trouble has created a strong precedent for the future. To date, no Labour Prime Minister has died still in office, or resigned leaving his Party with a majority in the Commons. Thus the conditions under which Mr Macmillan followed Sir Anthony Eden have not yet arisen for the Labour Party. After the royal nomination of Mr Macmillan the Party issued a statement to indicate that should a Labour successor be sought for a Labour Prime Minister, the Parliamentary Labour Party would first proceed to elect a new Leader who would then be ready to accept the invitation of the Crown to take office.[2] Thus the rights of Labour Members have been safeguarded in advance.

Not only the appointment of a Prime Minister but those of all Ministers is technically the prerogative of the Crown.[3] A Monarch can, in Bagehot's famous phrase, 'encourage, advise and warn' when Cabinet-making is in progress, but ultimate authority rests with the Prime Minister. Queen Victoria often expressed opinions on proposed appointments; her successors have intervened less frequently. The latest recorded instance of royal advice of this nature was the suggestion of George VI to Earl (then Mr) Attlee that Mr Ernest Bevin and not Dr Hugh Dalton should become Foreign Secretary.[4] The allocation of

[1] H. Dalton, *The Fateful Years* (Muller, 1957), pp. 467 and 473.
[2] *The Times*, January 22, 1957.
[3] Apparently this does not extend to Junior Ministers: H. Morrison, *Government and Parliament* (Oxford, 1954), pp. 59-60.
[4] Sir J. Wheeler-Bennett, *King George VI* (Macmillan, 1958), pp. 638-9. See also H. Dalton, *High Tide and After* (Muller, 1962), pp. 8-13.

offices initially proposed by the Prime Minister was altered and Dr Dalton became Chancellor of the Exchequer. Earl Attlee has since denied that royal advice was the decisive cause of his change of mind: in any case, the Prime Minister is constitutionally responsible for all appointments to his Government. George VI also objected successfully in 1951 to Sir Winston Churchill's proposal to nominate Earl Avon (then Mr Eden) as Deputy Prime Minister as well as Foreign Secretary.[1] Sir Winston had a respectable basis for his suggestion since the term Deputy Prime Minister had then been in common use for a decade; this status had been commonly attributed to Mr Attlee during the war and to Mr Morrison in the post-war Labour Government. There are, however, two objections to the concept. The first, essentially theoretical, is that it may be thought to imply some limitation on the royal prerogative to choose the Prime Minister. The other is important. Were the Prime Minister accorded a formal right to choose his deputy, it might add significantly to his power to determine his successor as party leader. *De facto* it is usually clear who is the second man in the Cabinet, for someone has to take the Chair at Cabinet meetings when the Prime Minister is absent. And the nomination of Mr Butler in 1962 as First Secretary of State comes near to formal recognition of his effective status as Deputy Prime Minister.

There are no restrictions on the prerogative power to appoint Ministers but both legal and conventional limitations exist over the Prime Minister's use of political patronage. The Ministers of the Crown Act, 1937, and the subsequent amendments thereto, control the size of and number of ministerial salaries. The House of Commons Disqualification Act, 1957, restricts the total of office-holders in the Commons. This Act codified a multiplicity of legal provisions passed during the previous 250 years designed to ensure that the House of Commons should not lose its independence of thought and action through being flooded with M.P.s holding official positions.

---

[1] Wheeler-Bennett, p. 797. In December 1956, when Sir Anthony Eden was convalescing abroad, a question was asked in the Commons whether a Deputy Prime Minister would be appointed. Mr Butler replied that this office was 'not known to our constitution'. H.C. Deb., Vol. 561, cols 1448-9.

Thus, subject to exceptions for members of the Government, those holding offices of profit under the Crown were debarred from the House. Newly-appointed Ministers had to vacate their seats and stand for re-election: this rule did not, in general, apply when a Minister was moved from one office to another, nor did it apply to the Chancellor of the Exchequer or to junior Ministers. The purpose was to prevent political conversion through the offer of ministerial posts, so an M.P. on becoming a Minister had to answer for his action to his constituents. This rule was clearly inconvenient for potential Ministers. Also it sometimes had an unfortunate effect on the construction of a Cabinet, since men sitting for marginal seats might be passed over in favour of those with large majorities. As party loyalties became more intense it became unlikely that a Prime Minister would or could suborn an opponent by the offer of ministerial office. The need for the safeguard was minimized so it was first limited, then abolished, by the Re-election of Ministers Acts, 1919 and 1926.[1]

Section 2 of the House of Commons Disqualification Act prescribes that not more than seventy M.P.s can hold office in the Government. Nor may the number of Ministers, including Ministers of State, in the Commons exceed twenty-seven.[2] A parallel restriction on Parliamentary Secretaries (excluding posts at the Treasury) limits this group to thirty-three.[3] It is, of course, possible that these totals will be adjusted in future if a Prime Minister and his colleagues become convinced of the need to create more ministerial posts. However, all parties recognize the case for controlling the number of office-holders in the Commons and any proposal to permit a significant increase would probably arouse substantial resentment.

It is traditional that members of the Government should belong to one of the Houses of Parliament. An exception to

[1] In 1929, W. A. Jowitt, the newly-elected Liberal member for Preston, accepted the post of Attorney-General in MacDonald's Labour Government. Jowitt thereupon resigned his seat, although requested by the Preston Liberal Association not to do so. At the ensuing by-election he was successful as a Labour candidate. Jowitt's action, not legally necessary in 1929, was in accordance with the spirit of earlier legislation.

[2] These are the offices listed in Part I of the Second Schedule to the 1957 Act: see p. 270 *infra*.

[3] Ministers of the Crown (Parliamentary Secretaries) Act, 1960. S.I.

this principle is the Solicitor-General for Scotland, and also (1963) the Lord Advocate, owing to the limited availability of suitable Scottish lawyers. When these posts are filled from outside Parliament, attempts are made to find seats for the holders. Similarly when non-parliamentarians such as Mr Ernest Bevin and Sir James Grigg joined the war-time Churchill administration, they soon entered the Commons through convenient by-elections.

The distribution of Ministers between Lords and Commons is an important matter. One effect of the Ministers of the Crown Act, 1937, was to ensure that at least three senior Ministers would always sit in the Lords. But subsequent legislation has removed this requirement. It is still necessary for a Government to have sufficient spokesmen for their Lordships' debates. There are also specific restrictions that a Prime Minister must heed when allocating portfolios. The Lord Chancellor sits always in the Lords. The Foreign Office and the Ministry of Agriculture always have representatives in the Lords. As the Commons has primacy in finance, the Chancellor of the Exchequer, the Financial Secretary of the Treasury and the Financial Secretary of the War Office must be in the Commons. A Government will also want to have its Chief Whip, the Parliamentary Secretary of the Treasury, in the Commons. With the rise in the authority of the Commons, and the decline of the Lords, it has also been widely assumed that the political heads of major Government departments should be directly answerable to the House of Commons—an extension of the doctrine that the Prime Minister must belong to the democratic assembly. In recent years Ministers in the Lords have tended to hold such semi-sinecure posts as Lord President of the Council, Lord Privy Seal and Paymaster-General, or have supervised departments not thought to be of first class importance, e.g. Education, Science, Power and Commonwealth Relations. This situation can cause real difficulty to a Prime Minister. In 1955 Sir Anthony Eden wished to appoint Lord Salisbury to be Foreign Secretary as he had far greater experience of foreign affairs than any other possible candidate for the post. Sir Anthony's memoirs[1] contain a full statement of why

[1] *Full Circle* (Cassell, 1960), pp. 273-4.

he thought it impossible for the Foreign Secretary to be in the Lords. Important statements on foreign affairs could not be made to the Commons by a Junior Minister. A Minister of Cabinet rank must represent the Government in all important debates and—in Sir Anthony's view—that would have to be the Prime Minister himself. Sir Anthony was unwilling, quite rightly, to take on this added burden. Nor would a Foreign Secretary find it tolerable for major debates in his sphere of responsibility to take place in an assembly to which he did not belong.[1] Accordingly, Lord Salisbury was passed over and Mr Macmillan went to the Foreign Office.

A few months after the publication of these memoirs in 1960, Mr Macmillan, as Prime Minister, chose Lord Home to be Foreign Secretary and another member of the Cabinet, Mr Edward Heath, the Lord Privy Seal, was nominated as Foreign Office spokesman in the Commons. Lord Home's appointment caused a minor political storm, but there were few protests other than those from the opposition parties. To discuss the varied implications of this event would be outside the present purpose. Here it is important to note that the patronage power of the Prime Minister was able to upset easily a principle which had been widely regarded as a very necessary convention of the constitution.

What considerations guide a Prime Minister when selecting the members of his Government? The outside observer can answer this question only from observation, but certain broad tendencies are clear. First, the element of personal preference is important; a Prime Minister has his favourites, his likes and dislikes. Mr Macmillan's favours fall on the *alumni* of Eton and Harrow rather than those of Redbrick and business. In 1951 Sir Winston Churchill surrounded himself, as far as possible, with his old war-time colleagues. It is inevitable that a Prime Minister will know some of the leading members of his Party better than others; this is partly a matter of luck and partly the result of having common interests.

The extent to which the members of the present Cabinet are

[1] *Full Circle*. Lord Strang, an ex-Permanent Under-Secretary at the Foreign Office, also thought it would be impossible to have a Foreign Secretary in the Lords: cf. his *Home and Abroad* (Deutsch, 1956), p. 300.

related to each other has attracted considerable comment. The Prime Minister's son-in-law, Mr Amery, is the Minister of Aviation; his wife's nephew, the Duke of Devonshire, is the Minister of State for Commonwealth Relations. Other more distant relations of the Prime Minister are Lord Dilhorne, Lord Chancellor; the Earl of Home, Foreign Secretary; Mr Sandys, Minister for Commonwealth Relations; Mr Soames, Minister of Agriculture; Mr Wood, Minister of Power; the Marquess of Lansdowne, Minister of State for Colonial Affairs; the Marquess of Salisbury, ex-Lord President of the Council, and Lord John Hope, ex-Minister of Works. In addition, our Ambassador in Washington, Mr Ormsby-Gore, is the brother of the Prime Minister's daughter-in-law. No doubt Mr Macmillan has a conscientious conviction that all these men are admirably fitted for the jobs that they occupy, but no one can pretend that family associations have not given them some advantage in the process of catching the Prime Minister's eye. It is also of interest that these relations seem to prefer diplomacy to the administration of social services; those who live in country mansions may well feel more at home with international affairs than they do with, say, rules governing pensions. The influence of family in Cabinet-building, however, may soon decline, for none of the more important of the younger Conservative Ministers belong to the Macmillan network.

When a vacancy occurs in the lifetime of a Cabinet, it is likely that the post will be filled by a man thought to have done well in a job of lesser responsibility. Recruits to the Cabinet come normally from Ministers in charge of departments not permanently represented in the Cabinet or from the Ministers of State. Recruits to the latter categories come from among the Junior Ministers. Mr Alan Lennox-Boyd (now Viscount Boyd of Merton) is an illustration of such a career pattern: between 1938 and 1945 he was a Junior Minister in four different Government departments, subsequently he was Minister of State, Colonial Office, 1951-52, Minister of Transport (then a non-Cabinet post) 1952-54, Secretary of State for the Colonies 1954-59 and was elevated to the Lords in 1960. But this is an ideal example rather than a typical one. Not all

Junior Ministers reach Cabinet level. Some do not show the requisite ability; some lose interest in ministerial life because they can obtain greater financial rewards elsewhere; some quit office owing to disagreements with their colleagues; some fall out when the political pendulum swings against their party; some leave because of ill-health or, occasionally, because of personal disgrace. Alternatively, some Cabinet members may miss the junior Minister stage altogether. e.g. Mr Macleod and Mr Heathcote-Amory (now Viscount Amory).

In the case of junior vacancies, a Prime Minister is less likely to have personal knowledge of possible candidates. He will, therefore, take advice from his senior colleagues. A Minister may be consulted on who should fill the junior post(s) in his department. The Chief Whip may possess considerable influence, for he should know which of the backbenchers have the greatest promise. Backbenchers may come into prominence through the quality of their contributions to debates or through their activities on unofficial backbench committees. They may achieve a reputation through work as parliamentary private secretaries—unpaid and semi-official assistants to ministers. The P.P.S. to the Prime Minister has a high chance of a place in the Government. Lord Commissioners of the Treasury, the whips, are recruited from the unpaid assistant whips.

Certain jobs in the Government demand a particular type of background. The Law Officers must be lawyers of the highest calibre: sometimes they are translated to the judiciary, and this tradition is strong with the Scottish posts. The Scottish Office is usually represented in the Commons by M.P.s sitting for Scottish constituencies. A section of the Ministry of Housing and Local Government is concerned with Welsh affairs and it is desirable for it to be headed by a Welshman. As so few Conservative M.P.s are elected in Wales this creates a difficulty for a Conservative Prime Minister: Mr Macmillan's solution in 1957 was to nominate a newly-created peer, Lord Brecon, as Minister of State for Welsh Affairs.

When a fresh administration is being formed by an incoming Prime Minister there are other general considerations for him to keep in mind. He may wish to have representatives of various shades of opinion in his party included in the Cabinet. A Conservative Prime Minister is likely to include a Liberal National element into his team. A Labour Prime Minister must allocate some senior positions to trade unionists and adherents of the Co-operative Party. Since the majority of the electorate are female, a few posts are reserved for women in each Government, usually as junior Ministers. Whether a forceful advocate of extreme opinions will be less trouble inside or outside a Cabinet is a recurrent problem. On the occasions when a coalition has been formed, the distribution of offices is a matter of exceptional delicacy; the coalition Government of 1915 was nearly stillborn because of a dispute over the Irish Chancellorship.[1] It is also essential that a Prime Minister should build for for the future and give young men an opportunity to show their capacities in places of secondary responsibility. At the other end of the life-span a Prime Minister must—in the classic phrase—be a good butcher. Men of failing health can do great damage to public well-being, and if the infirm show no disposition to retire voluntarily it is the unpleasant duty of the Prime Minister to displace them.

When a party is returned to power after a long period in opposition there will be a shortage of men with experience of office. Had Earl Attlee not promoted a number of young men, the Labour Front Bench would by now be bare of ex-Cabinet Ministers. The extreme case of this nature is a party forming a Government for the first time; the MacDonald Cabinet of 1924 were nearly all newcomers to ministerial life. A party in opposition, however, prepares itself for office by forming a 'Shadow Cabinet' consisting of its leading members each of whom are deputed to speak on particular topics. A Prime Minister's choice of Ministers is not predetermined by these Shadow Cabinet responsibilities but, naturally, an M.P. who has carried a shadow portfolio successfully is a strong candidate for inclusion in the Government should his party come to power. When the Conservatives are in opposition their Shadow Cabinet, known as the 'Consultative Committee', is appointed by the Leader with whom ultimate authority rests. The Consultative Committee is also assisted by a larger body called the 'Business

[1] Lord Beaverbrook, *Politicians and the War* (Oldbourne, 1960), p. 139.

Committee' which includes the leading officials of the committees formed by backbenchers to specialize on different subjects. No limitations exist on the right of the Leader to select his colleagues and prospects of appointment depend in great measure on the personal favours of the Leader. A Labour Shadow Cabinet, the Parliamentary Committee, has a more democratic basis. It is composed of three Peers and fifteen M.P.s including the Leader of the Party, the Deputy Leader and the Chief Whip, elected annually by the Parliamentary Labour Party. The function of this Committee is to determine the policy and tactics which the Party will adopt in Parliament. The Labour Leader also nominates a Shadow Government in which one or more M.P.s are allocated a watching brief over each ministry. The Shadow Government is much larger than the Parliamentary Committee and numbered forty-six in 1959. Thus in a Labour opposition, a process of election helps to determine both the colour of Party policy and the selection of its spokesmen. A comparison of voting figures at the annual elections can be used to show whether advocates of a particular viewpoint are gaining in popularity, and this imposes a type of pressure on a Labour Leader unknown to a Leader of the Conservatives. A Labour Prime Minister still has complete discretion to choose members of his Government as he sees fit, but it is also true that when Labour backbenchers elect their Parliamentary Committee each year they are, in fact, selecting potential Ministers. There is no indication, however, that the British Labour Party will ever follow the practice of their Australian brothers by which a Labour Cabinet is chosen at a party meeting and the authority of the Leader is limited to deciding the size of his Cabinet and the allocating of portfolios.

The table on page 74 shows that in 1936 there were twenty-two members of the Cabinet, and in 1962 it numbered twenty-one. This could leave a mistaken impression that the size of the Cabinet had been constant throughout the period. In fact, there have been considerable changes in its size and structure as different Prime Ministers have had varied ideas on how best to conduct ministerial business. The Cabinet consists of such members of the Privy Council as the Prime Minister chooses to invite, so he can, without constitutional hindrance, manipulate it to suit his wishes. The Churchill war-time Cabinet initially had five members, four of whom —following the Lloyd George precedent of 1916—were free of departmental responsibilities. Gradually the pattern changed and the war-time Cabinet grew to ten ministers each of whom had specific responsibilities, but the Government departments that had no major rôle in the war effort were not represented in the Cabinet. From 1945 to 1959 Cabinets were smaller than pre-1939 and had between sixteen and eighteen members; the number did not reach twenty again until 1960. The 1951 Churchill Cabinet was peculiar by reason of its system of 'Overlords'. The 'Overlords' were Peers responsible for representing departments in the Cabinet and for co-ordinating their work. They were, therefore, the 'Overlords' of Ministers not included in the Cabinet: the Minister of Defence supervised the three Service Departments, the Lord President of the Council had special responsibility for the Ministries of Food and Agriculture and the Secretary of State for the Co-ordination of Transport, Fuel and Power had a title both novel and self-explanatory. Since the Ministers excluded by this device from the Cabinet were said still to be wholly responsible to Parliament for the work of their departments, the Overlord system was confusing and gave rise to much criticism. After two years it broke down. Yet the 1951 Cabinet is a patent demonstration of how a Prime Minister, firmly in charge of but a slim Parliamentary majority, can manipulate both the personnel and structure of his Cabinet to suit his personal wishes. At one stage seven out of the seventeen members of this Cabinet were peers, thus forming the most aristocratic Cabinet of the twentieth century.

How the Government has grown in recent years can be seen from the table on page 74.

In addition to the positions listed it is the custom to nominate some unpaid assistant whips in the Commons; there were two in 1936 and six in 1962. Reference to the table will show that the major contribution to the rise in numbers has been the increase in non-Cabinet Ministers. This has two causes. More Ministers in charge of departments are omitted from the Cabinet: in particular, the three Service Ministers

THE SIZE OF THE GOVERNMENT
1936 AND 1962

Category	1936 In Commons	1936 In Lords	Total	1962 In Commons	1962 In Lords	Total
Cabinet Ministers	17	5	22	18	3	21
Non-Cabinet Ministers	4	1	5	10	8	18
Law Officers	3	—	4*	3	—	4*
Junior Ministers	19	4	23	30	4	34
Lords Commissioners (Whips)	3	—	3	5	—	5
Officers of the Household†	3	5	8	3	5	8
Totals	49	15	65	69	20	90

* The Solicitor-General for Scotland was not a member of either House of Parliament.

† In 1924 the Labour Prime Minister Ramsay MacDonald proposed that all Household appointments become non-political. The King arranged for other party leaders to be consulted on this question. Asquith agreed with Lloyd George, but Balfour thought these posts were useful sops for rewarding supporters unfitted for ministerial office. A compromise was reached that six Household posts should be political (H. Nicolson, *King George V*, pp. 390-1). The number was raised as soon as the Conservatives returned to power. The Household Officers act as whips, and in the Lords, where whipping duties are light, they are also used as Government spokesmen.

have not been included since 1946. Also there has been the post-war invention of the Minister of State as second-in-command of a department. This device was originally used to give higher status to Junior Ministers who were often required to represent this country abroad, but it has now extended to Ministers concerned with domestic business.

Outside the Government, three important posts filled by M.P.s are those of Speaker and his two deputies, the Chairman of Committees and the Deputy Chairman. Technically these are filled by a vote of the Commons but the effective selection is in the hands of Ministers. The Speaker is, by tradition, politically neutral and takes no part in controversial business. His task is to apply the rules of the Commons impartially to all members. Since he is accepted as a non-party man he does not lose his place when the political complexion of the Government ment changes. On the resignation of a Speaker the office is filled from the majority party in the Commons; there has not yet been a Labour Speaker as no vacancy has occurred when Labour held a majority. No clear rules guide the choice of a Speaker. In the first half of this century the post was filled by the promotion of a Deputy Speaker, but in 1951 the Churchill Government chose Mr W. S. Morrison, who had no experience of the Chair, but who had occupied a variety of ministerial posts in Conservative and Coalition governments prior to 1945. This was the first time since 1872 that a man with ministerial experience had become Speaker. In 1959 the Solicitor-General, Sir Harry Hylton-Foster, was chosen. On this occasion it was understood that the Government were willing to nominate Sir Frank Soskice, a member of the Opposition Front Bench and a Law Officer in the Attlee Government; but Sir Frank declined. Since the duty of a Speaker is to protect the rights of private members of the House it would seem unfortunate for a man with a ministerial background to be chosen. However, of all Ministers, a Law Officer is the least objectionable; as a legal adviser to the Government he should be well-versed in the art of separating the legal and political aspects of any issue. Certainly the Speakership should not be used to accommodate senior ex-Ministers who, for one reason or another, are no longer required in the Cabinet. It is often said that a Government should be guided by Parliamentary opinion as to the most suitable occupant of the Chair. But when, as was the case in 1951 and 1959, the Speaker retires at a dissolution and a new Parliament chooses the successor, it is not easy to consult Parliamentary opinion. In any case, such consultation must always be informal and private, so can there be any guarantee that it is genuine and not merely a cover to provide an appearance of support for the ministerial nominee?

The Deputy Speakerships are political prizes in the sense that they change hands when the party in office is replaced by another. Thus two supporters of the Government, back-benchers with considerable Parliamentary experience, are chosen for these posts. There have been two recent exceptions to this rule: in 1950 the Labour Government chose a Conservative to be Deputy Chairman and in 1951 the Conservatives chose a Liberal. The reason was the narrowness of the Government majority after the elections of 1950 and 1951. The Speaker and the deputies never vote and the Government could not afford to 'waste' three of their supporters in these positions. More recently, in 1962, it was reported that Mr W. R. Williams (Lab., Manchester, Openshaw) had refused the post of Deputy Chairman. According to *The Observer* (January 21, 1962) the Prime Minister had made this offer to smooth the path of Government legislation through the Commons. The move to appoint Mr Williams can be interpreted as a demonstration of political goodwill or of support for the tradition of political impartiality by the Chair, but the appointment could scarcely have had any significant effect on the behaviour of the Opposition. Yet the circumstances surrounding this business are curious. It seems that the offer was made twice; first, the invitation went via Mr Gaitskell as Leader of the Labour Party, who consulted Mr Williams before sending a negative response, and then a direct approach was made to Mr Williams which produced a second refusal. Party manoeuvre and suspicion have become very prominent since 1951 in relation to the occupancy of the Chair—a most unhealthy development.

It has already been noted that an M.P. who is appointed to an Office of Profit—as defined by The House of Commons Disqualification Act, 1957—automatically loses his seat. Thus the Government cannot purchase support in the House through the use of patronage. During the war this principle was waived by an Act of 1941 which exempted from disqualification M.P.s who received a certificate from the Prime Minister that their appointments were required in the public interest to assist the prosecution of the war. A Select Committee of the House had agreed previously that the normal disqualification rule should not operate in the war-time emergency, but it was also deeply concerned to preserve the independence of the House. It recommended that M.P.s holding extraordinary war-time posts should refrain from addressing the House and from voting on matters connected with their official duties, unless convinced that their so doing would receive the general assent of the House or was urgently

Political Appointments

APPOINTMENT OF M.P.s TO
NON-MINISTERIAL POSTS
1945-62

LABOUR GOVERNMENT

Year	Name	Constituency	Pty	Prev. Post(s)*	New Appointm't
1946	E. J. Williams	Ogmore	Lab.	Minister of Information	High Commissioner, Australia
	Mrs J. Adamson	Bexley	Lab.	—	Deputy Chairman, National Assistance Board
	F. C. R. Douglas	Battersea N.	Lab.	—	Governor of Malta
	Sir Ben Smith	Rotherhithe	Lab.	Minister of Food	Chairman, W. Midland Divisional Coal Board
1947	T. Smith	Normanton	Lab.	—	Labour Director, N.E. Regional Coal Board
	G. R. Thomson, K.C.	Edinburgh E.	Lab.	Lord Advocate	Lord Justice Clerk
1948	G. Buchanan	Glasgow, Gorbals	Lab.	Minister of Pensions	Chairman, National Assistance Board
1949	J. S. C. Reid, K.C.	Glasgow, Hillhead	Con.	Solicitor-General for Scotland, 1936-41	Lord of Appeal
	J. J. Lawson	Chester-le-Street	Lab.	Secretary of State for War, 1945-46	Vice-Chairman, National Parks Commission
1950	T. N. Donovan, K.C.	Leicester N.E.	Lab.	—	High Court Judge
1951	Sir Ronald Cross	Ormskirk	Con.	High Commissioner in Australia, 1941-45	Governor of Tasmania
	Sir Ronald Ross	Londonderry	U.U	—	Northern Ireland Government Agent in London

77

APPOINTMENT OF M.P.s TO
NON-MINISTERIAL POSTS
1945-62
(continued)

CONSERVATIVE GOVERNMENT

Year	Name	Constituency	Pty	Prev. Post(s)*	New Appointm't
1954	Sir Geoffrey Hutchinson, Q.C.	Ilford N.	Con.	—	Chairman, National Assistance Board
	J. Wheatley, Q.C.	Edinburgh E.	Lab.	Lord Advocate, 1947-51	Senator of the College of Justice in Scotland
	J. L. Clyde, Q.C.	Edinburgh N.	Con.	Lord Advocate	Lord Justice General and President of the Court of Session
1956	B. Nield, Q.C.	Chester	Con.	Recorder of Salford	Recorder of Manchester
1957	P. Buchan-Hepburn	Beckenham	Con.	Patronage Secretary, 1951-55	Governor-General of West Indies
1960	W. R. Milligan, Q.C.	Edinburgh N.	Con.	Lord Advocate	Judge of the Court of Session
	P. I. Bell, Q.C.	Bolton E.	Con.	—	County Court Judge
	A. Robens	Blyth	Lab.	Minister of Labour, 1951	Chairman, National Coal Board
	A. Head	Carshalton	Con.	Secretary of State for War, 1951-56; Minister of Defence, 1956-57	High Commissioner, Nigeria
	S. G. Howard, Q.C.	Cambridgeshire	Con.	—	High Court Judge
1961	D. H. Johnston, Q.C.	Paisley	Lab.	Solicitor-General for Scotland, 1947-51	Judge of the Court of Session

Year	Name	Constituency	Pty	Prev. Post(s)*	New Appointm't
	C. J. M. Alport	Colchester	Con.	Minister of State Commonwealth Relations Office	High Commissioner, Central African Federation
	W. D. Ormsby-Gore	Oswestry	Con.	Minister of State Foreign Office	Ambassador to the United States
	W. D. Sumner	Orpington	Con.	—	County Court Judge
	G. de Freitas	Lincoln	Lab.	Junior Minister, 1946-51	High Commissioner, Ghana
1962	Sir Jocelyn Simon, Q.C.	Middlesbro' W.	Con.	Solicitor-General	President, Probate, Divorce, Admiralty Division
	Sir Edward Wakefield	Derbyshire W.	Con.	Government Whip	High Commissioner, Malta
	Sir Lynn Ungoed-Thomas, Q.C.	Leicester N.E.	Lab.	Solicitor-General, 1951	High Court Judge
	W. Grant, Q.C.	Glasgow, Woodside	Con.	Lord Advocate	Lord Justice Clerk

* This column is not exhaustive: it records only the most important or most relevant posts. If no date is given the post immediately preceded the appointment.

necessary in the national interest.[1] Between 1945 and 1955 a number of cases arose in which an M.P. was found to be disqualified through some petty office, e.g. membership of a rent tribunal,[2] and the 1957 Act was passed to clarify the law.[3] Another safeguard is that an M.P. cannot be appointed to a disqualifying office without his consent.

None of this, however, would prevent a Government from distributing lucrative jobs, or honours, to M.P.s as a reward for

[1] Report, para. 86; 1940-41 (120) iii.
[2] For details see my *Honourable Members* (Faber, 1959), pp. 60-1.
[3] The present list of disqualifying officers is given in the Appendix, pp. 259-71.

loyal support in the past: the knowledge that such rewards were commonly available could well influence political conduct. Honours are dealt with in a subsequent chapter. Here it is necessary to show the position in relation to jobs. On pages 77-9 is a list of cases since 1945 in which the appointment of a member of the Commons to an office of profit has necessitated a by-election. This list does not include vacancies caused by elevation to the peerage, nor does it include appointments received by M.P.s after retirement from the Commons.[1]

In these thirty-one cases, two main categories are discernible. There were fourteen legal appointments, exactly half of them in Scotland. The other group are the nine overseas appointments, mainly for ex-Ministers. Among the remaining posts the only one that has any resemblance to a political 'prize' is the Chairmanship of the National Assistance Board. Both Labour and Conservative Governments occasionally offer jobs to their opponents; the appointment of Mr Robens to the National Coal Board being an outstanding example. Between 1945 and 1959 the appointments averaged roughly one per year. In the 1960s the figure has risen sharply. It is impossible to judge whether this change is fortuitous or whether it has arisen from a deliberate change in policy. A party that has been in office for a long period must find increasing difficulty in providing rewards for its leading supporters. And a party with a majority of 100 seats in the Commons will be less concerned by the prospect of extra by-elections. In any case, jobs are not offered to Members with marginal seats; this is not through machiavellian calculation but because the representatives of marginal constituencies tend to be less senior parlia-

---

[1] The most controversial appointment for an ex-member in recent years was that of Lord Dunrossil (previously Speaker Morrison) to be Governor-General of Australia. A Speaker, in common with the Prime Minister and the Lord Chancellor, receives a pension upon retirement in recognition of past services and in order to obviate any need to seek further employment. In the case of the Speaker the pension also ensures that financial pressure will not cause him to seek the favour of Ministers. The post of Governor-General of Australia is a Crown appointment, but is made on the advice of Australian Ministers and is in no sense the responsibility of the British Cabinet. Even so, there was much feeling on the Opposition benches that this appointment was unfortunate. (Cf. H.C. Deb., Vol. 613, cols. 610-20, 1170-238; and Vol. 614, cols. 219-45.)

mentarians.[1] The table shows that the sneers sometimes heard
in the post-war period about 'jobs for the boys' had an
extremely slender basis as far as M.P.s were concerned. Yet
the more recent tendency to allot diplomatic and judicial posts
to our elected representatives has obvious dangers.

II

For over two and a half centuries statutes have restricted the
number of office-holders who can sit in the Commons. All
shades of political opinion accept that these measures are
essential to preserve the independence of the legislature. The
law on this subject was codified afresh in 1957 and is rigidly
adhered to. But there are two types of position which, not
being offices of profit, fall outside the disqualification law but
which are also inimical to its purpose. The two positions are
unpaid-assistant whip and Parliamentary Private Secretary.

The duties of unpaid whips are similar to those of the whips
holding office. They have a group of about twenty-five M.P.s
to 'look after': they are expected to know the physical where-
abouts of members of their flock, to have a fair idea of their
opinions on most subjects and to be able to get the flock into
the right division lobby at the right time.[2] Since the war there
have always been three or four unpaid whips but recently the
total has reached six. It must be a matter of conjecture whether
the extra men (female whips are unknown) were required to
deal with the additional twenty-three Conservatives returned
at the 1959 Election, or whether the Government decided that
yet more intensive whipping was needed to cover current
political stresses. In future, will one whip be appointed for
each twenty-five seats a Government wins at a General Election? There is no statutory barrier to this happening. It can
be urged that a Government is less in need of efficient whip-

[1] In 1962 Government candidates at by-elections fared extremely badly.
Three of the contests that caused the greatest embarrassment for Ministers
were caused by Government appointments, i.e. Orpington, Middlesbrough
West and West Derbyshire. But in the exceptional conditions of 1962 a large
majority of Conservative seats became marginal.
[2] For a fuller discussion of the activities of whips see my *Honourable
Members*, pp. 143-6.

ping as the size of its Parliamentary majority increases—but it does not follow that a Chief Whip would view the situation in this light.

A vacancy for a paid whip is filled by the unpaid whip with the longest period of service. Thus the unpaid whips form a queue waiting for office. They have, of course, no formal promise of office but they tend to be a group of probationers with high prospects of advancement if they do well enough and wait long enough. Already they appear in the list of Ministers officially published in Hansard. It is very arguable that these appointments are contrary to the spirit of the House of Commons Disqualification Act, and as the queue of unpaid whips lengthens another difficulty emerges. Unless vacancies occur regularly, so that the queue can move forward, an assistant whip will remain unpaid for many years. Since they are not barred, as are office-holders, from other remunerative activities, the slowness of promotion might not matter much in financial terms. But there can be no doubt that a Conservative Government feels some obligation to these men, and it is met, in part, by the promotion of paid whips to other junior ministerial posts when opportunity offers. Thus the Conservative Whips' Room is a recognized channel of political promotion.

Another large group of M.P.s, the Parliamentary Private Secretaries, are closely associated with the Government. A P.P.S. is a personal assistant of a Minister; the post is unpaid and carries no official status. His general function is to provide the Minister with information on opinion in the Commons on matters relating to the latter's department.[1] Backbenchers who wish to raise a problem with a Minister often make their approach through his P.P.S. These liaison duties are another training ground for future office-holders. The P.P.S. to the Prime Minister has a great likelihood of entering the Government and those serving other senior Ministers often do so. An M.P. who becomes a P.P.S. must accept certain limitations that are conventional. He must not speak in the Commons on the work of the department with which he is associated; on other

[1] For a fuller discussion of the rôle of the P.P.S., see *Honourable Members*, pp. 207-8.

matters he should show restraint. The doctrine of collective responsibility—which binds Ministers to support each other on all occasions—now tends to engulf P.P.S.s; the five who voted against the Labour Government in 1948 on the Government of Ireland Bill did not keep their positions.

Ministers in the Commons, the Law Officers and some Junior Ministers each have a P.P.S. The total is now about thirty-five. It is easy to understand why the P.P.S. system has grown. Ministers find the service useful; for new backbenchers it provides wider experience and perhaps opportunity; it eases the task of the whips. The disadvantage is that by adding to the total of M.P.s attached to the Government, the P.P.S. system weakens the prospect of initiative and criticism from Government supporters in the Commons. In a period when the Government has a firm Parliamentary majority, this is particularly undesirable. Disquiet about the increase in P.P.S.s was expressed by the Select Committee on Offices of Profit in 1940,[1] and the Attlee Labour Government limited them to one per department.[2] Under the Conservatives this rule has disappeared. It should be re-introduced. And why does a Law Officer need a political *aide*?

The House of Commons Disqualification Act limits the total of office-holders in the Commons to seventy. But when the unpaid whips and the P.P.S.s are added to the members of the Government, the number of M.P.s associated with the Ministry is seen to be about 110. The Disqualification Act is partially ineffective because the limitation it imposed is based on receipt of financial reward. In modern conditions financial reward is no longer a main inducement to achieve political office because the salaries offered have not been adjusted to accord with changes in the value of money. The Lord Chancellor with £12,000 p.a. enjoys the highest ministerial salary; this figure is made up by a judge's salary of £8,000 together with another £4,000 as Speaker of the House of Lords. The Prime Minister receives £10,000, the other Ministers get £5,000, Ministers

---

[1] Report, para. 24; 1940-41 (120) iii.
[2] Cf. E. C. S. Wade and G. G. Phillips, *Constitutional Law*, 4th Ed. (Longmans Green, 1950), p. 85.

of State £3,750, Junior Ministers £2,500 and whips £2,000.[1] In addition, Ministers who sit in the Commons have an extra £750 p.a. which is a part of the normal M.P.'s pay of £1,750. Since 1956 the pay of a Minister in charge of a department has been below that of the top civil servant in it, the Permanent Secretary. Before 1957 the total remuneration of Junior Ministers was as low as £2,000 p.a. and for many years they have received less than under-secretaries, the third rank in the Civil Service hierarchy. The pattern is indefensible. A man in a position of authority should not be treated worse than his advisers. One is reluctant to urge anything that would add to the weight of patronage: nevertheless, a Minister should have a higher salary than his Permanent Secretary. Some improvement for Junior Ministers is also due.

The other major financial drawback of political office is that members of the Government have to abandon all other lucrative employment, including company directorships except those connected with the maintenance of private family estates or with philanthropic undertakings.[2] A Minister must also give up the controlling interest in any company and sell any shares he may hold in companies concerned with the business of his own department.[3] Thus to accept ministerial office may entail financial sacrifice. A steady trickle of Conservative Ministers return to business or the Bar: money is now an inducement to leave office—not to seek it. M.P.s still have political ambitions, but these are activated by a desire for influence or prestige or

[1] The annual salaries of the Law Officers are: Attorney-General £10,000, Solicitor-General £7,000, Lord Advocate £5,000, Solicitor-General for Scotland £3,750. The three Junior Ministers at the Treasury, the Parliamentary, Financial and Economic Secretaries, get the pay of Ministers of State.

[2] For a full examination of this topic see D. C. M. Platt, 'The Commercial and Industrial Interests of Ministers of the Crown' in *Political Studies*, Vol. IX, pp. 267-90.

[3] On January 28, 1960, Mr Marples, who had become Minister of Transport three months earlier, explained to the Commons that he was taking steps to sell his shares—which constituted a controlling interest—in Marples, Ridgway and Partners, a firm concerned with civil engineering. Mr Marples also told the House that 'the prospective purchasers have required me to undertake to buy the shares back from them at the price they are to pay if they ask me to do so after I have ceased to hold office'. (H.C. Deb., Vol. 616, col. 381.) In these circumstances Mr Marples still appears to have an interest in the financial success of this firm.

perhaps a selfless urge to serve their fellows. Under these circumstances, legislation about offices of profit cannot effectively restrict the growth of ministerial influence over the back benches. What is needed is a self-denying ordinance by Ministers to curtail the number of unpaid semi-official posts made available for M.P.s.

It cannot be doubted that the Prime Minister's patronage power helps to strengthen Party solidarity among M.P.s supporting the Government. A journey through the wrong division lobby is not likely to increase the chances of securing political advancement. This might be made clear by a whip to an M.P. contemplating rebellion. On the other hand there are important limits to any attempt to apply pressure of this kind. Office cannot be a normal reward for loyalty because there are insufficient offices to go round, although there are quite enough to feed the hopes of the ambitious. Some M.P.s who have been on the backbenches for many years know they have no chance of joining the Government and others may not want to. In 1962, after the Macmillan massacre, there were no fewer than forty-eight ex-Ministers on the Conservative benches, some of whom had left office for financial reasons. Thus the carrots of patronage are limited in both number and sweetness. They may also be used for political purposes in quite another way: a Prime Minister might decide to try to stifle the most damaging critics in his own party by the offer of a place in the Government. This technique has obvious dangers. It might well encourage M.P.s with strong ambitions to try to make sufficient nuisances of themselves to attract the gag of office. Certainly, Mr Macmillan has shown no tendency to ostracize those who have disagreed with him in the past. Thus three Ministers, Sir Edward Boyle, Mr Thorneycroft and Mr Powell, who had previously resigned on issues of policy, have been asked to return to his Government. Sir Edward Boyle's resignation was in protest against the British intervention in Suez; on returning to the Government Sir Edward stated that he recanted nothing of his views on that matter.[1] But the central fact is that in a two-party system the Prime Minister is

[1] *The Times*, January 19, 1957.

normally so secure politically that he can choose his Ministers without reference to such tactical considerations.

Many works on British Government describe the Prime Minister as *primus inter pares* with his Cabinet. By this is meant that the Prime Minister is not chosen personally by the electorate, like a President of the United States, and that the Prime Minister is responsible together with his Ministers to Parliament for all his actions. Yet *primus inter pares* is a serious underestimate of the Prime Minister's position. Because of his office, all his activities are news. The techniques of modern publicity build up his personality so that voters may feel well acquainted with him. His qualities are blazoned abroad; his weaknesses, if he has any, tend to be covered by the decencies of public life. He is identified indissolubly with the public image of his party; should he be judged a failure, the party suffers. There is, in consequence, much reason for all party supporters to keep their leader's reputation shining bright. Other Cabinet Ministers can disappear from office with scarcely a ripple of interest—for example the eclipse of Lord Salisbury in 1957. Not so the Prime Minister, for his pinnacle commands a degree of attention unique among politicians.

The Prime Minister's position in relation to senior members of his party is strengthened further by the patronage power. Harold Laski argued 'that about half the Cabinet nominates itself by the standing of its members in the eyes of the party'.[1] This is true for the moment at which a Prime Minister first forms his Cabinet—but not afterwards. Once established in Downing Street, the Prime Minister, to borrow Greaves' phrase, ceases to be the creature of his creators.[2] He has a much freer hand to deal with the vacancies that occur. He can cling to his old friends or promote younger men. He can surround himself in the senior Cabinet positions with those whom he judges will not seriously oppose his will. He can create an informal 'inner Cabinet' that is highly influential. He may, as Mr Gaitskell put it, 'refuse to exercise unfair discrimination against relatives'.[3] He may, indeed, transform the Government

[1] *Parliamentary Government in England* (Allen & Unwin, 1938), p. 239.
[2] *The British Constitution* (Allen & Unwin, 1938), p. 115.
[3] H.C. Deb., Vol. 629, col. 18 (November 1, 1960).

overnight. The Cabinet reshuffle of July 1962 provides a dramatic illustration of the Prime Minister's authority: seven out of twenty-one members of the Cabinet were removed, together with many other Ministers in lesser positions. Granted a firm party majority in the House of Commons, the Prime Minister's position is unassailable unless he is repeatedly and patently unsuccessful.

Only once in this century has a Prime Minister been displaced by a revolt among his Cabinet or his party. The fall of Asquith in 1916 is the single example.[1] It is also peculiarly instructive. The Cabinet of 1916 was a coalition and the Prime Minister was replaced by the combination of his Liberal second-in-command, Lloyd George, with the Conservative Leader, Bonar Law, who felt jointly that Asquith was ineffective in his direction of the war effort. When Asquith resigned office he appears to have believed himself irreplaceable, and expected to be re-summoned by the King to form a new Government. However, once he resigned he forfeited the patronage power, which passed to his opponents. A group of senior Conservative ministers who, in the immediate past, had been extremely hostile to Lloyd George as an intriguer, agreed to serve under the Welshman. Asquith miscalculated because he failed to recognize the influence of patronage. Had he not resigned, it is by no means clear, in retrospect, that Bonar Law and Lloyd George could have forced him out of office.

There has also been a single case where a party leader in office, but not a Prime Minister, was overthrown by his followers. In 1922 Austen Chamberlain ceased to be the Conservative Leader after a meeting of Conservative M.P.s at the Carlton Club refused to accept his advice that they should fight the coming election under the banner of the Lloyd George coalition. The meeting decided by a majority of more than two to one that the Conservatives should go to the electorate as a separate party, and Bonar Law replaced Chamberlain as Leader. Chamberlain's situation in this conflict was weakened by two factors. He did not possess the prestige and patronage

---

[1] Mr Ramsay MacDonald may have been 'persuaded' to retire in 1935. But in reality, he had been a prisoner of the Conservative majority in the Commons and Cabinet ever since the Election of 1931.

of a Prime Minister, and his policy ensured that there was no prospect that he would obtain that office in the foreseeable future. Those who opposed him were urging a policy which could, and did, bring their party the full fruits of victory. Thus, in these peculiar circumstances, the compulsion of patronage worked against and not in favour of the original Leader.

It is notable that party leaders in opposition are most subject to attack in the period immediately after the loss of a general elecion, as witness the experience of Balfour in 1912, Baldwin in 1930 and, more recently, Mr Gaitskell. The prestige of a leader who has lost an election is necessarily somewhat battered and he is unusually vulnerable. Also he has no chance of obtaining the Premiership for, at best, three years, therefore there is no immediate prospects that he will be able to distribute ministerial offices. But the Leader of the Opposition is not without patronage: he can assign 'shadow' portfolios which are often an important stepping stone in a political career. The right of a Labour Leader to nominate 'shadow' ministers is restricted a little by the Party's system of electing its Parliamentary Committee or Shadow Cabinet, but now that the total size of the 'shadow' Government is about forty-six, the Leader can offer partial promotion from the back-benches to roughly thirty M.P.s It is arguable that this had a marginal influence—but certainly not a decisive one—on Mr Gaitskell's victory over Mr Wilson in the contest for the Leadership in 1960.

To summarize, the argument of this section has been that patronage, even with unpaid posts, is used to strengthen ministerial control over the Commons to an unhealthy degree. Further, in combination with other factors, patronage helps to promote the authority of the Prime Minister over his Cabinet colleagues. This has led to an increasing concentration of power with its obvious disadvantages. M.P.s may select their leaders with great shrewdness, but once established the latter are difficult to replace. A Prime Minister may make serious errors because he is aged or ailing; his judgment of men may become less acute; he may fail to detect sycophants. It is important that these dangers are recognized, even if no new safeguards against them appear politically practicable.

CHAPTER FIVE

Administrative Boards

⊙

It is a commonplace that the great expansion in the activities of the State during this century has led to vast developments in the machinery of public administration. In consequence there has been growth in the number and size of ministerial departments. There have been created also many boards and commissions with differing degrees of independence from ministerial supervision. Whether functions should be removed from direct ministerial authority has been a matter of controversy. The Haldane Committee firmly opposed the creation of administrative boards,[1] but their opinion has been ignored consistently. On some matters Ministers have thought it politic to avoid the possibility of detailed Parliamentary questioning. Public opinion has also welcomed boards as a device for checking the growth of power in the hands of Ministers. Practical advantages may accrue from the dispersal of administrative functions and also from the introduction of persons into the public service who are neither politicians nor established civil servants. Thus the boards have grown and prospered,[2] and they form an important branch of ministerial patronage.

There is great variety in the constitution and functions of administrative boards. No complete list can be given. Some idea of their range is obtainable from the Appendix which shows the offices that involve disqualification from the House of Commons. For the most part, these constitute 'offices of profit', but the list includes a few bodies membership of which, although unpaid, is thought to be incompatible with a seat in the

[1] Machinery of Government Committee. Report, p. 11; 1918 Cd. 9230, xii.
[2] For greater details see F. M. G. Willson, 'Ministries and Boards: Some Aspects of Administrative Development since 1832' in *Public Administration*, Spring 1955, Vol. XXXIII, pp. 43-58.

Commons; leading examples are the Public Works Loan Board and the Forestry Commission.[1] The boards defy generalizations. In some cases membership implies full-time service; more frequently it involves part-time duties. It has already been noted that some positions are paid and some are not. Naturally, the whole-time jobs are salaried. With part-time posts the question of remuneration seems to depend on the extent of the duties and the purpose of the organization. It is usual for trading concerns—the public corporations—to pay their part-time members, but social welfare institutions, e.g. Hospital Boards, may run on voluntary service. Certainly this is a field that bristles with anomalies, both as to amounts of payment and whether payment is made at all. Many of the full-time posts go to those already in the public service and this category includes, of course, those promoted from a board's own staff. Usually the whole of a board is appointed by one Minister but there are cases where more than one Minister is concerned or where part of the board is not nominated by a Minister. The constitution of the Racecourse Betting Control Board combines these possibilities: two members are appointed by the Home Secretary, one each by the Chancellor of the Exchequer, the Secretary of State for Scotland and the Minister of Agriculture, while the other seven members are chosen by the Jockey Club, the National Hunt Committee, the Racecourse Association Ltd and Tattersall's Committee. There are also 104 public companies which have Government-appointed directors on their boards; some of these are research organizations, e.g. the Plant Breeding Institute, but others are large industrial firms like British Petroleum: the people chosen are either civil servants, acting *ex officio*, or 'outsiders' usually businessmen or scientists.[2]

The largest group of administrative boards is that concerned with commerce, finance and industry. Agriculture and fishing

[1] The Chairman of the Forestry Commission receives a salary. There is also power under the Forestry Act, 1945, to pay salaries to other members. Thus if Forestry Commissioners were not disqualified it would be open theoretically for a Government to pack the Commission with back-bench supporters and pay handsome salaries as a price for political loyalty.
[2] Cf. H.C.Deb., Vol. 620, cols. 193-204. The Government also appoints directors to some private companies under the Distribution of Industry Acts.

have also produced a substantial crop. The social welfare group is rather smaller and covers the National Assistance Board, the National Parks Commission and, at the local level, the Regional Hospital Boards. The New Town Development Corporations may be thought of as a welfare service or a trading undertaking; as each town is completed its Corporation will be disbanded and the assets handed over to the Commission for New Towns. Three other main groups of administrative agencies may be distinguished; nationalized industries, wages councils, whose task is negotiation rather than administration,[1] and institutions that can be classified only as miscellaneous. Into this category fall the War Works Commission, the Arts Council and the British Council. The latter is an interesting illustration of how a voluntary body financed by private donations can become virtually a Government agency, for its revenue is derived almost entirely from public funds and a number of Departments nominate members of the Council.

The table overleaf shows the appointing authority for the more important boards and the statutory limits imposed on their size. In a few cases the dignity of the Crown is invoked in the machinery of appointment and the nominations are made on the advice of the Minister most closely concerned with the particular organization. The University Grants Committee is a case apart, as there is no statutory basis for its existence. It was created in 1919 to advise the Treasury on the distribution of public funds to universities; since then the importance of its work and the scale of its activities have increased greatly, but have never been given legal definition. This omission is deliberate. To make more specific the powers of the U.G.C. might well damage the independence of universities.

Statutes do not normally prescribe the salaries paid to board members; these are left to be determined by the Treasury. However, the National Assistance Act, 1948, provides that the total salaries of members of the National Assistance Board shall not exceed £12,000 p.a. Pensions rights are also available for

---

[1] There are about 60 wages councils appointed by the Minister of Labour which contain representatives of both sides of industry and some 'independent' members on each. These 'independents' total about 180. Cf. 'Government by Appointment', *Planning*, No. 443, p. 212 (P.E.P., 1960).

APPOINTMENTS TO THE MAJOR
ADMINISTRATIVE BOARDS

Authority	*Created**	*Appointed by*	*Number of Members*
Agricultural Land Commission	1947	Minister of Agriculture	4-7
Atomic Energy Authority	1954	Minister for Science	8-11
Bank of England	1946	Her Majesty	18
British Broadcasting Corporation	1926	Her Majesty	9
British European Airways Corporation	1946	Minister of Aviation	6-12
British Overseas Airways Corporation	1946	Minister of Aviation	6-12
British Transport Commission	1947	Minister of Transport	5-15
Colonial Development Corporation	1948	Colonial Secretary	6-12
Commission for New Towns	1959	Minister of Housing and Local Government	up to 15
Cotton Board	1948	Board of Trade	11
Crofters Commission	1955	Secretary of State for Scotland	up to 6
Electricity: Central Generating Board	1957	Minister of Power	8-10
Area Boards†	1947	Minister of Power	each 7-9
Forestry Commission	1945	Her Majesty	up to 10
Gas: Area Boards	1948	Minister of Power	each 7-9
Herring Industry Board	1935	Minister of Agriculture Secretary of State for Scotland	up to 8
Independent Television Authority	1954	Postmaster-General	5-8
Iron and Steel Board	1953	Minister of Power	10-15
Iron and Steel Holding and Realization Agency	1953	Treasury	4-7
London Transport Executive	1947	Minister of Transport	5-9

Administrative Boards

Authority	Created	Appointed by	Number of Members
National Assistance Board	1948	Her Majesty	3-6
National Coal Board	1947	Minister of Power	9-12
National Dock Labour Board	1946	Minister of Labour	10-12
National Film Finance Corporation	1949	Board of Trade	5-7
National Parks Commission	1949	Minister of Housing and Local Government / Secretary of State for Scotland	no limit
New Town Corporations	1946	Ministry of Housing and Local Government / Secretary of State for Scotland	each up to 9
Sugar Board	1956	Minister of Agriculture	up to 5
University Grants Committee	1919	Chancellor of the Exchequer	no limit
White Fish Authority	1951	Minister of Agriculture / Minister of Transport	5

* The date in this column shows when the authority acquired its present constitutional structure.

† The South of Scotland Electricity Board and the North of Scotland Hydro-Electric Board are appointed by the Secretary of State for Scotland.

members of a few of the newer boards, e.g. the Commission for New Towns. For a majority of boards in the table above, the statutes provide that the conditions of appointment shall be determined by the Minister in the terms of each individual appointment; elsewhere a period of years, often five years, is laid down, subject to eligibility for re-appointment. A Minister reserves the right to terminate an appointment at any time but in some cases possible causes of dismissal have been given statutory definition. Thus members of the Herring Industry Board can become disqualified from their office through lunacy, bankruptcy, disclosure of confidential information about the Board and absence from Board meetings.

A variety of legal requirements govern the selection of board members. Occasionally there is a language qualification: one member of the Crofters' Commission must speak Gaelic. Regional knowledge may be wanted: one member of the Agricultural Land Commission must have experience of Welsh agriculture, and three members of the British Broadcasting Corporation and the Independent Television Authority shall be persons considered suitable to make the interests of Scotland, Wales and Northern Ireland their special care. Where a board is concerned with a particular industry, e.g. forestry, some members must know something of its technicalities. A board may be representative of particular interests and this is reflected in its constitution: the various sections of the cotton trade are represented on the Cotton Board. The National Dock Labour Board brings together employers and employees and includes four members from each side of industry. Another factor that demands attention is sex: one member of the National Assistance Board must be a woman. Financial interests in an industry affected by the operations of a board may be a *disqualification*; this applies, for example, to the Iron and Steel Board, the Independent Television Authority, the White Fish Authority and whole-time members of the Sugar Board. The statutes governing the National Parks Commission, the Tithe Redemption Commission and the Local Government Commission for England are silent on the question of qualifications and the rubric governing the others gives Ministers a very free hand. Thus members of the National Film Finance Corporation must have had experience and shown capacity in matters relating to finance, industry, commerce, administration or law. Requirements for the National Coal Board are typical of those for other nationalized industries: its members must have experience of industrial, commercial or financial matters, applied science, administration or the organization of workers. Within the framework imposed by these restrictions there remains the crucial tasks of choosing individuals.

How can it be done? For a few positions of major importance a Minister may have personal knowledge of some likely candidates. Clearly, Lord Robens was known to the Minister of Power before he became Chairman of the National Coal Board in 1961. When Dr Dalton left the Treasury in 1947 he left behind a note for his successor, Sir Stafford Cripps, on the suitability or otherwise of various people for the position of Governor of the Bank of England.[1] Since this post was not due to fall vacant until 1949, it is clear that Dalton had been giving substantial forethought to the appointment. Such a degree of personal ministerial attention is probably unusual. The problem of making appointments grows more acute as it grows in size, and the acquaintanceship of the most gregarious Minister must have limits, nor is it automatically composed of those well suited for high responsibility. The Minister of Power is responsible for over 200 salaried appointments to boards of nationalized industries; the Minister of Housing and Local Government makes over one hundred appointments to the New Town Corporations;[2] the Minister of Health must choose over 300 people to serve on Regional Hospital Boards. For this work Ministers must have help which comes largely from and through their civil servants. Local advice will be needed for local posts; one example of this nature, the Regional Hospital Boards, is discussed below. Often it will be necessary to seek the opinions of men outside the Civil Service who have specialized knowledge; such opinions may be highly influential. It is noticeable that the people finally chosen are commonly well known around Government departments, possibly through service on advisory committees. This situation is neither surprising nor necessarily regrettable. Especially in the case of unpaid posts, a department may wish to have some prior notification of whether an individual is prepared to devote time to voluntary service. Finally, if a department is not satisfied

[1] H. Dalton, *High Tide and After* (Muller, 1962), p. 287.
[2] A written Parliamentary answer (December 1, 1959) gave details of the qualifications of the thirty-two persons appointed to New Town Corporations in the previous twelve months. The list includes industrialists, local councillors, two ex-M.P.s, and ex-civil servants, including a former private secretary to Princess Elizabeth and two Prime Ministers. These are salaried part-time posts, Chairmen £1,700 p.a., deputy-Chairmen £700 p.a., other members £400 p.a. See H.C. Deb., Vol. 614, cols. *117-19.*

with its own sources of information about possible nominees, it can use the central list at the Treasury.[1]

Regional Hospital Boards provide a leading example of how people are selected for *local*, unpaid posts. There are fifteen such Boards in England and Wales appointed by the Minister of Health and another five north of the Border appointed by the Secretary of State for Scotland. The Boards normally have between twenty and thirty members, but are smaller in Scotland. When selecting members, Ministers consult universities, organizations representing the medical profession, local health authorities and other interested associations. There has been some controversy over whether the Boards should be chosen solely by a Minister or whether they should be made more representative in character by giving local authorities and the medical profession a right to appoint members. Since Ministers have ultimate financial responsibility for hospitals it is difficult to imagine they would agree to relinquish control in this way. The nature and extent of medical membership has also been a source of argument; the Guillebaud Committee recommended that normally it should not exceed one-quarter of a Board.[2] One further source of dispute has been the extent to which the personnel of a Board should overlap that of Hospital Management Committees, the next lower tier in the hierarchy of hospital administration.[3] The chairmen of the Boards have varied backgrounds—the Armed Forces, Civil Service, local government and the law. Many are company directors. One has the impression that often they are men of substantial means who are content to receive their reward, if any, through the Honours List.

It was noted above that appointments to boards are some-

[1] Cf. oral evidence to the Franks Committee (Administrative Tribunals and Inquiries. Third and fourth days; 1956 Non-Parl.) Q. 931. Sir Gilmour Jenkins of the Ministry of Transport was asked why the Treasury was consulted about the appointment of non-lawyers to tribunals. He replied, 'Because they have a comprehensive list of likely people to be used for this and various other kinds of public service'.

[2] Cost of the National Health Service. Committee. Report, para. 262; 1955-56 Cmd. 9663, xx.

[3] Cf. *Hospitals and the State: Groups, Regions and Committees.* (Acton Society Trust, 1957), Part II, pp. 5-8. The Committees are chosen by the Boards.

times on a whole-time, sometimes on a part-time basis. Naturally, the implications of 'part-time' vary considerably. An element of flexibility has now entered into the meaning of 'full-
time', for appointment to a full-time post no longer implies the
automatic surrender of company directorships or other employment. The change started in 1953 when the Iron and Steel
Act defined a whole-time member of the Iron and Steel Board
as one required to devote himself wholly *or mainly* to these
duties. The Chairmanship of the Board became a part-time post
(at £6,000 p.a.) in 1961. This pattern exists elsewhere; in the
Iron and Steel Holding and Realisation Agency and the
Colonial Development Corporation the chairmen give most of
their time to these institutions. Such arrangements have dangers
and disadvantages, but they do make it possible to obtain the
services of men with wide experience who would not be willing to incur the financial sacrifice involved in giving up other
interests.

Controversy about the salaries of members of boards has
centred on the public corporations of a commercial character.
Members of non-commercial boards are commonly unpaid.
The problem of how much to pay men in charge of the nationalized power and transport industries raises immediately the question whether their remuneration should be in keeping with com-
parable rates in private industry or the public service. Since the
gap between the two is wide, and tends to widen further, the
issue is acute. In 1946 the Labour Government fixed salaries
for chairmen of the major public corporations at £8,500 p.a.
and for full-time board members at £5,000 p.a.; these figures,
it was argued, were justified by the need to obtain men of first-
class ability to serve on the boards. Left-wing critics were not
appeased, but the Government was determined that its
nationalization programme should be a success and were therefore prepared to accept that salaries of board chairmen should
be substantially higher than those of Ministers and senior civil
servants. Under Conservative Governments these salaries remained unchanged until 1957. Inflation had eroded the value
of money and since 1946 salaries in the private sector had
steadily increased. The relative position of the members of
the nationalized boards had deteriorated substantially and some

of them, e.g. Sir Miles Thomas and Mr W. Straight, resigned to return to private industry. Three official inquiries urged that salaries be raised, the Beveridge Committee on Broadcasting,[1] the Fleck Committee on the National Coal Board[2] and the Herbert Committee on Electricity.[3] Upward adjustments were made in 1957 and full-time members of major boards received £7,000 p.a. and chairmen £10,000 p.a., figures analagous to conditions in neither the public nor private sectors of the economy.

The dilemma is very real. If public corporations are to be efficient and pay their way, they must be conducted in accordance with the best commercial practice. Yet men with experience of management in large-scale industry cannot be expected to serve on public boards if to do so involves substantial financial loss. But if commercial salaries are paid the disparity with Ministers and civil servants becomes increasingly impossible to justify. At the same time it is constant Treasury policy to hold down levels of public salaries in order not to provide more fuel for the fires of inflation. Further, not all members of a board need to have industrial experience; if industrial-style salaries were granted, should all members receive them? The idea of individual salaries as opposed to a 'rate for the job' can easily lead to embarrassment, yet why pay industrial-type salaries to ex-service officers, ex-civil servants and ex-trade union officials when they are reasonably content with far less? One way out of this problem was noted above, the tendency to replace full-time appointments with 'a large part of the time' appointments which permit the retention of outside financial interests. The nomination of Dr Beeching in 1961 to take charge of British Railways on a five-year contract at a 'commercial' salary of £24,000 p.a. finally cut the Gordian knot. As yet it is too early to say what effect this development may have on other public corporations.

---

[1] 1950-51 Cmd. 8116, ix. The salary of part-time members of the B.B.C., £600 p.a., is £100 p.a. *below* the original figure fixed in 1926.
[2] Report of the Advisory Committee on Organization (N.C.B., 1955), paras 76 and 78.
[3] Electricity Supply Industry. Committee. Report, paras 312-4; 1955-56 Cmd. 9672, xv.

The Government now publishes an annual White Paper which names the members of public boards of a commercial character and shows their remuneration and term of appointment. It takes special note of cases where a person holds more than one appointment. The document, however, would be far more valuable as a check against abuses of patronage if its scope were of a less limited character, for it includes only those boards which undertake substantial trading activities. Even so, the document gives a broad picture of the boards of nationalized industries with their large numbers of company directors,[1] men promoted from within an industry for their specialized technical knowledge, and some ex-civil servants. There is also a scattering of less radical trade union leaders who give part-time service, and some whole-timers who have left the union movement altogether. The current tendency, especially with area gas and electricity boards, is for internal promotion, and this policy was explicitly approved in the 1960 White Paper on the Reorganisation of the Nationalised Transport Undertakings. 'The Government consider it important that, so far as possible, the nationalized transport undertakings should produce their own leaders. Promotion from within the industry should be within the grasp of those who prove themselves capable.'[2] Such words are excellent for the morale of management. Internal appointments of this nature are likely to be uncontroversial and to avoid parliamentary challenge. Yet there is a danger that Ministers will be content, when things run smoothly, not to seek talent from outside. A self-perpetuating technocracy could develop.[3] This is a possibility to be closely watched.

There are divergent views about the advisability of including union officials on the boards. Some left-wing opinion has feared that a taste of the flesh-pots may have a corrupting

---

[1] C. Jenkins, *Power at the Top* (MacGibbon and Kee, 1959), argues that leaders of private enterprise should not control the nationalized industries as they will try to run them in the interests of the private sector of the economy.

[2] Cmnd. 1248, para. 33. The same paragraph added, 'At the outset, however, some major posts may have to be filled from outside'.

[3] R. Kelf-Cohen, *Nationalisation in Britain*, second ed. (Macmillan, 1961), p. 249.

effect—a possibility that would be less grave if union leadership were better paid or better endowed with talent of a high order. The T.U.C., to the contrary, expressed concern in a report in 1959 because the proportion of board members with a union background was falling. A meeting was sought with the Prime Minister to discuss the issue, but Mr Macmillan did not give the deputation any satisfaction.

Senior civil servants, notably Permanent Secretaries, sometimes receive a salaried post on retirement or, in the case of Sir Cyril Musgrave, on early retirement. There are two objections to this tendency. The first is age, for these men are asked to take on new responsibilities often unconnected with their previous experience, at a time when their intellectual vigour is declining. The second is that they will be so imbued with the conventions and methods of Whitehall that they will tend to restrict the independence and initiative of the boards. Professor Robson energetically rebuts this view by arguing that ex-civil servants are keen to be free of the fetters of ministerial responsibility and Treasury control.[1] There still remains, however, the danger that this tendency will degenerate into 'jobs for the old boys', especially if Ministers have an uneasy conscience about the levels of official remuneration.

Various alternatives have been suggested to the practice of ministerial nomination of boards, especially in relation to nationalized industries. As early as 1920 the Webbs considered the problem and concluded that appointments 'should be made by the appropriate standing committee of a new Social Parliament'.[2] In 1933 the Conservative Government adopted the device of appointing trustees for the London Passenger Transport Board in order to strengthen its independence from Ministers and to minimize the taint of socialism. These trustees were the Chairman of the L.C.C., a member of the London Traffic Advisory Committee, the Chairman of the Committee of London Clearing Bankers, the President of the Law Society, the President of the Institute of Chartered Accountants and the

[1] W. A. Robson, *Nationalised Industry and Public Ownership* (Allen & Unwin, 1960), p. 218.
[2] *Constitution for the Socialist Commonwealth of Great Britain* (Longmans, 1920), p. 147.

Chairman of the L.P.T.B. itself: on such a body it is not difficult to guess that the last named member might have substantial influence. These appointing trustees disappeared in 1947 when the L.P.T.B. was transformed into the London Transport Executive appointed by the Minister of Transport, and the device has not been used elsewhere although the Churchill Government made a proposal on these lines in 1952 in relation to the Governors of the B.B.C. To safeguard against the risk of the B.B.C. being used for political purposes the suggestion was that the power of appointing and removing Governors should be given to a committee consisting of the Speaker of the Commons (chairman), the Prime Minister, the Leader of the Opposition, the Lord Chief Justice and the President of the Court of Session. This proposal eliminated any possibility of Parliamentary challenge to appointments; as no Minister would have been personally responsible, no questioning would have been allowed. The resulting controversy caused the idea to be dropped as the non-political members of the proposed committee asked to be excused. Clearly it would be wrong to drag holders of high positions which are traditionally impartial into the arena of party conflict.[1] The independence of the B.B.C. can be served better by strict adherence to existing conventions than by new institutional arrangements. A compromise suggestion made in *The Economist* at this time was peculiarly ill-conceived.[2] It was that the Government should continue to appoint Governors subject to a requirement that an advisory council consisting of five or six distinguished holders of non-political offices must be consulted: this scheme would merely leave power in ministerial hands but provide an opportunity to blur responsibility.

[1] Cf. Memorandum on the Report of the Broadcasting Committee (1951-52 Cmd. 8550, xxv), para. 15 and H.C. Deb., Vol. 502, cols 238-42. It is odd that a Churchill Government should have been so concerned with the independence of the B.B.C. in view of Churchill's attempt to take over the B.B.C. during the General Strike of 1926. But *autre temps, autre moeurs.* In 1952 many Conservatives had an exaggerated view of the extent to which war-time broadcasting had helped Labour to power in 1945 and they feared presumably that a future Labour Government might use the B.B.C. for socialistic propaganda.
[2] June 21, 1952, p. 799.

Another school of thought, distressingly widespread, urges that boards of nationalized industries should have a voice in their own selection. Lord Simon of Wythenshawe was one advocate of this view.[1] The Fleck Committee suggested that the Minister appoint full-time members of the National Coal Board after consultation with the Board's part-time members. Since the members are normally appointed for a five-year term—and may wish to be reappointed—this could scarcely fail to have an unfortunate effect on the relationships between full-time and part-time members.[2] And why should part-timers have special access to the Minister's ear? Can it be that they have fuller knowledge of the coal industry than colleagues who devote their whole attention to its problems? Officially, at least, the Fleck suggestion was not adopted. A Minister, however, can consult with whomsoever he chooses; it may well be that he will discuss informally the filling of vacancies with a member of the Board, especially the chairman. But no formal channels should be laid down concerning the sources of a Minister's advice. Yet a Labour Party pamphlet has urged that a Minister should have sufficient confidence in a board to ask their advice before making a new appointment.[3] This is highly idealistic. The board may well have been nominated by a Minister's predecessor(s), and possibly by his political opponents. Further, were a Minister to ask a board for advice, and then did not like the advice received, the Minister would have the choice of making an appointment against his own judgment or of demonstrating to the board his lack of trust in their opinion.

The conclusion must be that a Minister should be allowed to go about the business of making appointments as he sees fit. Certainly, he will need advice. Much of this will come from civil servants in his department: the Prime Minister has a personal *aide* with the title Secretary for Appointments. In-

[1] *The Boards of Nationalized Industries* (Longmans, 1957), pp. 28-9.
[2] Report of the Advisory Committee on Organization (N.C.B., 1955), para. 67(c). For part-time members of the N.C.B. the Minister was recommended to consult a panel consisting of the Presidents of the Federation of British Industries and the British Employers' Federation, the Chairman of the Trades Union Congress and one or two other members.
[3] *Public Enterprise* (1957), p. 28.

evitably, at this stage, the cloak of anonymity falls. But the system ensures that a Minister is solely and clearly answerable for any appointment he makes, and Parliament may call him to account. The possibility of Parliamentary criticism, as in the d'Erlanger case,[1] is a valuable safeguard; a Minister will try to avoid a debate that might be embarrasing for him and his appointee. Equally, M.P.s should not assail appointments too frequently or without good cause, for men of distinction will not serve on public bodies if to do so involves a real risk of unpleasant controversy. As it is, the system works tolerably well. Some mistakes are made; some choices seem uninspired; some names have an 'Establishment' flavour. On other occasions—for example, the Local Government Boundary Commission, 1945-49—a board containing familiar faces may become too adventurous for the taste of Ministers. Friction between a Minister and a board is most likely to arise after a change in the political complexion of the Government, as with the conflict in 1952 between Mr Hardie of the Iron and Steel Corporation and Mr Sandys, Minister of Supply. These illustrations show that boards have some spirit of independence and they are a sign of health.

There is no case for special institutional arrangements to check the right of Ministers to make administrative appointments. This right is but one aspect of their responsibilities. If we accept that Ministers answerable to Parliament are entitled to govern us, we must trust them to select members of public boards.

---

[1] H.C. Deb., Vol. 551, cols. 1317-22.

CHAPTER SIX

Advisory Bodies

⊙

I

The large number of advisory committees and advisory councils constitute a major feature of contemporary public administration. Ministers would not create myriads of these bodies unless they were believed to be of benefit; it is necessary, therefore, to examine what benefits may accrue to Ministers through this form of patronage. First, however, a description of the main types of these advisory institutions must be given.

Royal Commissions

The appointment of a Royal Commission is traditionally the means adopted to pursue an investigation of major public importance. The Domesday Book may be regarded as the first report of a Royal Commission.[1] Both Tudor and Stuart kings made great use of Commissions and they became discredited as an unpopular emanation of royal authority. Partly for this reason they declined in the eighteenth century, but were revived again after the first Reform Bill as Ministers tried to grapple with the social and economic problems of an industrial society. The massive Blue Books of the Victorian period provided a major stimulus to change and are today an invaluable quarry for the social historian. In our own century Royal Commissions have again declined in importance, not because governments no longer seek advice, but because departmental committees are created to carry out the sort of task previously allotted to a Commission. A century ago it was not uncommon for half a dozen Royal Commissions to be established in a single year; in recent times the annual average has been one. Their

[1] For the history of Royal Commissions see H. M. Clokie and J. W. Robinson, *Royal Commissions of Inquiry* (Stanford University Press, 1937), Ch. II.

ponderous machinery is ill-suited to any problem on which early action is required, and its use tends to be reserved for long-standing questions, e.g. the taxation of profits and income, marriage and divorce, population, the Civil Service, the re-muneration of doctors and dentists, and the Press. It is not difficult to believe that all these subjects will still be matters of controversy a generation hence. A few Royal Commissions, notably those on Fine Arts, Historical Monuments and Foreign Compensation, are permanent bodies; such Commissions tend to have administrative as well as purely advisory duties. The Monopolies Commission is also permanent; it investigates monopolies, at the bidding of the Board of Trade, to ascertain whether their existence is contrary to the public interest.

Departmental and Inter-departmental Committees
These are established by a Minister or Ministers without the panoply of the Royal Warrant requisite for Commissions. Committees are sometimes created to inquire into relatively limited and technical issues but often deal with matters of general public concern. They provide the advantages of greater informality, speed and economy, for they do not—in contrast to Royal Commissions—hear the oral evidence they receive in public sessions, nor is this evidence usually published. These factors hasten the production of a report, but it is still true that committees dealing with complex problems are often occupied for more than two years, roughly the minimum period taken by a Royal Commission to reach any conclusions. Committee reports tend to be briefer, and with this slimming process the historic blue covers are used less frequently.

Working Parties
The next stage in streamlining led to the concept of a 'working party': this term was first used in government circles in 1945 when it was applied by the Board of Trade to a series of com-mittees charged with the consideration of post-war reorganiza-tion in particular industries. A working party does not normally take evidence at formal hearings and relies more on the personal experience of its members. It is thus yet more informal than a departmental committee and is suitable for

narrower and more specialized topics. Other ministries than the Board of Trade now use this device and two of many examples are the working parties on School Construction and Police Pensions.

The table below gives an indication of the scale of activity of Royal Commissions, Committees of Inquiry including departmental committees and working parties. It is based on the categories included in the Ford *Breviates*,[1] i.e. those dealing with problems of constitutional, economic, financial or social policy and legal administration. Thus the table excludes reports relating to both foreign and colonial policy and ecclesiastical and military matters. Also excluded by definition are purely factual papers, periodical reports required by statute and reports from standing advisory committees (which are considered separately below). The distinction between Parliamentary and non-Parliamentary papers was intended to be some measure of their urgency and importance. Parliamentary papers are issued free to Members of Parliament and are included in the annual sets of bound volumes; since 1921 they have been restricted to documents likely to be the subject of early legislation or whose contents were regarded as essential to the proper discharge of Parliamentary duties.

Parliamentary Sessions	Parliamentary Papers		Non-Parliamentary Papers		Calendar Years
	Royal Commission Reports	Committee Reports	Committee Reports	Working Party Reports*	
1917-18 to 1921	12	170	14	—	1917-21
1922 to 1926	12	87	40	—	1922-26
1927 to 1930-31	9	58	33	—	1927-31
1931-32 to 1935-36	7	55	31	—	1932-36
1936-37 to 1940-41	3	47	25	—	1937-41
1941-42 to 1945-46	2	69	34	7	1942-46
1946-47 to 1950-51	5	75	55	34	1947-51
1951-52 to 1955-56	6	65	45	24	1952-56
1956-57 to 1960-61	5	61	47	14	1957-61

* Four of the working party reports included in this column were issued as Parliamentary papers.

[1] P. and G. Ford, *A Breviate of Parliamentary Papers*, 3 Vols. (Blackwell, 1951, 1957, 1961). These volumes cover the period 1900-54.

How the end of two world wars has stimulated committee activity is shown clearly by these figures. The latest stage in the decline of Royal Commissions is also apparent.

Written answers to Parliamentary questions[1] have shown how long recent committees have taken to produce their reports. For committees appointed between 1955 and 1960 the extreme limits were one month—to inquire into the difficulties over tally-clerks in the Port of London—and the four years' labour of the Ingleby Committee on Children and Young Persons. Inevitably, the speed of committee work depends usually on the scope of the task embodied in the terms of reference.

Standing Advisory Bodies
While the various types of *ad hoc* inquiry already described are the most publicized advisory bodies, they are dwarfed in number by the array of permanent advisory councils and the committees attached to each Government department. According to the Financial Secretary to the Treasury,[2] in November 1958, there were some 850 advisory bodies of a central or national character assisting the Government. The P.E.P. report on this subject noted that this figure included sub-committees and advisory bodies connected with institutions outside the main care of ministerial departments: P.E.P. suggested 484 as a more realistic total.[3] All these estimates omit advisory bodies of a local or regional character, including the sixty Scottish committees that meet in Edinburgh, and the vast network of committees attached to the local offices of central departments, notably those dealing with employment, national insurance and public assistance.

Permanent bodies of this kind serve to keep Ministers and civil servants in regular touch with specialized opinion and experience. They form an important link between the executive and independent voluntary organizations concerned with particular aspects of State activity. Thus these committees and

[1] On March 3, 1960, and March 23, 1961: H.C. Deb., Vol. 618, col. *169*; and Vol. 637, col. 75.
[2] H.C. Deb., Vol. 595, col. 1305.
[3] *Advisory Committees in British Government* (P.E.P., 1960), pp. 10-11.

councils are one recognized channel through which 'pressure groups' may work. Because their function differs from that of Royal Commissions or committees with specific terms of reference, these standing bodies tend to have somewhat different constitution and procedure. They may be larger in size; for example, the National Advisory Council on Education for Industry and Commerce has seventy-nine members. It is also usual for civil servants to play a significant part at meetings, either as full members of the advisory body or as assessors. Evidence is not solicited from members of the public and, in most cases, formal reports are not published. There are, of course, exceptions to these generalizations: the Report of the Central Advisory Council for Education (England) *15 to 18* issued in 1959, was one of the most widely-discussed State documents in recent years, and in preparing this Report the Council received evidence from a large number of individuals and associations.

Local Advisory Committees

At a much more humble level the local offices of many Government departments have advisory committees which help to them to keep in touch with local opinion and local problems. Such bodies exist in the fields of national assistance, national insurance and employment. Some Post Office regions have advisory committees. The area gas and electricity boards have consumers' councils attached to them which investigate complaints. Perhaps the most important example is the county agricultural executive committees: during and after the war these bodies carried out important administrative tasks, which have since been taken over by the local officials of the Ministry of Agriculture, so the committees have now essentially a consultative function. All these committees are commonly recruited by asking local organizations—local authorities, trade unions, chambers of commerce, etc.—to suggest names of possible members and the Ministry then makes a final selection from the panel of nominees. Local authority representatives tend to dominate the gas and electricity consumers' councils; in the case of electricity between two-fifths and three-fifths of the councils must be drawn from panels nominated by the associations of local authorities, and for gas the proportion is higher, one half to three-quarters. The Agriculture Act, 1947, provided an even more precise constitution for the county agricultural committees. They have twelve members. Of these three are drawn from a panel suggested by farmers' representatives, i.e. the National Farmers' Union, two are to represent workers and two represent landlords, i.e. the Country Landowners' Association. The Minister appoints the remaining five members directly, one of whom is required to be a member of the county council; many of the Minister's nominees are farmers and this serves to make the farmers' hold on the committees much stronger than the formal constitution would suggest.[1] In theory, of course, all members of local committees serve as individuals in a personal capacity and not as delegates responsible to an organized sectional interest.

II

Recruitment of members to advisory institutions is a complex task, and one devoid of opportunities to dispense lucrative patronage. Normally these duties are unpaid, but travelling and subsistence expenses are usually met. On a few scientific bodies, e.g. the Aeronautical Research Council and the Interservice Metallurgical Research Council,[2] fees are paid on a daily basis and are thought of as payment for professional services. There are no salaries[3] or retaining fees. But the lack of remuneration creates no problem. Eminent persons show a remarkable willingness to undertake work of this kind—a willingness evoked by sentiments of flattery and *noblesse oblige*. Yet even if invitations to serve are generally accepted,

[1] For a full discussion of the composition of these committees see Peter Self and H. Storing, *The State and the Farmer* (Allen & Unwin, 1962), pp. 140-5. Farmers' and landowners' representatives are chosen at county level and normally the names submitted are twice as many as the places to be filled. The names of workers' representatives are proposed by the national headquarters of the trade unions concerned, the National Union of Agricultural Workers and the Transport and General Workers' Union: there appears to be little consultation with local branches and about half of those nominated are union officials.

[2] *Advisory Committees in British Government*, p. 53.

[3] The Monopolies Commission is an exception to this principle.

the conveners of advisory bodies must still decide what type of personnel to seek. Should the membership be expert or lay, representative or independent? Or is some combination of these possibilities the best arrangement? If a body is to be wholly or partially representative, there arises the delicate question of which interests shall be recognized and how a balance between them can be held; frequently this is done by the nomination of some 'independent' members, including an independent chairman.

As we have seen, representative membership is common on the permanent or semi-permanent advisory councils that provide liaison between Government departments and associations of all kinds, but its use on inquiries into specific matters is of doubtful value. This difficulty was put squarely by the Committee on the Procedure of Royal Commissions in 1910: 'A Commission selected on the principle of representing various interests starts with a serious handicap against the probability of harmony on its work. . . .'[1] To include people associated with widely divergent groups intimately concerned by the matters under discussion is virtually to preclude the possibility of the production of a unanimous report. Thus the membership of the Sankey Commission on the Coal Industry, which included both mineowners and mineworkers, ensured that the Commission could reach no agreed conclusions.[2] Alternatively, it may be argued that unanimity should not be regarded as an over-riding virtue; that what a government requires is a full and searching analysis of a problem, not merely a patched-up compromise solution. However, if members of a committee are too much at odds with each other, meetings will become valueless. This prospect must haunt any body of employers and employees set up to facilitate economic progress. A somewhat different example—of a personal conflict between experts—is provided by the Tizard Committee on our air defences.[3]

Another objection to representative membership, and sometimes to expert membership, is summed up in the phrase 'no

[1] Report, p. 6; 1910 Cd. 5235, lviii.
[2] Cf. its Reports; 1919 Cmd. 359, Cmd. 360, xi, xii.
[3] C. P. Snow, *Science and Government* (Oxford, 1961), pp. 24-36.

man should be judge in his own cause'. Where the terms of reference of an inquiry carry the merest hint of potential culpability, persons connected with the subject-matter should clearly be excluded. The inclusion of two eminent civil servants on the Committee on Ministers' Powers came near to a breach of this principle, for this Committee was established because of the fears that the executive branch of government had acquired excessive influence. Similarly, if an inquiry is established into a topic of current controversy, it is important that its members should not be publicly committed to an opinion on the matter. Again, a man with special knowledge of a problem, but who has been conditioned over the years to take a particular view about it, is not a good choice. Sir Richard Hopkins, an ex-Permanent Secretary to the Treasury, was a member of the Masterman Committee on the Political Activities of Civil Servants. The tendency to appoint civil servants or retired civil servants to inquiries into problems of central administration is unfortunate: it is not inevitable that such men will see nothing but good in existing practice, but it is improbable that they are in favour of radical change. Their mature experience should, of course, be utilized, but as witnesses rather than as members of the inquiring body.

How useful is the expert in public investigations? British tradition sets great store by the qualities of the knowledgeable layman and treats the claims of the specialist with healthy scepticism. But the expert cannot be confined to the witness-stand. Working parties and the standing advisory bodies do not normally invite evidence; they must, therefore, include persons fully competent in all technical and specialized matters that come before them. Even where witnesses are summoned there may well be a place for experts on both sides of the table. Only a man with substantial understanding of the intricacies of a subject can direct the questioning of experts to the best advantage, can assess the value of the information provided and interpret it for the benefit of lay colleagues. It is also important that the chairman of an inquiry should have a general mastery of its problems. No doubt this is why many chairmen are lawyers, and thus habituated both to the conduct of oral examinations and to the mastery of complex briefs.

One other major consideration governs the assembly of national advisory bodies: at least some of the members must have established reputations. Where a published report is a potential prelude to legislative action, the authority of those who sign it is of great significance. The desire to form a 'strong' committee containing personages of distinction helps to explain why some names have appeared almost regularly in connection with various inquiries, e.g. Lord Beveridge, Sir Ernest Gowers, Sir Harry Pilkington and Sir Edwin Herbert. Indeed, the chairmen of Royal Commissions and the major committees of inquiry are chosen from very narrow groups. Between January 1955 and March 1961 four Royal Commissions and seventy-six committees were appointed to investigate social and economic questions in this country. Almost without exception their chairmen fell into four categories: peers, lawyers, knights or baronets (often with a Civil Service background) and university professors.[1,2]

Advisory bodies are recruited in three ways that may be described briefly as representation, nomination and direct approach.[3] Alternatively, a combination of these methods may be used, especially where independent members are included to give prestige or balance to a representative committee. The method by which any particular body is brought together acts as a valuable guide to how the sponsoring department views its purpose.

The representation technique is simple. Various organizations are asked to send one or more people along to serve on an advisory council. In this case there is no ministerial control over who comes or the extent to which individual membership is continuous. The system recognizes that the Government is willing to consult with interested parties to a problem: it implies also that the organizations represented are recognized as effective spokesmen of the interests concerned. Bodies drawn from both sides of industry often fall into this category.

[1] H.C. Deb., Vol. 618 col. *169*; and Vol. 637, col. *75*.
[2] Plurality of membership on standing advisory bodies arises for a different reason. Here nominations are often invited from various organizations, e.g. associations of local authorities, and the latter may nominate the same individuals on a number of occasions.
[3] *Advisory Committees in British Government*, pp. 36-42.

The National Joint Advisory Council at the Ministry of Labour has six representatives of nationalized industries and seventeen from both the British Employers' Federation and the Trades Union Congress.

Nomination arrangements are more common and were noticed above in connection with local committees. Organizations are asked to suggest a number of names and subsequently one or more of these are chosen by the Minister. It follows that the Minister retains complete freedom of action and that members selected by this means are expected to act as individuals, not as ambassadors. In practice, however, the nominating bodies will propose only those in whom they have confidence so this pattern also provides for the representation of interested parties.

The personal approach is used for Royal Commissions and major inquiries. It depends on the knowledge of Ministers and their advisers about potential committeemen. This information is obtained in various ways. Civil servants will learn something of the qualities of those in the outside world with whom they do official business. Service on an advisory body as a representative or nominee may lead to further invitations to serve in a purely personal capacity. The abilities of ex-civil servants can also be easily assessed. If all else fails, use may be made of the central list at the Treasury.[1] The circle of people well known in Whitehall and the London clubs is quite large; it includes the leaders of all substantial sections of opinion—employers' organizations, trades unions, churches, local government and a mass of welfare associations. No doubt much talent is unknown and therefore unused, but men without a wide reputation are less valuable on a committee in so far as they can add nothing to its prestige and authority. The danger of this system is not that useful people will be overlooked; rather it is that useful people may be avoided because of the awkward—or supposedly awkward—character of their opinions. A radical and stimulating mind is not always welcome. How easy it is to pass over a possibly 'difficult' name and come to rest upon that of a committee-server of long standing.

[1] See p. 96.

The inclusion of M.P.s and civil servants raises special problems. Members of the Commons are barred by the 1957 Disqualification Act from the few advisory bodies on which service attracts remuneration. It can be fixed policy to appoint M.P.s, e.g. to the Advisory Panel on the Highlands and Islands of Scotland. Yet the general rule is for them to be neither excluded nor automatically included. Sometimes one is included because of qualifications or experience unconnected with his political status. Major inquiries into constitutional matters, e.g. the Committee on Ministers' Powers and the Committee on Administrative Tribunals and Inquiries, normally include an M.P. from each party. What is desirable practice in this matter? Herbert Morrison is in favour of Parliamentary representation on committees for it provides valuable experience and improves contributions to Parliamentary debate.[1] But can advisory responsibilities conflict with the over-riding duties of a legislator? If a committee has access to confidential information, an M.P. would be inhibited when discussing the business of the committee in Parliament. No M.P. should remain on a committee if he feels that to do so would seriously limit his freedom of political action. Members of the Lords are used frequently on major inquiries, but in their case this issue does not arise to the same degree: the Lords are not representatives of the people and the political importance and the political tensions of their House are much less.

Civil servants face an allied prospect of conflict of status. The permanent servants of the Crown who aid Ministers are anonymous, politically impartial, and must never be credited publicly with opinions of their own. Service on an advisory body need not clash seriously with these principles so long as no published reports are issued which contain recommendations on matters of policy. It was noted above that civil servants are most often associated with standing advisory committees and the majority of these bodies do not publish their conclusions. But conflict arises where an official is a member of a body that announces its views. He cannot sign the report as a representative of his department, for this would

---

[1] *Government and Parliament* (Oxford, 1954), p. 275.

imply prior ministerial approval of any proposals made. If the proposals are in concert with Government policy, the suspicion arises that the official members have steered the committee to convenient ideas. If the official signs as an individual, the traditions of anonymity and impartiality are jettisoned. The classic example of this difficulty arose over the famous war-time Beveridge inquiry on Social Insurance. Originally this was established as an inter-departmental committee composed, except for the chairman, of officials chosen from the various ministries concerned with the investigation: the constitution of the committee was the logical consequence of the Government view that the inquiry would centre on matters of administrative detail. Under the guiding hand of Lord Beveridge, fundamental issues of policy were quickly raised and it became clear that the report of the committee would raise highly controversial issues. It was therefore decided that the Chairman alone should sign the report and that the other members should be regarded as assessors or assistants to the Chairman.[1] Perhaps Civil Service anonymity should be regarded as less than sacrosanct, but it is still wrong to expose officials in matters that are politically contentious.

III

The value of advisory bodies is a matter for some argument. The permanent bodies have an established niche in our methods of administration: they let the Civil Service and other organized bodies talk with each other, and from this talk comes fuller understanding, tolerance and compromise. But the use of inquiries into social and economic affairs can be questioned. They may be established as a piece of smart political tactics; their reports are sometimes ignored either altogether or for long periods. In such cases are the eminent and busy citizens who serve on inquiries wasting their time? Dame Irene Ward has urged the Government to guarantee that the Commons

[1] Lord Beveridge, *Power and Influence* (Hodder & Stoughton, 1953), p. 298, and the Report (1942-43, Cmd. 6404, vi), para. 40, in which the position of the officials is explained.

should always have an opportunity to debate Reports reasonably soon after their publication.[1] Naturally, the Government has not done so. A Report may be pushed aside for various reasons. Ministers may disagree with it in principle. The topic may have lost urgency. Its adoption might cost money that the Treasury are unwilling to find. The requisite legislation may not find a gap in the crowded Parliamentary timetable. And action on reports that raise moral issues is always an invitation for a political storm. In spite of all these obstacles, it is not true that a majority of reports rot in pigeon-holes. Between 1951 and May 1960 as many as 151 reports were issued on domestic matters and of these 83 have been 'largely implemented and 22 implemented in part'.[2]

Why are advisory bodies established? The range of possible reasons is wide, and a combination of them will apply in each particular case. But the ostensible reason—that Ministers need advice—is rarely the full explanation. On highly specialized and unfamiliar matters Ministers and their permanent servants may feel the need for extra aid and experience; one illustration is the succession of committees on broadcasting in its early days[3] and another is the more recent inquiry into decimal coinage. The most common reason has been discussed already —the desire to negotiate or consult with particular interest groups. 'Decision only after discussion' is now a broadly accepted maxim in public administration. If an organized section of the community is adversely affected by Government action—other than tax changes—without a prior opportunity to express its own viewpoint, the lack of consultation will be high on its list of complaints. Consultation is now so frequent that its absence wounds pride. The advisory bodies can have a negative purpose, to mollify or remove an added sense of injury. When dealing with outside organizations a government may also have a more constructive purpose: it may wish to promote thought. Thus the idea behind the Local Government Manpower Committee was to discover how local

---

[1] H.C. Deb., Vol. 649, col. 1785.
[2] Mr Macleod, Leader of the House, *ibid.*, col. 1790.
[3] Broadcasting. Departmental Committee. Report; 1923 Cmd. 1951, x. Broadcasting. Committee. Report; 1926 Cmd. 2599, viii.

authorities could economize in their use of administrative manpower.[1]

It has become traditional to have periodic inquiries to look at some of our public institutions, notably the Civil Service and broadcasting. Investigations into public services are useful both to allay anxieties and to provide remedial action, e.g. those into transport disasters and the Curtis Committee on Child Care.[2] A Cabinet intent on reform may appoint an inquiry as a prelude to action, a prelude designed to educate public opinion in the need for change. The two Royal Commissions on Justices of the Peace would fall squarely into this category.[3]

Alternatively, the purpose of a government may not be so vigorous or honourable. The establishment of a committee is a useful delaying tactic; as Mr Gladstone noted in 1869, 'A committee keeps a cabinet quiet'.[4] It also helps to keep Parliament quiet by throwing a kind of *sub judice* veil over a subject. It becomes unreasonable to expect the Government to declare a policy until it has had a chance to consider the committee's report. Delay can be desired for a number of reasons. A government may wish to gain a little time to do some thinking itself, e.g. into the administrative problems of creating New Towns; it may need an escape from an immediate political difficulty, e.g. the controversy over tithe redemption in 1934;[5] it may procrastinate through lack of enthusiasm for reform combined with unwillingness to announce that no changes will be made. The cynic could produce any number of candidates for inclusion under the last heading; among the clearest cases are the Committee on Pleas against the Crown[6] and the Royal Commission on Marriage and Divorce.[7] Professor Wheare remarks that delay has its uses, including the possible education

---

[1] The Committee became largely an inquest into central departmental control over local authorities. It issued two Reports; 1950 Cmd. 7870, xiii; 1951-52 Cmd. 8421, xvi.

[2] Care of Children. Committee. Report; 1945-46 Cmd. 6922, x.

[3] See Chapter Nine.

[4] Lord Morley, *Life of Gladstone* (Macmillan, 1912), Vol. I, p. 691.

[5] H. M. Clokie and J. W. Robinson, *Royal Commissions of Inquiry*, pp. 136-7.

[6] The Committee sat for six years, 1921-27. Action was taken twenty years later in the Crown Proceedings Act, 1947. Report; 1927 Cmd. 2842, viii.

[7] Report; 1955-56 Cmd. 9678, xxiii.

of public opinion.[1] Hesitation may also stoke higher the fires of controversy and make action still more difficult.

When Ministers are convinced that reform is inevitable in a field in which opinion is sharply divided, possibly across party lines, the report of an inquiry can provide useful shelter for the Government, by showing that any legislation produced is largely the result of careful, independent investigation. Responsibility remains with Ministers, but they can argue fairly that they are not just forcing their own ideas on to the statute book; recent examples are gambling and the reform of London government. Alternatively, a committee can be used to cover retreating footsteps. In 1953, after a public outcry, the Government withdrew the proposed 10 per cent cut in the grants for adult education and established instead a committee to inquire into the adult education service: the subsequent report[2] commented on the value of the work already done by the extra-mural departments of universities and the W.E.A. and urged that this might be extended. Finally, a committee may be used to kill an idea. This technique is dangerous for two reasons. First, to establish an inquiry into any scheme tends to enhance its importance; it is an admission that it merits serious consideration. Second, the report might be unexpectedly favourable and thus increase, rather than reduce, the political difficulty of rejection.

For Ministers, there is always the risk that a report will prove unacceptable or otherwise politically embarrassing. The Devlin Report on Nyasaland[3] is a useful reminder of this possibility. Yet this is an infrequent occurrence. The ability to choose the members of inquiries—the power of patronage—is a powerful weapon with which to avoid the unexpected. The Webbs put the point well. 'When we are told that a particular person has been appointed on a Royal Commission or Government Committee ... on the ground that he is, or claims to be, an impartial party, we may rest assured that the selector and the selected agree in their bias.'[4] It was noticed above that the

[1] *Government by Committee* (Oxford, 1955), p. 91.
[2] Organization and Finance of Adult Education in England and Wales. Committee. Report; 1954, Non-Parl. Min. of Education.
[3] Nyasaland. Commission. Report; 1958-59 Cmnd. 814, x.
[4] *Methods of Social Study* (Longmans, 1932), p. 45.

chairmen of major inquiries are chosen from restricted social categories, and their general predelictions will be well known to Whitehall. The influence of the chairman is important: his status, personality and experience can all be used to secure compromise and unanimity. One or two colleagues may stand out against him and produce a minority report (that can be easily disregarded), but it is rare indeed for a chairman to be forced into a minority position. The inclusion of critics on a committee may serve to silence or mollify them—especially in the case of permanent advisory councils that publish no reports.

Advisory bodies are useless on issues where there is a straightforward division of opinion between the major political parties: an investigation into the reform of the Second Chamber is unlikely to prove fruitful. On other matters they can be of the greatest service to a government and the right to create them and select the membership is an important political asset. The most valuable forms of patronage may carry no price-tag.

CHAPTER SEVEN

Judicial Appointments

⊙

I. HER MAJESTY'S JUDGES

The need to protect the independence of the judiciary was established by the Act of Settlement, 1701, with the classic formula that judges should remain in office *quamdiu se bene gesserint*. A judge can be removed from his post after an address has been presented to Her Majesty by both Houses of Parliament. No English judge has been removed in this way and the details of the procedure that would be involved are by no means clear.[1] Judges' salaries are a permanent charge on the Consolidated Fund and thus do not require annual Parliamentary confirmation. But salary levels, pensions and other conditions of service are all governed by legislation. It is possible, in theory, for Parliament to reduce the salary of a judge as a mark of displeasure; such action, however, would be without precedent and be widely regarded as unconstitutional. Further, it is a convention that the actions of a judge may not be criticised except in debate on an address for his removal as, for example, that on the conduct of Lord Justice Abinger in 1843.[2] More recently, in 1924, George Lansbury tabled a motion about Mr Justice McCardie because of remarks made by the latter to the jury in a libel case, *O'Dwyer v. Nair*.[3] It will be seen that the machinery that exists to enable Parliamentary discussion of judicial conduct is almost never utilized. Judgments of the courts may be criticized, but the challenge must be to the law, and not to a judge. The judiciary is, therefore, reasonably

[1] R. M. Jackson, *The Machinery of Justice in England*, 3rd ed. (Cambridge, 1960), p. 233.
[2] Parl. Deb., 3rd Series, Vol. 66, col. 1037 *et seq.*
[3] After a statement by the Prime Minister at question time the motion was withdrawn. Cf. H.C. Deb., Vol. 175, cols. 6-8.

secure from interference by the legislature and it need pay no regard to the political convenience of Ministers. Any attempt, or suspicion of an attempt, to trespass on judicial independence is certain to arouse stern opposition: thus the calm of the House of Lords was deeply disturbed in 1934 by the clause in the Supreme Court of Judicature Bill to allow the Government to appoint a Vice-President of the Court of Appeal.[1]

The appointment of judges is still, however, in the hands of Ministers. The Lord Chancellor nominates the fifty-eight puisne judges and the Prime Minister appoints to the more senior posts—the Lords of Appeal in Ordinary, the Lords Justices of Appeal, the Lord Chief Justice, the Master of the Rolls and the President of the Probate, Divorce and Admiralty Division. Similarly, for Scotland, the Prime Minister is responsible for the senior posts, while the Lords Ordinary in the Court of Session together with the Sheriffs are nominated by the Secretary of State. Minor appointments are in the hands of the Lord Advocate. Since 1948 the Lord Chancellor has filled the chief judicial appointments in the armed forces— the Judge Advocate General and the Judge Advocate of the Fleet. Technically, of course, all these appointments are made by the Crown on the advice of Ministers.

The Lord Chancellor personifies the British rejection of the theory of the separation of powers. He is the head of the judiciary and plays a dominant rôle in the selection of its members; he presides over the House of Lords; he is a senior member of the Cabinet. His appointment is essentially political and he leaves office when the political complexion of the Government changes. The Lord Chancellor is a barrister and usually a man who has had a successful political career and previous experience of ministerial office. It is true that there are exceptions: Lord Maugham (Lord Chancellor 1937-39) and Lord

[1] The Vice-President would have presided over the No. 2 Appeal Court, a task which traditionally fell to the senior appeal judge. At that time the senior judge, Lord Justice Greer, was ill and the next most senior, Lord Justice Slesser, had been deputising. The clause appeared to be an attempt to by-pass Slesser and, as Slesser had been a Labour supporter, it also had political implications. The Lord Chief Justice, Lord Hewart, strongly upheld Slesser's rights and no Vice-President has ever been appointed. R. Jackson, *The Chief: The Biography of Gordon Hewart* (Harrap, 1959), Ch. 13. H.L. Deb., Vol. 95, cols. 219-39 and 366-420.

Simonds (Lord Chancellor 1951-54) had had no connection with party activity, but these cases are contrary to the general practice. Normally, then, the Lord Chancellor is a politician, and the danger emerges that the judicial appointments he authorizes will be made on a political basis. If this should happen, and if the same political party remained in power for a lengthy period, the independence of the judiciary could be undermined in spite of the legal and conventional safeguards.

As the present system is open, at least in theory, to abuse, it is important to examine whether any other method of appointment might be preferable. The two broad alternatives are nomination and election. It is difficult to envisage that any form of election could produce satisfactory results. Election by Parliament would tend to degenerate into a political contest and would do nothing to strengthen the independence of the judiciary. The electorate at large has no substantial understanding of the qualities required in a judge and no knowledge of the prospective candidates for the office. A democratic election of judges must become, as it is in the U.S.A., another opportunity for party conflict, and the impartial application of the law can only be hampered if those who administer it are chosen on a basis of popularity. The remaining possibility is that of nomination, and the central issue becomes—nomination by whom? A constitutional monarch, by definition, is debarred from such an obligation. The Privy Council is too large and effete a body for the task. It is more practicable to suggest that the duty be assigned to those members of the Privy Council who are judges—i.e. the Lord Chancellor, the Lord Chief Justice, the Master of the Rolls, the President of the Probate, Divorce and Admiralty Division, the Lords of Appeal in Ordinary and the Lords Justices of Appeal. Such a body would have full knowledge of the candidates for promotion to the Bench and expert appreciation of the qualities needed. But such a scheme would entail that judges become a self-perpetuating oligarchy responsible to no one for the way in which they filled their own ranks. If we are not prepared to allow judges to be a separate, powerful estate of the realm, this arrangement is unacceptable. Thus we are forced back to the present technique of nomination by Ministers. In the *Grammar of Politics*

Laski accepted ministerial nomination as the means of selecting men for the Bench, but urged that a standing committee of judges be established to advise on appointments.[1] The danger of advisory bodies is that they may be used to blur responsibility. As it is, the Lord Chancellor is probably well informed about judicial opinion on the calibre of leading barristers without the aid of formal institutions, for the legal world is remarkably compact and centralized. And when new judges are appointed there is no scintilla of doubt on who is responsible for what has been done.

Equally, there is no doubt that during the nineteenth century politics played a large part in the choice of judges. Laski has shown that of the 139 judges appointed between 1832 and 1906, 80 were appointed directly to the Bench from the House of Commons and a further 11 had been Parliamentary candidates.[2] Sixty-three of the 80 M.P.s who became judges attained the office while their own party was in power. Under Lord Halsbury (Lord Chancellor 1885-1905 with interruptions) the distribution of political favour was unusually obvious. Authors of the standard works on British government of this period accepted that political activity could be a useful aid to a legal career. Thus Redlich recorded that promotion to the Bench was 'often—perhaps too often—the reward for political services'.[3] Similarly, Viscount Bryce recorded that traces of the spoils system could still be discovered in Britain, especially in relation to legal posts.[4] This was most noticeable in the case of the Law Officers who managed to establish a strong claim to judicial preferment: Lloyd George regarded the Attorney-General as entitled to the post of Lord Chief Justice should that office become vacant. Nothing could be more inimical to the concept of judicial independence. The duty of a Law Officer is to provide legal advice and representation for the government of the day on all matters, including those which arouse political passion.

[1] 4th ed. (Allen & Unwin, 1941), p. 548.
[2] *Studies in Law and Politics* (Allen & Unwin, 1932), p. 168.
[3] *The History of Local Government in England* (Macmillan, 1903), Vol. II, p. 371.
[4] *Modern Democracies* (Macmillan, 1921), Vol. I, p. 132.

Is such a man automatically the best suited for high judicial office, the duties of which include the task of ensuring the equal administration of the laws including, where necessary, their equal administration as between government and people?

Events in 1921 show how undesirable it is for the selection of judges to be entangled by political considerations. In that year the Prime Minister wished to appoint Lord Reading, the Lord Chief Justice, to be Viceroy of India. The Attorney-General, Sir Gordon Hewart, was anxious to leave political life and return to the law. Thus he welcomed the prospect of filling the vacancy. At this stage, a difficulty arose. The Prime Minister, Lloyd George, did not wish to lose the services of his Attorney-General; he regarded Hewart as a major asset to the coalition government and often sought his advice. Hewart, however, did not wish to lose his chance of the Chief Justiceship. To escape the dilemma, Lloyd George proceeded to nominate Mr Justice Lawrence (aged seventy-seven) to be Lord Chief Justice on the condition that the latter should retire whenever the Prime Minister required in order to make way for Hewart. The appointment of a judge on these terms would appear to be a breach of the irremovability during good behaviour guaranteed by the Act of Settlement. Hewart and the Lord Chancellor, Lord Birkenhead, were both unhappy about the arrangement. However, the plan went through: Mr Justice Lawrence replaced Lord Reading and next year read his own resignation in *The Times* just before the break-up of the Lloyd George Cabinet.[1]

In recent years the picture has changed. When Mr Gerald Howard, M.P., became a judge in 1961, it was the first time an M.P. had joined the English Bench for eleven years; however, there were two further such appointments in the early months of 1962. Only about one-tenth of the judges on the English Bench have sat in the House of Commons. The pattern relating to the Chief Justiceship altered in 1946 when Mr Attlee appointed Lord Goddard to the post—and not a lawyer-politician. When the retirement of Lord Goddard was thought to be near in 1958, letters appeared in *The Times*

[1] A full statement of this incident is given in R. Jackson, *The Chief: the Biography of Gordon Hewart* (Harrap, 1959) Ch. 7.

urging that he be succeeded by another judge; the choice of Lord Justice Parker seems to show that Mr Macmillan shared this view. On the other hand, the last two vacancies in the Presidency of the Probate, Divorce and Admiralty Division (1933 and 1962) have been filled by the translation of the Solicitor-General. It is to be hoped that these two precedents will not be used to claim that a new tradition has been established. The 1962 appointment can be excused partly by the fact that the Solicitor-General of the day, Sir Jocelyn Simon, happened to be a specialist on divorce law; even so, it is surely probable that one or more of the judges already on the Bench could have filled the vacancy with at least equal distinction. Scottish Law Officers and ex-Law Officers are also regularly elevated to the Scottish Bench. This could be justified by a greater scarcity of Scottish lawyers of high quality. Certainly, these particular appointments are not dominated by party considerations as it is common for ex-Law Officers to be nominated to the Scottish Bench by their political opponents —e.g. Mr Johnston in 1961 and Mr Reid in 1949. However, Dr Thompson, a Labour backbencher, suggested to the Commons in May 1960 that the dispensation of judicial patronage in Scotland was influenced by political considerations: this view was rejected by the Lord Advocate.[1]

When dealing with legal appointments, the Lord Chancellor enjoys very real advantages. He is, in contrast to other Ministers, an expert on the business of his department. Legal patronage must be dispensed within a limited professional circle: Lords of Appeal and Lords Justices of Appeal must be barristers of 15 years standing, for puisne judges the qualification period is 10 years, for County Court judges 7 years and for recorders 5 years.[2] Furthermore, the members of this professional group regularly meet each other on circuit and in London. Opinions about individual members are both easy to

---

[1] H.C. Deb., Vol. 623, cols. 172-3.
[2] Any period of time spent in practice as a qualified solicitor will be counted for the purpose of the period of qualification: Barristers (Qualification for Office) Act, 1961. Similarly, for a solicitor any period spent as a barrister is allowed. The 1961 Act may encourage solicitors to transfer to the Bar, and may help to bring the two branches of the legal profession more closely together.

gather and well informed. Thus the Lord Chancellor can seek advice on the suitability of candidates for the Bench from the Lord Chief Justice, the Master of the Rolls or any judge in the knowledge that the advice received will be based on reasonably intimate acquaintance with the barrister under review. Of course, the kindness of heart of the adviser may have to be discounted; according to the Lord Chancellor's Permanent Secretary—'some of the greatest judges seem to find it virtually impossible to speak ill of any possible candidate'.[1] In addition to this aid, the Lord Chancellor will have personal experience of the legal profession to guide him. He remains a bencher of his Inn and is still 'subject to the professional and social criticisms of his intimates, with whom and against whom he fought during his days at the bar'.[2] Thus he is closely in touch with the limited community within which legal appointments must be distributed, and a barrister's reputation among his colleagues has a dominant influence on his chances of a judgeship. A Lord Chancellor may well have his own ideas on who is suitable for elevation to the Bench; members of the circuit to which he used to belong may enjoy a slight differential advantage. The safeguards against eccentric choices are that a man likely to make such will not become Lord Chancellor and, secondly, that Lord Chancellors respect the opinion of the legal profession. And the legal profession is aware—of what may not be widely realized—that a great advocate may not make a good judge. Thus some men who have enjoyed great popular prestige, e.g. Marshall Hall, never transfer to the Bench.

It is true that judges, like bishops, tend to come from the limited section of society that manages to send its sons to public schools and the older universities. The root cause of this, however, is not any deliberate social exclusiveness in the process of selection. Rather is it caused by economic conditions within the legal profession: the young barrister must be able to withstand the early days of relative penury, waiting for occasional briefs and doing some ill-paid devilling for his

[1] Sir G. P. Coldstream, 'Judicial Appointments in England', *Journal of the American Judicature Society*, Vol. 43, p. 43.
[2] *Ibid.*, p. 42.

seniors. Those without some private source of income often seek alternative occupation that gives greater security.

The age of judges is now affected by new retirement and pension provisions.[1] The Judicial Pensions Act, 1959, introduced a retiring age for judges: those appointed after the passage of this Act, and those who elect that its provisions apply to them, will retire at the age of 75.[1] By the same Act, judges will receive a maximum pension of one half their salary on completion of 15 years' service and on reaching the age of 70; judges who retire after 5 years receive a pension of one quarter of their salary, and for between 5-15 years' service the pension is fixed *pro rata*. Thus above the age of 60 it becomes increasingly unlikely that a man will be made a judge, for he would automatically be barred from earning the maximum pension. Similarly, those appointed over 55 will have to work beyond 70 to enjoy the maximum pension, and they may be tempted to carry on, in spite of failing health, for financial reasons. It must be stressed, however, that the present situation is a vast improvement on that prior to 1959 when no retirement age existed at all. And, in fact, the current tendency is to choose younger men, about or below 55, for whom the temptation to stay on for a better pension cannot arise.

Judgeships are not always accepted by those who are offered them. A private law practice confers a substantial degree of independence: successful advocacy can produce much personal satisfaction. Vigorous men may not be willing to sacrifice these advantages. At least one leading Q.C., who is opposed to capital punishment, feels conscientiously unable to go on the Bench while the death penalty remains on the Statute Book. Usually the main reason for refusal is financial. By their early fifties the most successful Q.C.s have built up a practice which can provide an income in excess of the salary of puisne judges, now £8,000 p.a.; before the salary was raised from £5,000 p.a. in 1954 this was even more common. This higher income level can be maintained only through considerable exertions

[1] Both the St Aldwyn Commission of 1913 and the Peel Commission of 1936 recommended that judges should retire at seventy-two. Cf. Despatch of Business at Common Law, Royal Commission. Report, Ch. IX; 1935-36, Cmd. 5065, viii. Seventy-two was fixed as the normal retiring age for County Court judges in 1934.

and, as the years pass, the security and regular tours of duty on the Bench may come to appear more attractive.

Nomination to the highest offices raises additional issues. Here the Prime Minister is responsible. Since the Prime Minister is rarely a lawyer he lacks the personal knowledge of the Bar possessed by the Lord Chancellor. However, it is traditional that the Prime Minister should seek the Chancellor's advice, and, since it is increasingly the practice for superior posts to be filled by the promotion of puisne judges, it may be that the influence of the Lord Chancellor is substantial. Whether such a system of promotion is desirable, or whether superior posts should sometimes be filled straight from the Bar, is a matter for debate. It can be argued that a good trial judge is not necessarily a good appeal judge, that it is essential for judges to feel secure and independent and that they should not be encouraged to seek further favours from the executive in the form of promotion. Alternatively, it can be urged that there is no evidence whatever that hopes of advancement have led judges to curry favour with Ministers and, in any case, the financial increment gained by becoming an appeal judge (£1,000 p.a.) is relatively small. To raise men straight from the Bar to senior appointments would give exceptional opportunities for favouritism. On balance, the system of raising judges from a lower court to a higher court would seem to reduce, rather than increase, the probability that patronage might be used for political ends. Yet it also means that appeals will always be heard by older men who are perhaps more likely to hand down a harsher, more illiberal interpretation of the law.

There remains the central question of why political patronage has died out in this field. It has, no doubt, become accepted more fully that the operation of the law should be divorced from political associations; the rise of the Labour Party strengthened this tendency. The Labour Party also ended the alternation of Whig and Tory, Liberal and Conservative governments which meant that these parties could share the fruits of victory. A judgeship also became much less desirable financially, for the salary of £5,000 p.a. remained unchanged from the reign of William IV to 1954. Also the longer sessions of the House of Commons and the growing pressure of constituency business made it far more difficult than in pre-1914 days to combine a busy law practice with a political career. There are still many barristers in the Commons—the present total is a little over a hundred and the figure has shown a tendency to rise during the 1950s[1]—but, with a few exceptions, these men are not the leading figures of the Bar. They are more interested in a political than in a legal career. Many of them are, or have been, Ministers; many will become Ministers. Many are, or will be, company directors—another source of income not available to a judge. Thus the busy lawyer has not the time to spend on politics, and the successful politician may not seek the relative isolation of the Bench. Politics and law have drifted a little apart from each other through a combination of political and economic pressures. And this is not a matter for regret.

II. LESSER JUDICIAL APPOINTMENTS

All lesser judicial appointments are now controlled by the Lord Chancellor's Department, but before 1950 the appointment of recorders and metropolitan and stipendiary magistrates was in the hands of the Home Office. There is now a concentration of judicial patronage in one department. Apart from the benefits that normally accrue from unification of parallel activities, the changes in 1950 had the further merit of removing the power to make judicial appointments from the department responsible for the police and thus achieved a fuller separation of the prosecution function from adjudication.

These appointments fall into two categories, full-time and part-time. The full-time posts are those of Crown Court recorders, County Court judges, metropolitan and stipendiary magistrates.[2] Recorders and chairmen and deputy chairmen of

---

[1] As a higher proportion of Conservative M.P.s than Labour M.P.s are barristers, this rise is partly a reflection of the increase of Conservative strength in the Commons.

[2] Registrars and masters, concerned with the organization of the work of the courts and minor, incidental matters of adjudication, are not considered here.

quarter sessions serve on a part-time basis. There are also a great number of posts, mostly part-time, associated with various administrative tribunals, but these will be considered separately in the following chapter. Barristers who wish to obtain an appointment commonly make application to the Lord Chancellor's Department. Such applications are helpful for otherwise the Department would not know who was interested in the various types of position. One barrister may be keen to obtain a recordership but not be willing to abandon his law practice entirely; another may welcome full-time salaried employment. Applicants are asked to name referees—preferably judges who have seen them in action in the courts: unless they are already well known to the Department they may also be asked to attend for an interview. But, as noted above, the law forms a close professional community and it is relatively easy to obtain well-informed opinions about the qualities of those available for a particular post. It is customary, provided that a suitable candidate is available, for a provincial appointment to go to a barrister who has practised in the area as a member of the local circuit. This is partly a matter of tradition and convenience, but it does also ensure a fair distribution of patronage as between those who work on the different circuits.

In the past, all judicial salaries paid out of national funds were fixed by statute. This is still the position for the superior judges discussed in the previous section. However, under the Judicial Offices (Salaries and Pensions) Act, 1957, the pay of the Recorders of Liverpool and Manchester, County Court judges and metropolitan magistrates may be increased by an Order submitted to Parliament by the Lord Chancellor and approved by resolution in both Houses. Thus these salary levels became more flexible and they were raised in 1957 and 1959. A common retiring age of 72 has also been established for these posts.

County Court judges now (1961) receive a salary of £4,400 p.a. There are 74 of these appointments at present, but a maximum of 80 is permitted by the County Courts Act, 1955. These numbers tend to mount with the growth of civil litigation; in 1934 the establishment was fixed at 60 and this was raised to 65 in 1950. County Court judges must be barristers of seven years' standing, and may be dismissed by the Lord Chancellor for inability or misbehaviour. Only a minority are Queen's Counsel and they are generally regarded as less than the cream of the legal profession. It is fairly unusual for a County Court judge to be promoted to the High Court. Recently two Conservative M.P.s have become County Court judges.

Full-time appointments are made in relation to criminal business as well. To relieve pressure on unpaid lay justices, 14 stipendiary magistrates are appointed in the provinces and up to 35 metropolitan magistrates. The latter receive a salary of £4,100 p.a. It is rare for a Queen's Counsel to accept one of these posts. There are also full-time recorderships at London, Liverpool and Manchester. At Liverpool and Manchester the Recorder presides over the new Crown Courts established by the Criminal Justice Administration Act, 1956,[1] to ease congestion of business. The salary of these two recorders, £5,250 p.a., is the highest obtainable in a provincial post. Opinion is divided on whether the system of Crown Courts in more or less continuous session should be extended to other heavily-populated areas. Prospects of its immediate extension are not strong. The Streatfeild Committee emphasized the social and judicial isolation of Crown Court judges, the monotony of criminal cases and the consequent risk that their judges would become stale.[2] However, there are already a handful of full-time appointments connected with the busiest quarter sessions, e.g. London and Middlesex, and in 1961 Lancashire Quarter Sessions decided that it needed a full-time deputy chairman.

Chief among the part-time judicial posts is the office of recorder. A recorder presides over a borough quarter sessions and sits alone on the bench. He must be a barrister of five years' standing and—apart from the three full-time recorders mentioned above—he can continue in private law practice.

[1] This Act followed the Report of a Departmental Committee on a Central Criminal Court in South Lancashire; 1952-53, Cmd. 8955, xiv.
[2] Business of the Criminal Courts. Interdepartmental Committee. Report; paras 132-8; 1960-61, Cmnd. 1289, xiii.

The post is salaried and the remuneration varies with the extent of the duties: before 1962 the sum was fixed by the local authority, but is now determined by the Lord Chancellor. In fact the pay has not been over-generous and did not always compensate the recorder for the loss of earnings suffered by his private practice. Yet there is a degree of honour associated with the position of recorder which helps to make the financial sacrifice less unacceptable. Some recorders are relatively young and are first appointed in their thirties and forties; these men are often promoted at a later stage to be High Court judges. It is also common for the recorder of a small borough to be transferred to a larger borough quarter sessions in the same area. The total of recorderships, including the 3 full-time posts and 6 honorary posts,[1] is now 102: the Justices of the Peace Act, 1949, abolished separate quarter sessions in towns with a population below 20,000, and eliminated thereby about 20 recorderships. A few quarter sessions in smaller towns were saved, however, by a special dispensation from the Lord Chancellor.

Pressure of work in the courts has led to the development of sub-species of recorders. A recorder may nominate a deputy to take his place or a deputy may be appointed by the Lord Chancellor. Further, assistant recorders may be appointed at busy sessions. Nominations made by the recorder are subject to the approval of the Lord Chancellor. Finally, if a recordership becomes vacant unexpectedly, it may be necessary for the Lord Chancellor to make a temporary appointment to fill the gap until a new man is chosen, in order to ensure that prisoners do not languish unreasonably in jail.

One peculiarity attaching to the office of recorder deserves special mention. Although it is an office of profit under the Crown, a part-time recordership does not disqualify its holder from service in the House of Commons—except that a re-

[1] Six boroughs have the right, by Charter, to appoint recorders although they have no Quarter Sessions. It follows that these recorderships are essentially honorary. One example is Kingston-on-Thames where a Law Officer of the Crown has often been chosen for the position. The salary, according to the Borough Charter, is six sugar loaves per annum: this has fallen into disuse but recently recorders have been presented with two sugar loaves on appointment.

corder may not represent any part of a borough in which he has judicial responsibilities. It is thus a small piece of ministerial patronage that can be held by sitting Members: at present, seven M.P.s occupy recorderships but there is no suspicion that these are distributed as political favours. The same position also applies to chairmen and deputy chairmen of county quarter sessions appointed by the Lord Chancellor.[1]

The composition of county quarter sessions is more complex. Originally it consisted of the county justices meeting at county headquarters to deal with administrative business. Thus the magistrates of quarter sessions were laymen who did not necessarily have the appropriate skill to give proper direction to juries. Criticism developed over the varying quality of the work of these courts, and the problem was aggravated by the need to reduce, as far as possible, the lists of cases to be dealt with at Assizes. The burden on Assizes could be reduced only if quarter sessions were given wider powers, but the 1936 Committee on Quarter Sessions reported that it was not in favour of such extended jurisdiction unless all chairmen of quarter sessions were legally qualified.[2] Many quarter sessions had adopted the practice of inviting someone with substantial legal experience to act as chairman, but this arrangement was not uniform. In the heavily populated counties it was not easy to find suitable men who were willing to sacrifice sufficient time for this work. London, Lancashire, Middlesex and Hertfordshire obtained powers by Private Bills to pay salaries to their chairmen and deputy chairmen, and these developments were noted with favour by the Royal Commission on the Despatch of Business at Common Law which also

---

[1] Also excluded from the Parliamentary disqualification normally attaching to offices of profit are Crown briefs, the employment of counsel to represent Government departments in lawsuits. Crown briefs are in the gift of the Attorney-General, but it is clear that political considerations do not affect their distribution. Yet there has been some concern on the Labour benches about this form of patronage and an unsuccessful amendment seeking to stop it was forced to a division at the Committee stage of the 1957 House of Commons Disqualification Bill. (See Minutes of Evidence of the Select Committee on the House of Commons Disqualification Bill Q.s 669-71; 1955-56 (349), ix. See also H.C. Deb., Vol. 566, col. 357 *et seq.*)
[2] 1935-36, Cmd. 5252, viii.

urged that all chairmen of quarter sessions should have legal qualifications.[1]

The Administration of Justice (Miscellaneous Provisions) Act, 1938, gave wider powers to quarter sessions provided they have a legally qualified chairman. (Broadly the position is that quarter sessions can deal with any form of offence except those carrying the death penalty or life imprisonment on first conviction.) The legally qualified chairman can be appointed in one of two ways. Quarter sessions can invite, as before, someone who holds high legal office, a High Court judge, a County Court judge or holders of other offices specified in the Act, to preside over them. Alternatively, quarter sessions can invite the Lord Chancellor to appoint a barrister or solicitor[2] of not less than ten years' standing as a qualified chairman or deputy chairman who may receive a salary. As a result of the 1938 Act, all quarter sessions had qualified chairmen, for the few counties that were reluctant to have such appointments ultimately submitted to persuasion from the Lord Chancellor's Department. Another consequence of the 1938 Act was to create a new category of salaried appointment. There are now (1961) eighty-eight paid chairmen and deputy chairmen of quarter sessions and the number grows steadily. The payment varies from £5,000 p.a. paid to the full-time chairman of the London Sessions to the £100 p.a. paid to the chairman of Rutland Sessions. For the rest, the sums paid are various; those that have been fixed in recent years tend to be more generous. Some counties, including a few of the larger ones, e.g. Norfolk and Somerset, still obtain qualified assistance on a voluntary basis. A High Court judge is often willing to serve in his home county and some County Court judges are able and ready to help. But while the spirit of voluntary service still exists in quarter sessions, one has the impression that, as far as legally qualified justices are concerned, it is on the decline.

In 1958 the Government appointed a committee under the chairmanship of Mr Justice Streatfeild to consider *inter alia* how the work of the criminal courts might be speeded up so

[1] P. 71; 1935-36, Cmd. 5065, viii.
[2] The choice of a solicitor is very uncommon.

that the delays suffered by those awaiting trial might be reduced. The committee reported in 1961;[1] their recommendations were transformed into legislation with unusual speed and a number of useful changes in the powers and organization of quarter and borough sessions were effected by the Criminal Justice Administration Act, 1962. Sessions can now deal with cases of night poaching, bigamy and sexual offences against a girl between thirteen and sixteen years of age. The acceptance of a legally qualified chairman is now enforced by this statute and not—as previously—through the persuasions of the Lord Chancellor. Quarter sessions can meet not merely quarterly, but as often as is necessary. In the boroughs, the appointment of an assistant recorder no longer requires the authority of a local council resolution. All these provisions will tend to increase the number of salaried posts at sessions. This the Streatfeild Committee regarded as inevitable and it also felt that the remuneration paid by local authorities was often inadequate. Under the 1962 Act the scale of payment for recorders and salaried posts at quarter sessions is fixed by the Lord Chancellor.

At a time when the demand for lawyers to preside over courts and tribunals is increasing, it is odd that the number of practising barristers should be falling. Their decline is substantial—from 2,010 in 1954 to 1,919 in 1960. A discussion of the reasons for this fall would take us beyond our present subject. However, it does increase the probability that a successful barrister will be able, if he wishes, to obtain a salaried post from the Lord Chancellor's Department. He may not, of course, be able to get exactly the sort of post he wants. It is commonly said that a Queen's Counsel can always get a County Court judgeship. Lesser men, generally, must be content with less. The stage has not been reached when the number of judicial jobs exceeds the number of lawyers looking for them. But it is important that the Lord Chancellor should have sufficient choice of men when exercising his patronage powers. The present margin is not excessive and appears to be getting smaller. If unchecked, the decline in those practising

[1] 1960-61 Cmnd. 1289, xiii.

at the Bar could have a serious effect on the future quality of the judiciary, especially in the minor posts.

By way of a tailpiece, notice must be taken of the power of the Lord Chancellor to nominate Queen's Counsel. Originally, Queen's Counsel were appointed to do legal work for the Crown, but now it has become a senior grade of barrister whose position is governed by the conventions of the legal profession. When a Q.C. appears in court he is assisted always by a 'junior' barrister, and except for writing opinions he is relieved of much paper work. Yet, for the barrister, the decision of whether or when to apply for 'silk' is delicate. It means the surrender of the type of practice that he has built up as a 'junior' and a wait for briefs from those clients who are able and willing to pay for the services of a 'leader' and a 'junior' together. The advantages of 'silk' are that the pressure of work will be less severe and the chances of obtaining a full-time salaried post are substantially increased. 'They won't let a Q.C. starve.' The total of Q.C.s in practice has been growing in recent years, because of the increase in the total of judicial posts. It now fluctuates around 180 or rather less than one-tenth of the barristers in practice. Not all of those who apply for silk are successful, at least in the first year they apply. A code of secrecy surrounds these applications; requests for silk are sent to the Lord Chancellor's office, and include the names of referees. No formal qualifications are laid down but it is understood that a minimum of ten years' experience of the Bar is necessary. The opinion of judges who know candidates are scrutinized with care. Copy books are scanned for blots.[1] Note is also taken of the supply of Q.C.s in the various circuits and specialities of the law—Chancery work, taxation, divorce, etc. It is also said that the Lord Chancellor makes inquiries about the financial status of applicants in order to eliminate those who may be seeking 'silk' as a tactic in job-hunting. In the past an M.P. was able to become a Q.C. whether or not this was justified by his standing in the legal profession. There is reason to believe that this practice has been stopped and this will help to widen the healthy gap between law and politics.

[1] Cf. 'More Silks than Ever' in *The Observer*, April 2, 1961.

CHAPTER EIGHT

Administrative Tribunals

⊙

An administrative tribunal is a body, other than a regular court of law, which is established to adjudicate on a particular type of dispute. With two chief exceptions, the Agricultural Land Tribunals and the Rent Tribunals, they deal with cases in which an individual is exercising a right to appeal against a decision of a Government department. Opportunities for the individual to come into conflict with Government agencies have multiplied as the range of State activity has broadened. The tribunals have been created to try and ensure that the powers of the State are used properly and fairly. Their number is now in excess of 2,000 and there are at least forty-two separate types. A new species of tribunal appears almost every year. In some cases where the statutes made no provision for appeals against departmental decisions, arrangements for such appeals have been made administratively, extra-legally. Thus if a farmer is dissatisfied with the amount of the subsidy payment received from the Ministry of Agriculture, he may state his objections to the local county agricultural executive committee. The committees have no statutory powers to determine subsidy payments but their rulings are almost always accepted by the Ministry.[1] Clearly, Ministers find the tribunal system to be convenient. It acts as a lightning conductor for complaints and enables minor administrative errors to be corrected. It also limits the responsibility of Ministers in individual cases, for the tribunals are independent bodies. And since the tribunals must operate within a framework of policy enshrined

[1] JUSTICE. *The Citizen and the Administration* (Stevens, 1961), p. 13.

137

in ministerial regulations, there is little likelihood that their decisions will cause major political embarrassment.

The omnibus phrase 'administrative tribunal' covers a great variety of institutions. Much variation exists in their functions, powers, personnel and pressure of business. Some tribunals meet regularly, perhaps more than once a week; some meet infrequently; some exist only in the statute book and have never yet been brought into being.[1] A few people doing this type of adjudication hold full-time salaried posts, e.g. the umpire and deputy umpires who deal with National Insurance appeals. Some members of tribunals have legal qualifications and some have not, but the chairman is usually a solicitor or barrister. Fees are paid to all members of some tribunals; elsewhere only the chairman is paid; elsewhere no fees are payable but expenses may be claimed. All persons holding full-time salaried posts are, of course, in occupation of offices of profit and barred from membership of the House of Commons, and the same rule applies to some, but not all, of the part-time fee earners. This is a field where no consistency is to be found. Thus the part-time chairman of a local National Insurance tribunal is paid and holds an office of profit, while members of a rent tribunal are also paid but are not disqualified from the Commons.[2]

It will not be possible here to give a full description of every kind of tribunal, but the following paragraphs contain an outline survey of some of the more important species and show the differing means whereby their members are recruited.[3]

---

[1] An example of the last category is the tribunal concerned with the registration of children's homes: under the Children Act, 1948, homes provided by voluntary bodies for the care of children must be registered with the Home Office, and if the Home Secretary refuses to put or retain a home on the register an appeal may be made against this decision to a specially constituted tribunal. So far this body has never had cause to meet.

[2] Difficulties caused through membership of tribunals were a major cause of the passage of the House of Commons Disqualification Act, 1957. See my *Honourable Members*, pp. 55, 60-1. The 1957 Act contains a list of disqualifying offices which is reproduced in the Appendix *infra*, pp. 259-71.

[3] Chapter 3 of Professor Robson's *Justice and Administrative Law*, 3rd edn. (Stevens, 1951), describes the work of the tribunals. The chapter was 228 pages long and then was not comprehensive.

Licensing Authorities for Public Service Vehicles

These bodies, often known as Area Traffic Commissioners, control road passenger transport. Various types of licence are issued to ensure the safe and economical operation of stage and express services. England, Wales and Scotland are divided for this purpose into eleven regions in each of which the Minister of Transport appoints a licensing authority consisting of a full-time chairman and two part-time members, except in London where the chairman acts alone. The chairmen are often drawn from the Civil Service, they retire at the age of seventy and their salary varies according to area but in 1961 is about £3,000. p.a. The part-time members, appointed for a three-year term, are drawn from two panels, one nominated by the county councils in the area and the other by the boroughs and urban districts. No commissioner may have a financial interest in a passenger transport undertaking. The explanation of the close association of local government with these bodies is historical; before the Road Traffic Act, 1930, their licensing functions were carried out by local authorities themselves.

Prevention of Fraud

This is an example of the lesser known and lesser used tribunals. Under the Prevention of Fraud (Investments) Act, 1939, investment dealers must obtain a licence from the Board of Trade. Members of Stock Exchanges and other reputable bodies are exempted from these provisions. A refusal or the revocation of a licence may be the subject of an appeal to a tribunal of three persons. The chairman and one other member must belong to the legal profession and are nominated by the Lord Chancellor. The third member is chosen by the Treasury, must have experience of finance and accountancy and must not be in the service of the Crown. Members of the tribunal are paid for their services.

The General Commissioners of Income Tax

Appeals against assessments for income tax and profits tax by the Inland Revenue go before the local General Commissioners of Income Tax. In some cases the taxpayer may choose that his case be heard by a central body, the Special Commissioners, who also have jurisdiction over surtax.[1] The Special Commissioners are whole-time civil servants in the Inland Revenue department, but they act independently when exercising their appellate functions.

Although the method of appointment of the General Commissioners was changed as recently as 1958 it is still not wholly satisfactory. Before 1958 the Commissioners were appointed by the Land Tax Commissioners, normally from among their own members.[2] The Land Tax Commissioners were charged with the administration of the ancient land tax, the compulsory redemption of which was provided for in the 1949 Budget. Thus the primary duty of this body is disappearing, and this alone necessitated a reconsideration of the method of choosing the General Commissioners. Justices of the Peace were *ex officio* Land Tax Commissioners but other commissioners were obtained from lists of persons nominated in a periodic Act of Parliament known as a 'Names Act'. The last such Act was passed in 1938. Thus by the 1950s nearly all Land Tax Commissioners and, therefore, all General Commissioners, were justices. There was also a property qualification for the General Commissioners—personal estate of £5,000 or an income of £200 p.a. from real or personal estate: this qualification was abolished by the Tribunals and Inquiries Act, 1958, in accordance with the recommendation of the Royal Commission on the Taxation of Profits and Income. The 1958 Act also transferred responsibility for appointing General Commissioners to the Lord Chancellor. The latter now carries out this duty through machinery similar to that used for the appointment of Justices of the Peace in the counties, i.e. the nominations come through the Lord Lieutenant who is aided by a local advisory committee. However, the advisory committee to deal with General Commissioners cannot be the same as that used for justices, for the latter is representative only of county (not borough) areas. But the difference is one of detail.

---

[1] There are no General Commissioners in Northern Ireland where their functions are carried out by Special Commissioners.

[2] This account is based on the Final Report of the Royal Commission on the Taxation of Profits and Income, paras. 958-67; 1955-56, Cmd. 9474, xxvii.

One suspects that the General Commissioners may be regarded as a self-co-opting body. Most of them are company directors, farmers, businessmen or retired officers.[1] The General Commissioners differ from other tribunals in that their quorum is two. Like the justices they are unpaid, although they may (since 1958) receive travelling expenses and, where appropriate, a lodging allowance. Unlike the justices there is no likelihood of this type of appointment being used as a political prize, for General Commissioners sit in private and enjoy no publicity or prestige. Here is a pure example of voluntary service without any return tangible or intangible.

The constitution of the General Commissioners is unsatisfactory because they are subject to no age limit. Since 1949 justices may not sit in judgment after the age of seventy-five, but as General Commissioners they may serve until death intervenes; frequently they are willing to continue this duty as it is often their last link with public responsibilities. Thus General Commissioners tend to be older than members of any other type of tribunal: at the time of writing the chairman of my local commission is eighty-two years of age. The imposition of retiring ages on those who exercise judicial powers is now general and it is hard to see why the General Commissioners have escaped. The danger is that an elderly body may have insufficient mental vigour to master the details of a complex case. They may also rely unduly on their clerk, especially when he is legally qualified.

Independent Schools Tribunal

Under the Education Act, 1944, independent schools must be registered with the Ministry of Education. Registration may be refused on a number of grounds, the unsuitability or inadequacy of school premises, inefficient or unsuitable instruction and the unsuitability of the proprietor or any teacher. An appeal against a refusal to register a school goes before the Independent Schools Tribunal. This body has three members drawn from two panels. The first is a list of persons with legal

[1] H.C. Deb., May 9, 1960, written answer col. *23*, gives an occupational analysis of the General Commissioners appointed since the Tribunals and Inquiries Act, 1958, came into force.

qualifications nominated by the Lord Chancellor from which the chairman is chosen. The second panel supplies the other two members of the tribunal and is chosen by the Lord President of the Council from persons with experience of teaching or the management of schools. Members are paid for their services. They are deemed to hold offices of profit and are, therefore, barred from the Commons: as the tribunal meets infrequently (only once in 1960), this seems a little unnecessary.

National Health Service Tribunal

The establishment of the National Health Service in 1948 made necessary some method of dealing with complaints against the various practitioners employed—medical, dental, optical and pharmaceutical. These complaints are heard by so-called service committees of the local health executive councils. As the health executive councils are essentially administrative organs, their composition will not be considered here.

The local executive councils are not empowered to dismiss a practitioner from the Health Service. This extreme penalty can be imposed only by a national body, the National Health Service Tribunal, and is subject to an appeal to the Minister of Health. Cases can be brought before the Tribunal either by local executive councils or by private individuals. It is rare for an individual to take a case to the tribunal and, in practice, the tribunal is the ultimate means whereby executive councils can discipline practitioners. In the first ten and a half years of the National Health Service the Tribunal had 74 cases, concerning 14 doctors, 42 dentists, 16 opticians and 2 pharmacists: in 52 cases the practitioner was barred from further employment under the Health Service or was allowed to resign.[1] The tribunal has three members. The chairman is a barrister or solicitor appointed by the Lord Chancellor. The other members are appointed by the Minister of Health. One is drawn from a panel nominated by the local health executive councils; the second is a person from the same profession as the individual whose conduct is under consideration and who is drawn from a panel representing the professional associations concerned.

[1] Ministry of Health. Annual Report for 1958, p. 143; 1958-59, Cmnd. 806, xv. Out of fourteen appeals to the Minister, two succeeded.

National Insurance and Industrial Injuries

Claims arising out of the National Insurance Acts are subject to a three-tier system of adjudication. Initially, applications for benefit go to an insurance officer appointed by the Ministry of Pensions and National Insurance. This officer has independent status within the Ministry and cannot be over-ruled by his superiors. He can determine an application himself or—and this is rare—he may send it on to the local tribunal. An appeal from the decision of the officer also goes to the local tribunal. Finally, appeals from local tribunals go before the National Insurance Commissioner or one of his deputies: these officials hold full-time salaried posts, they are legally qualified, represent no sectional interest and are independent of ministerial influence. Their status is shown by the fact that the commissioner and the majority of the deputies are Queen's Counsel.

The jurisdiction of the local tribunals is not unlimited, e.g. a dispute as to whether a claimant has satisfied the contribution requirements for benefit goes not to the tribunal but to the Minister. Since 1959 these tribunals have dealt also with appeals against a refusal to grant family allowances. The 204 tribunals are very busy. In 1958 they heard 39,017 cases under the National Insurance Acts and a further 6,839 industrial injury cases.[1] A tribunal has three members but the chairman alone receives a fee.

Chairmen have been nominated by the Lord Chancellor since 1958. They serve for a three-year term, are eligible for reappointment but must retire at age seventy-two. A total of 288 chairmen have been appointed for the 204 local tribunals. When more than one is appointed to a local tribunal they are invited to sit in rotation:[2] this prevents any possibility of the Ministry quietly 'dropping' a chairman who has become *persona non grata*, a device sometimes used by the Ministry of Labour in the pre-war tribunals. Officials of the Ministry of Pensions and National Insurance undertake the initial stages in the selection of chairmen and a confidential code issued by

[1] Ministry of Pensions and National Insurance. Report for 1958, para. 197; 1958-59, Cmnd. 826, xviii.
[2] This safeguard was introduced at the suggestion of the National Insurance Advisory Committee. Cf. W. A. Robson, *Justice and Administrative Law*, 3rd edn., p. 205.

the Ministry lays down various desiderata which govern this process.[1] Chairmen must be legally qualified (an almost invariable rule), and be prepared to master the law relating to National Insurance. They must have a knowledge of industrial and working-class conditions and should combine the qualities of independence and impartiality. Lower and upper age limits on first appointment are set at thirty-five and sixty-five. To ensure impartiality, people with strong political attachments are excluded from consideration; M.P.s, Parliamentary candidates, party officials and political speakers are thus disqualified. When a vacancy occurs, the regional office of the Ministry makes inquiries among those who have knowledge of the local personnel of the legal profession, e.g. the Registrar of the County Court, the Town Clerk or the Clerk to the Justices. A senior official then interviews possible candidates and the opinion of the chairman of the local advisory committee of the Ministry may be sought. Next, the names of at least three candidates in order of preference are sent forward from the region to Ministry headquarters. What happens then is obscure, except that the Ministry submits names to the Lord Chancellor. The Lord Chancellor's Department, as already noted, has its own sources of information about the legal profession, but presumably the recommendation of the Ministry is not overturned unless there are good reasons for so doing.

The other members of a tribunal are drawn from two panels, one representing employers, the other employees. The panels contain over 6,000 names and are revised every three years. They are nominated through the local advisory committees of the Ministry and, in practice, by the same organizations that nominate members to the advisory committees, i.e. various local employers' organizations, Chambers of Commerce and local trade unions through the Trades Council. One aspect of this arrangement must be noted. A claimant appearing before a tribunal is entitled to assistance from another person, possibly a solicitor but more often a trade union official. Thus it

[1] For a fuller description of the code and its operation see Susan McCorquodale, 'The Composition of Administrative Tribunals', in *Public Law*, Autumn 1962, pp. 298-302.

can and does happen that the same man will be, on one occasion, a member of a tribunal and, on another, will appear before the same tribunal as an unpaid advocate. In theory, this arrangement is offensive: in practice, it appears to work well.

The system of adjudication of claims for industrial injuries benefits is parallel to that for National Insurance claims and does not demand separate description. In addition, however, disputes about the extent of a disablement go before a medical board. Either party may appeal from the decision of a medical board to a medical appeals tribunal. There are thirteen of these tribunals which are organized on a regional basis. As usual, they consist of three persons. The chairman must be a lawyer, is often a Queen's Counsel, and is chosen from a panel nominated by the Lord Chancellor. The other members are medical men of high professional standing; they are appointed by the Minister of Health after recommendations have been received from the Royal College of Physicians and Surgeons for the London tribunal, and from the Heads of Medical Faculties of local universities for the provincial tribunals. All members are paid and the volume of work involved is substantial.

Agricultural Land Tribunals

The Agricultural Land Tribunals were instituted by the Agriculture Act, 1947. Initially they had wide powers which included appeals against supervision orders by county agricultural executives to ensure the efficient management of farms, and appeals over dispossession orders against landowners made by the Minister of Agriculture in the interests of good husbandry. These sanctions were widely unpopular, much criticized and decreasingly used before their termination in 1958. Part of the criticism arose from the *Woollett* case which concerned the method of appointment of the tribunals. An Agricultural Land Tribunal had upheld a dispossession order against Mrs Woollett who owned a smallholding of four acres in Essex. Mrs Woollett appealed to the High Court against the decision principally on the ground that the members of the tribunal had been improperly appointed. The members of the tribunal, other than the chairman, were to be appointed by the Minister of Agriculture from panels representing farmers and landowners. In this instance they had been chosen by the secretary of the tribunal, a civil servant, who was unable to show that he had received authority to act for the Minister. However, as the Agriculture Act provided that the decisions of a tribunal should be valid, notwithstanding a defect in the appointment of its members, Mrs Woollett lost her case.[1] The Minister appreciated the widespread feeling that she had been unjustly treated and let her have the land back. The Agriculture (Miscellaneous Provisions) Act, 1954, attempted to remedy this situation by transferring responsibility for maintaining the farmer and landowner panels to the Lord Chancellor, and the selection of members for each sitting was vested in the chairman. In practice this made no difference as *ad hoc* members continued to be chosen by the clerk.[2]

The functions of these tribunals were greatly reduced by the Agriculture Act, 1958. They now deal with disputes between landlord and tenant about the occupation of agricultural land. On the application of a landlord the tribunal may dispossess a tenant on one of three grounds, sound estate management, good husbandry or balance of hardship as against the owner. There are nine such tribunals. The chairman, the only member to be paid, must be a barrister or solicitor of seven years standing and is appointed by the Lord Chancellor. The other two members are drawn from two panels, one representative of farmers, the other of landowners, nominated respectively by the National Farmers' Union and the Country Landowners' Association. When asking for nominees the Lord Chancellor may be fairly precise in his requirements: thus he has told the Lancashire N.F.U. that there should be men on tribunals with 'experience of the smaller type of farm, including milk producers and producer-retailers'.[3]

[1] Initially, Mrs Woollett won the case in the High Court where Mr Justice Stable held that the saving clause to cover defects in appointment could not apply because no appointments had been made. The Court of Appeal did not accept this argument.
[2] H. Storing and P. Self, 'The Birch in the Cupboard' in *Public Law*, Winter 1960, p. 377.
[3] McCorquodale, p. 313. For further comment on the personnel and method of appointment of these tribunals, see below, p. 150.

Rent Tribunals

Due to the severe housing shortage in the post-war period
Rent Tribunals were established in 1946 to control rents of
furnished accommodation. Similar tribunals had existed in
Scotland since 1943, and the 1945 Report of the Interdepartmental Committee on Rent Control proposed the extension of
this system south of the Border.[1] The jurisdiction of Rent Tribunals was extended in 1949 but curtailed in 1957. The forty-
three remaining tribunals are less used than formerly. They
are, however, of special interest for two reasons. First, they
deal with disputes between private individuals and not, as with
other tribunals, between an individual and some ramification
of the state. Second, there has been substantial dissatisfaction
with the quality of their personnel. The work of Rent Tribunals might well have been allocated to the existing courts,
probably the County Courts. Reasons for creating separate
Rent Tribunals were *inter alia* that they would be quicker and
cheaper. Also, according to Mr Key, speaking in the Commons, people would be less frightened of going before them
especially 'if they consist of ordinary people'.[2] In the same
debate Mr Bevan, Minister of Health, suggested that tribunals
would work 'more justly and fit in more snugly with local
circumstances if the chairman of the tribunal is usually a lay
person'. In spite of this view of the responsible Minister, a
clear majority of the chairmen appointed were legally
qualified.

The principles by which members of Rent Tribunals were
chosen have never been wholly clear. Members were not to
represent the interests of any particular section of the community, so the technique of the representative panel was not
appropriate. Lords Lieutenant and the advisory committees
for the appointment of Justices of the Peace were not consulted: possibly Mr Bevan viewed them with some political
suspicion. Furthermore, the Rent Tribunals had to be established in a hurry, and one has a firm impression that the administrative officers of the Ministry of Health were left to do
the best they could. 'Bodies such as local authorities, the Bar

[1] 1944-45, Cmd. 6621, v.
[2] H.C. Deb., Vol. 415, col. 2015. Mr Key was then the Minister of Works.

Council and the Law Society were invited to submit names. In addition, a number of persons offered themselves as candidates.[1] Many councillors and retired officials of local authorities were appointed, but the choice of councillors is open to serious objection because local authorities can and do refer cases to the tribunals. Thus the principle 'no man shall be judge in his own cause' is open to violation. The Franks Committee reported that they had received more criticism of Rent Tribunals than of any other type of tribunal, and noted that some Rent Tribunal decisions had been quashed in the High Court due to irregularities of procedure.[2] The Committee therefore recommended that all chairmen be legally qualified, and as the appointment of chairmen was transferred to the Lord Chancellor in 1958 it is unlikely that any further lay appointments will be made. Members of Rent Tribunals are paid but the fee is modest; the Franks Committee thought fees should be increased to attract the services of members of the right quality.

It will be apparent from these descriptions of particular tribunals that no general statements about the constitution of tribunals can be made. The most common features are that a tribunal has three members; that the chairman is legally qualified and is appointed by the Lord Chancellor; that the other members are selected from panels which represent the profession or the section of the community most closely concerned.

In 1955 the Government appointed a committee to undertake a full investigation into administrative tribunals and inquiries. This body—usually known as the Franks Committee —reported in 1957 and made a number of basic recommendations concerning the appointment of administrative tribunals. It proposed the establishment of two councils, one for England and Wales and the other for Scotland, to keep the working of tribunals under continuous review. It urged that the appointment and removal of tribunal chairmen be the responsibility of the Lord Chancellor, or in Scotland of the Lord

---

[1] Robson, *op. cit.*, p. 248.
[2] Administrative Tribunals and Enquiries. Committee. Report, para. 161; 1956-57, Cmnd. 218, viii.

President of the Court of Session or the Lord Advocate; that chairmen of appellate tribunals should be legally qualified; that other chairmen be legally qualified as a general rule. The report suggested that the new councils should appoint the other members of tribunals. The councils should also review rates of remuneration where this was payable.

Many of these suggestions were adopted by the Government. A single Council on Tribunals with a Scottish sub-committee was established by the Tribunals and Inquiries Act, 1958. The same Act entrusted the Lord Chancellor with the appointment of chairmen for many more tribunals, including those for national assistance, national insurance and industrial injuries, some National Service tribunals and the Rent Tribunals. In Scotland similar powers go to the Lord President of the Court of Session and in Northern Ireland to the Chief Justice of Northern Ireland. Thus these posts are placed squarely in the hands of the legal fraternity. But the recommendation that the Council on Tribunals undertake the nomination of the rank-and-file tribunal members has not been adopted. Mr Butler explained to the Commons that this duty, in addition to its other tasks of general supervision, would be beyond the resources of the Council.[1] Members of the Council serve on a part-time basis, but the making of appointments—there are about 19,000 names on the various panels—would require daily attention. It follows that these appointments, in general, continue to rest with the Minister most closely concerned with the work of a tribunal. However, by Section 4 of the 1958 Act, the Council can make general recommendations about appointments to tribunals. So intervention is possible at any time it should feel that this amorphous system of patronage is working ill.

The annual reports of the Council on Tribunals show that it has not yet made any great use of the powers under Section 4. There has been no attempt so far to make a general survey of the techniques of appointment, to consider if they are satisfactory or whether improvements might be made. Members of the Council do attend tribunals to assess whether the proceedings are well conducted: notice of these visits is given

[1] H.C. Deb., Vol. 590, col. 1615.

to tribunals, so there is no 'snooping'. The Council has been occupied mainly with tribunal and inquiry procedure, with questions of accommodation and individual complaints. Its criticisms on personnel have concentrated on the Agricultural Land Tribunals. The Council proposed age limits for this tribunal—that the chairmen should be appointed for a three-year term and not be reappointed above the age of 72, while other members should retire at 70 as it is essential that they have a full understanding of modern methods of farming. It also proposed that a land agent who is on the panel from which a tribunal is formed should be barred from appearing before it professionally. The Lord Chancellor accepted these recommendations.[1] The Council were concerned at the quality of membership of Agricultural Land Tribunals and their Second Report throws further light on the methods of selection. Most appointments to tribunals for which the Lord Chancellor is responsible are reviewed every three years: up to 1960 this had not been done with agricultural tribunals—but will be in future. 'The Lord Chancellor has since informed us that all future nominations to these panels will be carefully scrutinized by the chairmen who are in a position to make local inquiries of their own; and he has assured us that if nominating bodies put forward names of people who turn out on further examination to be unsuitable, he will take the matter up with them.'[2]

No action, so far, has been taken to follow up the Council's own intimation in its First Report that an investigation would be carried out into rates of payment to members of tribunals. Here one suspects very strongly the restraining hand of the Treasury. Publication of the varying scales would invite embarrassing comparisons and financial demands from the more lowly paid. Adjustments to fees have been made recently, but anomalies still exist. The newer tribunals tend to receive the more generous treatment for the fees paid are related to current money values: scales of payment laid down in earlier years may remain unchanged. There is also the wider issue of

[1] Council on Tribunals. First Report, p. 22; 1960 Non. Parl. Lord Chancellor's Department.
[2] Second Report, p. 20; 1961 Non Parl. Lord Chancellor's Department.

when tribunal service should be gratuitous. The principle appears to be that expert—notably legal and medical—members are paid while those who serve in a representative capacity are not. This distinction is awkward to apply to rent tribunals; in this case the definition of 'expert' must be a little elastic.

The control of appointments to tribunals raises two separate problems—the choice of chairmen and the supervision of the panels from which other members are drawn. Chairmen are now, almost always, legally qualified, and their selection has been centralized in the Lord Chancellor's office. The task is similar to that of making the local judicial appointments described in the previous chapter. Opinions of trusted members of the legal fraternity can be collected and choices made on the basis of these recommendations. However, many tribunal chairmen are solicitors, so that the range of choice is wider and information about potential candidates may be more dispersed. Even so, the posts available must be distributed within a strictly defined professional circle. No such limits apply to the panels. The descriptions of particular tribunals have shown how various organizations are invited to submit nominations. Here the initiative may rest with limited groups of people— members of a committee of the organization concerned. There is a danger of self-nomination by local cliques. If a panel is reconstituted every three years, renomination may tend to be automatic. What check can be made on the suitability of nominations? For a Government department to institute inquiries about each name submitted would be an excessive task. The solution is for chairmen to be asked to report—as is being done with the Agricultural Land Tribunals—on the suitability of panel members. Since the selection of members, other than chairmen, to adjudicate at each hearing is left normally to the clerk of a tribunal it would be possible for an eccentric member to be quietly dropped. While this could be admirable in practice, for a civil servant to be able to exercise such a power over a quasi-judicial body is objectionable. Members should always be asked to serve on a rota. In fact, some panel members sit more often than others, usually because it is known that they are generally able and willing to do so.

The key to the quality of a tribunal is the chairman. If he is lacking in good humour, patience, sympathy or understanding, it will be impossible for the other members to cover over these deficiencies. The converse is not so true. A member prone to ask absurd questions or make irrelevant observations may be smothered by firm chairmanship. But the calibre of panel members is still of importance. Not all chairmen are capable of dealing firmly with an unintelligent colleague, and any chairman sitting with two unsuitable colleagues would be in an impossible situation. This raises the problem of how to deal with unsuitable members. To give Ministers unfettered discretion to dismiss them would be to undermine the independence of tribunals. Section 5 of the Tribunals and Inquiries Act, 1958, ensures that a tribunal member cannot be dispensed with unless consent is obtained from the Lord Chancellor, and in some cases from the Lord President of the Court of Session or the Chief Justice of Northern Ireland. Such procedure would be used only *in extremis*. The simpler way to control personnel of tribunals is to make all appointments for a limited period of, say, three years. Increasingly this is common practice. There can, however, be two views on whether it is desirable, for here again is danger to the independence of tribunals. Since 1958 the Council on Tribunals has provided an alternative safeguard. The examples given above show that the Council's watchdog service has had some useful results and the very knowledge that it exists may help to prevent abuses. Other matters it has dealt with by informal consultation and negotiation which—granted the conventions of behaviour among public servants—will not be officially recounted. Thus the extent and the value of the work of the Council cannot be fully judged from the limited contents of its formal reports.

The patronage associated with the tribunals is of interest more because of its extent and diversity than because of its inherent importance. To make the large number of appointments required, Government departments must have local help. This could come from specially created advisory committees or from the existing committees that nominate J.P.s. Alternatively, local organizations can be asked to submit nominations. The latter method is the one most used—and for good reasons. Administratively it is far simpler, for it avoids the initial problem of assembling *ad hoc* local committees. Secondly, it gives frank recognition to the fact that particular tribunals are of special concern to limited sections of the community. Finally, it helps to get away from some of the secrecy and the political ties which govern the selection of Justices of the Peace.

CHAPTER NINE

The Selection of Justices of the Peace

⊙

I

For six centuries the Justice of the Peace has occupied an influential place in our public affairs. The scope of his duties —administrative and judicial—grew steadily until the rise of the popular demand that expenditure of public funds should be controlled by persons selected by a system of popular election. Thus justices surrendered the supervision of poor relief to Boards of Guardians, although the justices became *ex officio* guardians, and in 1888 the bulk of the administrative business of quarter sessions passed on to the new county councils. But the justices still retain their original duty, responsibility for public order: their office commands a degree of respect which today is far higher than that accorded by Shakespeare to Justice Shallow or by Dickens to Mr Nupkins. The status of the justice is a reflection of the probity of public life; it is an acknowledgment that their willingness to sacrifice time on communal responsibilities is untainted by any opportunities for personal gain.

Each county council and each borough with a separate body of justices has a Commission from the Crown and, technically, the names of the members of each Bench are placed on a schedule to its Commission. This is commonly known as 'being put on the Commission'. Appointment is normally for life, but can be terminated by the Lord Chancellor at any time; and a justice loses his position should he move to another district. Women have been eligible for appointment since the Sex Disqualification (Removal) Act, 1919.

The right to appoint county justices has always belonged to the Crown, but the channels through which nominations

154

have had to pass were varied at different periods. The later Stuarts used these appointments as a means of attempting to strengthen the political position of the monarchy. After 1688 the practice was established whereby the Lord Chancellor obtained nominations from the Lords Lieutenant of the counties: the right of the Lord Chancellor to add or delete names was never renounced although it fell into disuse during the eighteenth century. The Lord Lieutenant was normally the most powerful landowner in a county and held his office for life. Although an *ex officio* justice, he frequently remained completely aloof from county administration. One of his few duties was to appoint the Clerk of the Peace for the county and this official sometimes played an important part in the choice of new justices. More often, the Lord Lieutenant consulted with the Chairman of Quarter Sessions and the latter, in turn, might consult his fellow justices. Thus a tendency developed for the magistracy to become a self co-opting body and abuses grew alongside the possibilities of peculation. Apart from demanding a fee for any service requested of him, such as signing papers, a justice could allow monetary considerations to sway his judgment in imposing punishment or granting licences. The trading justice was the product of a system which aimed at making the administration of justice a self-supporting occupation.[1] In Middlesex the corruption of the justices was widely known. Burke described them in the House of Commons (1780) as 'generally the scum of the earth —carpenters, bricklayers, shoemakers; some of whom were notoriously men of such infamous character as that they were unworthy of any employ whatever, and others so ignorant that they could scarcely write their own names'.[2] The growth of public works—for which the magistrates were responsible —further added to the chances of illicit profit through the placing of contracts large and small. For some forty years after Burke's denunciation, the Mainwaring family in Middlesex and Merceron from Bethnal Green continued to reach a

[1] S. & B. Webb, *The Parish and the County* (Longmans Green, 1906), p. 326. This work contains the classic account of the corruption of county government in the period before 1835. Originally, justices were paid 4s a day but, with the decline in the value of money, this custom fell into disuse.
[2] *The Parliamentary History*, Vol. xxi, p. 592.

high level in the art of misappropriation of public funds. Jobbery of this nature was difficult to stop, not least because honest men were unwilling to become tainted by association with public administration. Ultimately the problem was solved by the appointment of paid justices, the forerunners of the present Metropolitan magistrates. Originally their salaries were paid from Secret Service funds. Middlesex was not, of course, a typical county. In the majority of shires the squirearchy dominated the local Bench and provided honest, if conservative and uninspired government. The difficulty in the more urbanized areas was the lack of sufficient men of good estate to provide sound community leadership.

The unscrupulousness of—to use the Webbs' phrase—the Justices of Mean Degree led to demands that the property qualification for their office be raised. An act of 1439 stated that justices be 'of the most sufficient knights, esquires and gentlemen of the law' and must own estate within the county of their appointment of not less than £20 a year, but the Lord Chancellor was also given discretion to waive the property barrier in the case of persons of suitable experience. In 1731 the qualification was raised to the possession of landed property worth £100 a year, but men lacking such assets still occasionally contrived to get appointed in urbanized districts, either because the law was not enforced or because it was circumvented by the possession of mortgaged property. And since prosperity was not an infallible guarantee of probity, the 1731 legislation did not achieve its purpose everywhere. However, during the latter half of the eighteenth century the larger landowners began to take public responsibilities more seriously and the Benches were dominated by the rich. Together the Anglican gentry and some Anglican clergy ruled the county— tithe charges being the basis for the clergy qualification. During the reform agitation of the 1830s the class exclusiveness of the justices caused widespread criticism: Lord Brougham, the Lord Chancellor, warned Lords Lieutenant in 1830 that he would interfere with their selections unless they chose from a wider category of persons.[1] Three years later the

[1] Selection of Justices of the Peace. Royal Commission. Report, p. 5; 1910 Cd. 5250, xxxvii.

nomination of a Wesleyan landowner who had, in past years, owned a shop, caused a 'strike' by the Merioneth magistrates.

A major complaint against county benches was their severe enforcement of the Game Laws. Objection was also taken to the inclusion of the large number of clergy, whose influence was increased by their more regular attendance at sessions. In favour of the clergy it might be said that they took a more balanced view of poaching than did landowners. From a debate in the House of Lords in 1875 it appears that the choice of clergy was often due to the lack of other suitable, qualified and willing candidates; this shortage caused a cut in the property qualification to the occupation of a dwelling-house assessed to the inhabited house duty at not less than £100.[1] The restriction was swept away altogether by the Liberal Government of 1906, and the residential qualification was amended from 'within the county' by the phrase 'or within seven miles thereof'.

The system of appointing borough or corporate magistrates was wholly different. They were fewer in number, usually being from one to six of the chief office-holders in the Municipal Corporation. Thus they were chosen locally and symbolized the independence of their town from county administration. As borough quarter sessions were presided over by a recorder with legal qualifications, the attainments of borough justices were of less importance than those of their county fellows—as far as graver criminal business was concerned. The corporations themselves were largely self co-opting oligarchies, renowned for looking after the interests of their own members rather than for seeking to benefit the townspeople at large. Even so, criticism of borough justices was directed more to their standards of competence than standards of honesty, for the county gentry feared that shopkeeper magistrates would not control the riotous assemblies caused by the social and economic ills of the Industrial Revolution.

The proposals to reshape municipal institutions and place them on a democratic foundation created a problem over the

---

[1] Parl. Deb., 3rd Series, Vol. 223, col. 765 *et seq.* See also E. Halevy in *A Century of Municipal Progress* (ed. H. J. Laski; Allen & Unwin, 1935), p. 25.

future method of selecting magistrates. Were the rights of the corporations in this matter left unchanged, it followed that the magistracy would be chosen as a consequence of elections based on a ratepayer franchise. While Radicals welcomed this prospect, both Whigs and Tories opposed it in varying degree. In the unreformed corporations the justices were appointed independently of the majority of the townspeople they were called on to judge; once the corporations were popularly elected this relationship would be altered and the magistrates might be subjected to various types of local influence. On this issue the Webbs do not support the Radicals. To quote their view, 'The administration of criminal justice, in its humblest as in its most pretentious grades is emphatically a service of national interest, in which it is desirable that the interests and prejudices, the prepossessions and antipathies of the population of the particular locality should have the least possible play.'[1] In the original form of the Municipal Corporations Bill the mayor, annually chosen by the local council, was an *ex officio* justice, but the appointment of other borough justices was to be in the hands of the Crown, i.e. the Lord Chancellor, who was, however, to act on nominations received from local councils. This amounted to a system of choice by indirect election. It became one of the sources of contention in the battle between Lords and Commons over the Bill and, as a final compromise, Melbourne's Government agreed to the omission of any reference to nomination by town councils. For the remainder of their period of office the Whig Government, in practice, did invite formal nominations from local councils, but the custom was dropped by Peel in 1841 and never revived. Leading members of councils were still asked privately, however, to make suggestions about suitable appointees to their borough Bench.

Controversy over the method of selecting justices has tended to ebb and flow with the tides of national political opinion. When Conservatism has been in the ascendant, less

[1] S. & B. Webb, *The Manor and the Borough* (Longmans Green, 1908), p. 727. For a full description of the passage of the Municipal Corporations Act see *ibid.*, pp. 737-47. F. C. Mather, *Public Order in the Age of the Chartists* (Manchester University Press, 1959), pp. 52-73, gives an account of the appointment of—and the incompetence of—J.P.s in the Chartist period.

has been heard of the topic: with a Liberal or, more recently, a Labour administration in power, inquiries and important changes have taken place. Towards the end of the nineteenth century renewed criticism arose over the predominance of Conservatives among magistrates, a predominance much strengthened by the split in the Liberal Party in 1886 over Gladstone's Home Rule policy for Ireland. The Liberal view that Lords Lieutenant were Conservative in outlook and inspiration led the Commons to approve Sir Charles Dilke's motion in 1893 'that the appointment of county magistrates should no longer be made only on the recommendation of Lords Lieutenant'.[1] Lord Herschell, the Lord Chancellor, acted on this resolution, and a number of working men and people of modest means were subsequently appointed to the Bench. On these appointments Redlich and Hirst commented 'they prove that a popular government can . . . entirely alter the complexion of an institution . . . by assigning democratic officers to an oligarchic office'.[2] As a statement of theory this is entirely acceptable; in fact, these appointments did little to alter the established character of the benches. In Lancashire, where the Minister responsible is not the Lord Chancellor but the Chancellor of the Duchy, a series of changes in the process of selection were made between 1870 and 1908 owing to continual dissatisfaction over the character, and sometimes the number, of magistrates chosen.[3]

In 1906 the property qualification for county justices was ended. Three years later the Liberal Government followed this step by instituting a Royal Commission to inquire into the Selection of Justices of the Peace. Evidence presented to the Commission demonstrated how far the local administration of justice was in the hands of those with Conservative sympathies. Lord Loreburn described the consequence in this way: 'Social life in most counties among those who are well-to-do is mainly Conservative. . . . There is often a large field of selection (for justices) and it is natural that men should regard more favour-

[1] Parl. Deb., 4th Series, Vol. 12, col. 258.
[2] *The History of Local Government in England* (Macmillan, 1903), Vol. I, p. 205.
[3] For details see Selection of Justices of the Peace. Royal Commission. Report, p. 6; 1910 Cd. 5250, xxxvii.

ably those who are of the same opinion as themselves."[1] The Commission found that at least one Lord Lieutenant was assisted by an informal committee which made careful inquiry into conditions in each Petty Sessional division within his county to enable him to decide how many J.P.s were needed for each area. But over the greater part of the country no such careful scrutiny took place and each Lord Lieutenant consulted variously the Chairman of Quarter Sessions, Chairmen of Petty Sessions, the Clerk of the Peace, Clerks of the Justices or his personal friends about the need for new appointments and who might fill them. It is not surprising that the Commission reported that there was 'some grounds for the suggestion that opportunities of obtaining information afforded to Lords Lieutenant are not satisfactory'.[2] More support for this conclusion can be found in the figures relating to the religious affiliation of magistrates in Wales at this period; 478 belonged to nonconformist denominations and 1,006 to the Church of England—a proportion which quite failed to reflect the overwhelming Welsh allegiance to nonconformity.[3]

For the boroughs up to 1910 the Lord Chancellor had received a large number of recommendations from M.P.s, Parliamentary candidates, political associations and their agents. The inspiration behind these recommendations was obviously political—a desire to obtain favour for individuals prominently associated with a political organization, Conservative or Liberal. Some M.P.s had openly objected to the rôle they were expected to play in this system.[4] The Royal Commission reported that it was strongly opposed to the political basis for the selection of magistrates and to the submission of uninvited party nominations to the Lord Chancellor. It urged that working men with intimate knowledge of conditions of life among their own class should be appointed to county as well as to borough Benches. And while agreeing

[1] Royal Commission Report, p. 8.
[2] *Ibid.*, p. 7.
[3] Selection of Justices of the Peace. Royal Commission. Minutes of evidence. App. VI; 1910 Cd. 5358, xxxvii.
[4] Parl. Deb., 4th Series, Vol. 156, col. 612 (Mr Henderson), and at Vol. 155, col. 1544, Mr Luttrell urged that J.P.s be elected by county and borough councils.

that the Lord Chancellor, the Chancellor of the Duchy and the Lords Lieutenant should retain their existing responsibilities in relation to the selection of justices, the Commission proposed that advisory committees be appointed to assist Lords Lieutenant. The Lord Chancellor should also be empowered to create similar committees for boroughs. These committees, it was hoped, would produce a local magistracy drawn from all sections of the community; they would also have the tasks of advising on the total of justices required in their respective areas and the advisability of calling on justices to resign in cases of non-attendance. The Liberal Government authorized the establishment of these bodies which, however, failed to produce satisfactory results.

What guarantee could there be that advisory committees were themselves well-suited to carry out their task of nomination? The evidence of Mr Leo Page, a former Secretary of the Commissions,[1] to the Royal Commission of 1946-48 was not reassuring. In 1943 a borough with a population of over 60,000 had an advisory committee of 5 people. 'The chairman was a man well into his 70s who had been an invalid for a couple of years. A second member was 76 and also an invalid; a third member was 80, a doctor who had retired from all practice, and the only woman member was 80 years of age and almost stone blind. Another committee, this time in a county, consisted of 6 members in addition to the Lord Lieutenant. The first was 82 years of age, deaf and feeble; the second member was 80; the third was blind and out of touch with the affairs of the county; the fourth was ill and had taken no part in public work for some time; the fifth was an efficient member; and the sixth, the only woman, was over 90 years of age.'[2] This frightening picture of senility cannot be reflected today because age limits for committee members have since been introduced. Yet we can be certain that the 1910 Commission had no intention that such aged and feeble persons be entrusted with powers of patronage.

[1] The Secretary of the Commissions is the member of the Lord Chancellor's staff responsible for administrative work connected with Justices of the Peace.

[2] Justices of the Peace. Royal Commission. Minutes of evidence, App. III, p. 81; 1948 Non-Parl.

Only too often the Benches of magistrates themselves had much in common with the committees described by Mr Page. In the 1930s there was growing criticism of the work of lay justices. It is usual to associate this criticism with the growth of motoring and motoring offences, for this brought a new type of defendant before the courts—the middle-class car owner—who frequently had legal representation. Thus the well-to-do and the legal profession became more aware of the way in which petty sessions were conducted. Their concern was reflected in at least three authoritative works, *English Justice* by 'Solicitor' (1932), *Justice of the Peace* by Leo Page (1936) and *The Machinery of Justice in England* by R. M. Jackson (1940): these authors were men of differing political views and experience, yet their analysis of the shortcomings of magistrates' courts were remarkably similar. Many justices were too old, too deaf, too feeble or otherwise incapable of giving sustained attention to a long and difficult case. Defendants who pleaded 'Not guilty' were unpopular because they consumed more time: often they suffered a stiffer penalty than those who admitted a similar offence. Magistrates were often ignorant of the law, or depended too heavily on the clerk of the court. They tended to assume that police evidence must be true: they might resent cross-examination of evidence for the prosecution: they were unwilling to operate the provisions of the Poor Prisoners' Defence Act, 1930[1]: above all, they tended to be more concerned with the preservation of law and order and the protection of private property than with the impartial administration of justice.

Widespread complaints about the age and infirmities of some justices led the Lord Chancellor to issue a circular in 1938 which suggested that justices who were incapacitated for these reasons might apply to be transferred to a supplemental list. They would not then be summoned to sit in court but would still be available for minor duties as witnessing signatures on various official documents. Transfer to the supplemental list was voluntary: if a decrepit justice could not be persuaded into retirement, the sole remedy was for the Lord Chancellor to dismiss him from the Commission. And

[1] Now replaced by the Legal Aid and Advice Act, 1949.

the transfer was no bar to a justice subsequently reappearing in court should he decide to do so. In some areas the 1938 move had the reverse of the desired effect: aged justices, whose attendance at court had become infrequent, were often annoyed by the circular and proceeded to turn up regularly. Two years later the then Lord Chancellor, Lord Simon, initiated the practice of requiring newly appointed magistrates to give an undertaking to retire from active duty on reaching the age of seventy-five. The Justices (Supplemental List) Act, 1941, further strengthened the hand of the Lord Chancellor. The Act empowered him to translate a justice to the supplemental list and those on the list were prohibited from adjudicating in court, although they could still attend court to deal with administrative business. These useful reforms did not obviate the difficulty of how the Lord Chancellor was to obtain reliable information about the degree of infirmity suffered by ageing justices.

It was against this background that the Labour Government established a second Royal Commission on Justices of the Peace in 1946. Labour supporters were also still critical of the social and political composition of local Benches which they felt to be dominated by adherents of Conservatism. The Report of the Royal Commission[1] recommended a number of minor reforms, many of which fall outside the present subject —the technique of public appointment. These included the suggestion that a retiring age of seventy-five be made statutory, a proposal which was incorporated in the Justices of the Peace Act, 1949. The Report, together with the minutes of evidence, contained a frank explanation of how justices were selected and the extent to which political parties dominated the arrangements. To ensure the preservation of political balance, the Lord Chancellor kept a check on the political affiliation of those who served on local advisory committees: the position relating to the county committees in 1946 is set out in the table overleaf.[2]

[1] 1947-48 Cmd. 7463, xii.
[2] Justices of the Peace. Royal Commission. Minutes of evidence. App. I, p. 55; 1946 Non-Parl.

POLITICAL COMPOSITION OF
COUNTY ADVISORY COMMITTEES

Area	Cons.	Lab.	Lib.	Ind.
England and Wales (except Lancs.)	169	146	116	34
London	19	15	5	1
Scotland	85	67	67	7
Totals	273	228	188	42

Independents existed on less than one-third of the committees. No Liberal appeared in Northumberland or West Lothian, although the committees for both these areas contained a member styled as Independent. Through the Lord Chancellor's vigilance, nowhere did one party have an absolute majority on a committee. The presence of as many as forty-two Independents on county committees in 1946 was due to the efforts of Mr Leo Page who held the office of Secretary of the Commissions during the war.[1] Although full information is not available, it seems that the proportion of Independents was even lower in the boroughs than the counties. The Royal Commission was convinced of the value of non-party members and pointed out that independence did not necessarily imply that a person held no political views— more often it indicated that he was not unswervingly devoted to one party. 'We think that our national life is sufficiently rich in men and women who, whether they hold political views or not, have true independence of mind and a habit of acting impartially'.[2] It advocated that political influence on advisory committees be restricted and that the Lord Chancellor be free to form a committee without persons chosen for their political affiliations if, in any area, he thought he could form an effective committee on this basis. The Commission advised that directions be issued to advisory committees to emphasize *inter alia* the following matters: (a) that no member of an advisory committee should regard himself merely as a representative of a particular party; (b) that the paramount

[1] Cf. his evidence to the Royal Commission. (Minutes of evidence, App. III, p. 81.)
[2] Report, para. 80; 1947-48 Cmd. 7463, xii.

consideration in appointing justices was fitness to perform judicial duties and certainly not the extent of previous political services; (c) that justices should be drawn from all sections of the community. If the above principles were applied, no one political group would normally have preponderance on the Bench. Lists of nominations should be scrutinized to see if any one party predominated. If this should prove to be the case, a list should still stand, in the Commission's view, unless alternative nominations could be made of equal merit to those previously selected.[1] Thus the Commission was prepared to regard the political system of choosing justices as acceptable, providing that further endeavours were made to eliminate possible abuses. A Minority Report, signed by three members of the Commission, was more critical: it urged that members of advisory committees should be chosen irrespective of political considerations, as this would check the evil of political appointments to the Bench.

II

The Report of the Royal Commission contained much information about our magistracy, although as the years pass it becomes necessarily less valuable as a guide to the present. On some matters like the age and social classification of justices, the Report is still the most recent source of information available. It estimated the total of justices in England and Wales on the active list to be 16,800, comprised of 13,100 men and 3,700 women; approximately another 2,200 justices were on the supplemental list. In Scotland justices were said to number 6,248, exclusive of those *ex officio*: Scotland, quite clearly, had the more plentiful supply and Glasgow alone had above 500 magistrates. For male justices south of the Border the most common age group, in terms of 5-year spans, was 65-69; 28 per cent. were age 70 or over, 65 per cent. were age 60 or over, while a mere 10 per cent. had yet to score a half-century. One gentleman, still on the active list, had reached the age of 95. Women justices were somewhat younger, but at the time of the Commission's investigation

[1] Report, para. 84.

women had been admitted to local Benches for only a quarter of a century which may help to explain the disparity. The figures showing the extent of the justices' attendance at adult courts are most revealing. Over half the male justices in the counties went to court less than once a month, while 12.6 per cent. did not attend at all; 7.2 per cent. of women county justices did not attend. Percentages of absenteeism in the boroughs were 8.7 per cent. for men and 4.6 per cent. for women. It is apparent that a significant proportion of justices were prepared to enjoy the dignity and prestige of the designation J.P. without giving any real service to the community in return.

The table below, reproduced from the Commission's Report, shows the occupational categories of male justices on the active list:

OCCUPATIONS OF MALE JUSTICES
PERCENTAGES

Category	Counties	Boroughs	Total
Not occupied	3.9	2.5	3.5
Professional*	22.1	19.2	21.3
Employers†	29.6	31.4	30.0
Small businessmen†	17.5	13.3	16.5
Salary earners	13.0	16.1	13.7
Wage earners	13.9	17.5	15.0
	100.0	100.0	100.0

* This is an over-riding classification. Thus a solicitor may be salary-earning but he will be classed as a professional man.
† Employers are defined as those who employ at least ten people or who occupy higher managerial posts. Smaller businessmen are those in business on their own account and employ less than ten people.

Similar classification of women was more complex and perhaps less satisfactory. Over two-thirds of women justices were placed in the not-occupied category when judged in terms of remunerative activity; no doubt the majority of them were engaged, more or less busily, in running a home. If judged in terms of their husband's status, by far the largest group was in the professional category. Attendance records of women were rather better than those of men, and it is reasonable to connect this with the age differential. Among the men, those with the better attendance figures belonged to the larger employers, the salary earners and the wage earners: these groups may suffer less financially for devoting time to public responsibilities than do professional men and small businessmen.

In addition to the justices appointed in the ordinary way there were in 1948 roughly 2,500 *ex officio* justices. They fell into three broad classes. Those who held certain high offices of State; those who held judicial offices; those who held certain positions of local importance—mostly in local government. In the first division are the Lord Chancellor, the Lord Keeper and Privy Councillors,[1] all of whom are on the Commission of the Peace for each county. So also are the Judges of the Supreme Court and the Law Officers. Judicial office-holders appointed to the Commission for any area in which they adjudicate are county court judges, the chairman and deputy chairman of the County of London Sessions, chairmen and deputy chairmen of Quarter Sessions appointed under the Administration of Justice Act, 1938, recorders, stipendiary magistrates[2] and metropolitan magistrates.[3] Local dignitaries on the bench are the Keeper of Rolls of the county (*custos rotulorum*, usually the Lord Lieutenant), the mayor of a borough, the chairmen of county and district councils, aldermen of the City of London, the Archbishop of York and his Chancellor, the Bishop of Ely and his Steward, the Chancellor, Vice-Chancellor and Deputy Vice-Chancellor of the University of Oxford (the Oxford University (Justices) Act, 1886) and the Vice-Chancellor of the University of Cambridge (Municipal Corporations Act, 1882, s. 249). Before the Justices of the Peace Act, 1949, ex-

---

[1] It is rare for a Privy Councillor to exercise his right to act as a J.P. However, Lord Ogmore joined the Westminster Bench in 1960: *The Times*, January 13, 1960.
[2] There were sixteen stipendiary magistrates in 1948. Where stipendiaries are appointed, the work of lay magistrates is reduced, but not eliminated. Arrangements for sharing the work vary from place to place.
[3] There were twenty-six metropolitan magistrates in 1948. In London the work of lay magistrates consists largely of juvenile court work, licensing business and cases brought by local authorities for the recovery of rates, etc.

mayors remained on the bench for twelve months after surrendering mayoral office. The Royal Commission had also proposed that the chairmen of county and district councils should cease to be *ex officio* magistrates because the qualities needed to preside successfully over a local council were not necessarily the same as those required in a justice. Further, a local authority chairman who held his office for only a year could not gain enough experience to be a useful member of the local bench. There is, of course, nothing to prevent local chairmen being chosen as magistrates in the normal way: indeed, the Royal Commission found this was common practice and applied to 26 per cent of mayors and ex-mayors, 76 per cent of chairmen of county councils, 13 per cent of chairmen of urban districts and 24 per cent of chairmen of rural districts.

In Scotland, *ex officio* justices drawn from local authorities include the lord provosts and bailies of large burghs, and provosts and bailies of certain other burghs, the covenors (chairmen) of county councils and the chairmen of district councils. The Royal Commission recommended no changes north of the Border because there the status of justices is somewhat different to that in England and Wales. Much of the judicial business in Scotland is performed in the Sheriff's Court and the duties of the magistrates are correspondingly reduced. Yet, partly as a matter of law and partly as a result of tradition, there is more work for justices in 'signing papers'. Their office is regarded less as a judicial one but rather as a civic honour: in these circumstances it is appropriate that leading members of local authorities should be justices. For the rest, the Secretary of State for Scotland is advised about new appointments by local advisory committees as in England and Wales.[1]

The Lord Chancellor's department has to try to ensure that

---

[1] Responsibility for Scottish justices was transferred from the Lord Chancellor to the Secretary of State following the recommendation to this effect by the Royal Commission on Scottish Affairs (Report, paras 142-4; 1953-54 Cmd. 9212, xix). The Scottish Commission urged this course although it agreed that existing arrangements were satisfactory: nor did it seem to consider the argument of the 1946-48 Commission that such a change should not be made as the Secretary of State might be subject to greater political pressures over the appointment of justices than is the Lord Chancellor. (Report, para 321; 1947-48 Cmd. 7463, xii).

those nominated to become justices, and those *ex officio*, are not for any reason disqualified from becoming magistrates. Disqualification barriers are both statutory and non-statutory. The first group includes bankruptcy, corrupt practice at an election, or conviction of treason or felony for which the sentence imposed was at least twelve months imprisonment. Some justices are prohibited from adjudicating in a particular type of case, e.g. a member of a local authority may not sit on a bench which is hearing a rating appeal that concerns his authority. Similarly, a person with a financial interest in the drink trade may not sit for licensing business. A solicitor may not practise directly or indirectly before a bench of which he is a member. The numbers of these disqualifications in 1946 was reported by the Royal Commission as follows:[1]

Category	County	Borough	Total
Members of local authorities	3,743	1,449	5,192
Employed by local authorities	295	164	459
Disqualified for licensing business	552	408	960
Members of legal profession	368	115	483

In addition to these legal prohibitions the Lord Chancellor, in practice, has various grounds for objection to nominations. Others barred include those convicted of serious offences which fall outside the statutory restrictions, members of the police force, pawnbrokers,[2] brewers and licensed victuallers,[2] members of the Independent Order of Rechabites,[2] justices' clerks, probation officers, the blind and the deaf. M.P.s and Parliamentary candidates are not appointed as Justices for any area covering the constituency they represent or hope to contest.[3] It is unusual to appoint husband and wife to the same Bench: when it is done, they are asked to give an undertaking not to sit together. Finally, ministers of religion are not ap-

---

[1] Cf. Minutes of evidence, App. 4; 1948, Non-Parl.
[2] The Royal Commission felt that there should be no inflexible bar against these categories: Rechabites should not, however, participate in licensing business.
[3] If a justice is elected to the Commons for a constituency that comes within the area for which he is on the Commission of the Peace, he is invited by the Lord Chancellor not to sit while he is an M.P. Cf. H.C. Deb., Vol. 415, cols. 2089-90.

pointed unless no other suitable person is available in the locality. These various disqualifications have been thought necessary to eliminate the possibility of suspicion of bias in the local administration of justice. They represent a series of rules made by the central government to stop the patronage power of local advisory committees being used in a way that might damage the good reputation of the magistracy.

Reputation is also affected by the capacities of existing justices. Judicial authority should not be vested in those manifestly unsuited to its exercise through old age, decaying mental or physical powers. As noted above, the Justices of the Peace Act, 1949, ensured that justices are placed on the supplemental list on reaching the age of seventy-five. A justice may, of course, become seriously incapacitated at an earlier age: whether any action is taken in such a case will depend on the accident of how far reliable information is received by the Lord Chancellor. Alternatively, it may be found that some justices are morally, intellectually or temperamentally unfit to adjudicate. This raises more delicate issues. The Lord Chancellor can remove any justice for 'unsuitability', a power which is used, very properly, with great caution: the independence of the judiciary is regarded as the traditional safeguard of impartiality. To be dismissed from the Commission of the Peace could also do grave harm to the reputation of the individual justice concerned. But the Lord Chancellor must intervene when the continued presence of an undesirable person might damage the reputation of a local Bench.

The Lord Chancellor has a small staff to assist him with the appointment of justices.[1] At the head of this staff is the Secretary of the Commissions. The Royal Commission urged in 1948 that the status, i.e. the pay, of this official be improved and the number of his assistants, two or three, be raised. Little has been done on these lines and the Secretary of the Commissions—following the recommendations of the Royal Commission on Taxation of Profits and Income[2] and the Franks Report on Administrative Tribunals[3]—has become responsible

---

[1] In Lancashire the Chancellor of the Duchy works through his own staff.
[2] Final Report, para. 962; 1955-56 Cmd. 9474, xxvii.
[3] 1956-57 Cmnd. 218, viii.

for a wider range of appointments of a quasi-judicial nature to a variety of bodies. It can be argued that the meagre character of the administrative resources afforded to the Lord Chancellor has an important impact on the techniques of appointment. Political parties are firmly established as the main channels of influence through which the Secretary of the Commissions is accustomed to work: the organization of wider, alternative sources of information about the suitability of persons to become members of advisory committees would undoubtedly require more generous staffing in Westminster.

It is clear that the constitution and *modus operandi* of the local advisory committees are of the greatest significance in the appointment of justices. The committees are nominated by the Lord Chancellor; in counties the Lord Lieutenant is normally the chairman and in boroughs the Lord Chancellor selects a chairman. When vacancies occur on these bodies it is not uncommon for the existing members, especially the Lords Lieutenant, to suggest names for possible new members. The committees are usually small. The average size is about six or seven, but sometimes is as low as three—one representative each of the Conservative, Liberal and Labour parties. Those nominated to serve on advisory committees are themselves normally justices: thus local Benches are, in effect, self-co-opting. No one above the age of sixty-five is now chosen and if a new member is not already a justice, the practice is to add him to the local commission at the first convenient opportunity. Members are appointed for a six-year term and the maximum age for reappointment of an existing member is sixty-nine. The domination of political parties over these bodies has already been described. Explicit notice is taken of political sympathies in order to maintain 'balance': when a possible new member, Smith, is thought to belong to a particular party, the Lord Chancellor makes inquiries at the national headquarters of the party concerned to discover if Smith is still regarded as a supporter. Should the headquarters reply 'Smith belongs to our party, but we would prefer you to choose Jones'—Smith is still appointed. Even so, this practice is open to objection and the Royal Commission recommended unsuccessfully that it be stopped.[1] Membership of committees is secret[2] in order to prevent the possibility of unfortunate lobbying. Names of committee secretaries—usually the Clerk of the Peace for the borough or county—are now made public, and any representations about membership of the local Bench can be made through them. As all these proceedings are highly confidential it is not possible to discover how far associations, other than political parties, put forward names for consideration. However, one has the impression it is fairly uncommon for this to be done.

The functions of advisory committees go beyond the submission of names of potential new magistrates. They also consider how many magistrates are required for their area, and scrutinize the attendance records of existing magistrates. Should any question arise about the desirability of removing a magistrate from the Bench—because of his temperament, conduct or involvement in legal proceedings—the local advisory committee will review the case. Advisory committees are expected to be unanimous about the candidates they nominate: it seems an individual member of an advisory committee can exercise what is nearly a veto power. In many English counties, candidates considered probably suitable for appointment are placed on a waiting list. A borough usually has no waiting list as the advisory committee meets less frequently, but it is in the smallest boroughs that there is most difficulty in finding suitable persons. In some counties the chairmen of petty sessions are asked to suggest names for consideration by the advisory committee, and members of the committee may themselves make discreet inquiries.[3] Such preliminary investigation is less needed in boroughs when the committee members will tend to have—or think they know—the requisite information.

[1] Report, para. 78. Mr Dingle Foot, then a Liberal, was the sole dissentient to this view. It is, or was, sometimes difficult for the Lord Chancellor to discover whether a potential Liberal member was a Liberal or a Liberal National and, therefore, virtually indistinguishable from a Conservative.
[2] The pre-war practice of revealing membership of a particular committee in response to a parliamentary question has been stopped.
[3] A description of the proceedings of advisory committees is contained in the evidence submitted by the Lord Chancellor's department to the 1946 Royal Commission. (Minutes of evidence. App. 1; 1946 Non-Parl.)

The Lord Chancellor's department gives careful scrutiny to the names and numbers put forward by local committees. Westminster may take the view that too many, or too few, names are suggested. Attention is also given to the age of candidates: normally the maximum age is sixty-five and the Lord Chancellor is reluctant to appoint people over sixty. In the case of boroughs the Lord Chancellor insists that not more than one third of borough magistrates shall be members of the town council. It is also necessary to try to ensure that none of the nominees are disqualified for any reason. Finally, the Lord Chancellor requires to be satisfied about the qualifications of potential magistrates: it is accepted that the effect of political influence on the choices made is considerable. But the Lord Chancellor tries to establish that the new justices have engaged in some form of public service other than activity within a political party. For one reason or another roughly half the lists of nominees submitted by advisory committees are returned to them with critical observations or requests for fuller information. And the Lord Chancellor may submit names to a committee should he know that a particularly suitable person, e.g. a retired colonial judge, or a justice from elsewhere, has moved into its area. These representations are not always well received for a committee may consider a period of local residence to be an important qualification— a rationalization of dislike of 'outsiders'; local knowledge is as much a disqualification as a qualification to administer justice.

Once the Lord Chancellor has agreed to a list of new appointees his department writes to the persons concerned and asks if they are willing to serve. It is improper for an individual to be approached before he receives the formal request from the Lord Chancellor. Few invitations to join the local Bench are refused. No doubt this is a reflection of the status and honour associated with the letters J.P., but it is also the case that the majority of those approached are accustomed to spend an appreciable amount of time on public affairs. Yet some new magistrates find it less convenient to sit on the Bench than they anticipated. It might be better if the invitees considered the implications of becoming a magistrate more fully and for the Lord Chancellor to receive rather more refusals.

III

The Royal Commission of 1910 proposed the establishment of advisory committees, it will be recalled, to ensure that justices were not chosen solely from the dominant political and social circles in a local community. This has been achieved by getting a political balance on the committees and, therefore, among the magistrates they nominate. But while this process may help to satisfy those groups previously under-represented, it is quite irrelevant to the problem of obtaining justices of the highest calibre. The idea was widely held that a number of Left-wing or working class magistrates are required so that local Benches may be properly appreciative of conditions of life among the lower orders. Yet such magistrates, perhaps over-conscious of their own virtue, are sometimes more severe and merciless than their fellows. It is clear that local political personalities failed to provide the nation with a satisfactory local judiciary. The preceding pages have described some of the series of badly-needed reforms commenced in 1938. Other changes, the rules about the size and chairmanship of Benches[1] and the provisions made for new magistrates to receive instruction in their powers and duties, fall outside the scope of this study. The growing strength of the Magistrates' Association is another indication that justices now take their responsibilities more seriously. The President of the Association is the Lord Chancellor of the day. It issues a monthly journal and arranges meetings and conferences designed to assist justices in the performance of their duties. It also acts as a link between the magistracy and Government departments and may present evidence to official bodies inquiring into social problems. Since its foundation in 1920, membership has grown steadily, even during the war years, reaching 6,000 by 1946, 6,700 by 1948, 7,800 by 1950, 9,000 by 1952 and 10,000 by 1957.[2] Since then

[1] S.I. 1908 of 1950.
[2] I am indebted to Mr J. F. Madden, Secretary of the Association, for these figures.

an increase in the annual subscription from £1 to £2 has slowed the rate of increase. But in spite of the growing support, it would appear that roughly half of the justices on the active list are still unwilling to join the Association.

The substantial efforts made to reduce the shortcomings of lay magistracy have thus borne fruit. Yet the central issue remains, assuming lay magistracy is to continue, whether the present system of largely political appointments is the best that can be devised. Certainly, the problem of politics will not be solved by ignoring it; if no check is made on party affiliations there is a strong possibility that supporters of one group will dominate the Bench. Men and women who become prominent in public affairs, especially in boroughs, often do so in connection with political activity. There has been a notable change in Left-wing opinion on this issue. In 1910 it was highly critical of the technique of choosing justices; by 1946, with the advent of politically balanced Benches, it was in favour of the *status quo*. In Labour eyes, a person who does not support their party is classed as conservative, albeit with a small 'c'; most 'independent' members of local authorities do tend, in fact, to be conservative rather than socialistic in their sympathies.

Yet the idea of a politically balanced Bench creates a number of difficulties. What exactly is meant by balance? Does it mean that the local Commission of the Peace should reflect more or less accurately the results of the most recent Parliamentary election in the area? While the official answer to this question is 'no', it is also the case that election results do have some impact on the nominations made—witness the sharp rise in the proportion of Labour supporters chosen to be justices in Lancashire after 1945.[1] Again, the number of Liberals on advisory committees in 1946 was high compared with their voting strength. The number of Liberals has since fallen but, in keeping with the recommendations of the Royal Commission, an attempt has been made to increase the number of non-party independents on the committees and on the Bench. In particular, the advisory committee for London,

[1] Justices of the Peace. Royal Commission. Minutes of evidence, App. 2, p. 78; 1948 Non-Parl.

severely criticized by the Royal Commission,[1] was subsequently reconstructed.

Insistence on political balance in the choice of justices may well have adverse effects on the calibre of those appointed. There is no reason to assume that the candidates most suitable to join the Commission for any particular area distribute their political sympathies in the appropriate proportions. Suitability for a task of this kind is not a matter that can be precisely determined, but if political parties claim a quota of seats on the Bench it seems unlikely that the quality of their nominees will always be equal to that of many people who are willing to serve but are not considered. Devotion to a political cause might well be regarded as a disqualification for judicial work, except perhaps for those who have had a legal training. Political enthusiasm is not synonymous with a disinterested, unemotional or impartial outlook. Using the local Bench as a means of political reward also helps to keep the age of justices high, for a party may expect, say, twenty years of faithful support before the reward is offered. The principle of requiring advisory committees to be unanimous about the names put forward does help to increase the importance of their independent, non-party members. Without them, there is a real danger of horse-trading between the parties—'You agree to our list and we will not scrutinize yours.' The vigilance of the Lord Chancellor's staff is another safeguard against this possible abuse. Alternatively, should a local committee submit a list that is politically unbalanced the Lord Chancellor would, presumably, not reject it, at least on political grounds, for he would know that the political groups under-represented must have accepted it as containing the best possible nominations.

The chances of change in the present position are small. The Lord Chancellor's department has an attitude of positive acquiescence: the Labour Party is in favour of the existing arrangements as providing it with the best chance of a good place in this particular sun: Conservative opinion is more critical, but the Party seems unlikely to campaign to abolish a system which provides a form of honour for its active sup-

[1] Report, paras 294-303; 1947-48 Cmd. 7463, xii.

porters. Yet will the parties always be able to provide sufficient suitable justices? In some areas the Labour Party appears to have difficulty in providing its quota. Service as a justice involves minor out-of-pocket expenses and for wage earners it may lead to loss of remuneration. The Royal Commission of 1946 rejected the idea that subsistence allowances and compensation for loss of earnings should be paid as is now done for members of local authorities. It argued that such payment would detract from the authority and dignity of justices, that most justices would not welcome it, and that few persons, eminently suited to be justices, were in fact debarred from serving *solely* for financial reasons.[1] Labour circles do not agree, especially with the last conclusion, and in February 1959 the T.U.C. General Council sent a letter to the Home Secretary which urged that such payments be made.

Some justices, of course, have no connection with local politics and are chosen because of their record of activity in other types of public body. Obviously it would not be difficult to increase their number. Churches, social welfare and educational organizations, women's organizations, residents' associations and universities all contain persons unquestionably suitable to be justices. The objection to recruiting more in this way is that Benches would tend to become politically conservative again, although not consisting necessarily of active party supporters. How far this would happen, in fact, cannot be known, but the Labour Party believes it to be the case. The more significant question is whether the objection is relevant. As social distinctions disappear, is it still necessary to take special precautions to ensure that justices have knowledge of 'working-class conditions'—especially when these precautions have led to undoubted evils?

[1] Report, paras. 200-212; 1947-48 Cmd. 7463, xii.

CHAPTER TEN

Honours

⊙

I

The award of honours has been through the centuries a recognized method by which those in power have strengthened their authority. Medieval kings granted titles, property and privileges to their supporters. Tudor monarchs were somewhat chary of creating peerages, for they knew well how much trouble nobility could cause. The Stuarts, harassed by by the struggle with Parliament, were forced to grant honours more freely to try to gain money and support. The Order of Baronets was created by James I in 1611 for the express purpose of raising funds, not for his personal use but to assist with the administration and settlement of Ulster.[1] When it became difficult to find sufficient applicants for admission to the Order the price was reduced to attract more customers. Little secrecy was observed in these matters and Charles II employed agents to aid the sale of baronetcies. In the early part of the eighteenth century the centre of political power moved from the Crown to the Cabinet as the office of Prime Minister was developed by Walpole; the power to award honours moved as well and was used by Ministers to strengthen their position in Parliament. Before the passage of the Parliament Act, 1911, the traditional means to settle a dispute between Lords and Commons was for the Crown to create sufficient peers to give Ministers a majority in the Upper House. The ultimate sanction against their Lordships was the patronage weapon and the threat of its use was needed in 1832 to pass the Reform Bill and again in 1911 to pass the Parliament Bill. Every constitu-

[1] G. Macmillan, *Honours for Sale* (Richards Press, 1954), p. 225.

tional textbook quotes the example of how a dozen peers were created in 1712 to ensure that the House of Lords would ratify the Treaty of Utrecht as the precedent for the events of 1832 and 1911, yet at the time it was an orthodox use of patronage to ensure that the policy of the Queen and her Ministers was not obstructed by Parliament.

In modern times vast numbers of honours are distributed— the majority of them are appointments to the minor orders of chivalry—but most of the nominations are unconnected with party political considerations. Awards to foreign monarchs and statesmen are made for diplomatic reasons; medals and decorations are given for valour in times of war and emergency; civil servants, especially those holding senior posts, receive awards in recognition of devotion to their duties; voluntary public service of many kinds is also rewarded in this way on an increasing scale. Omitting purely military decorations, the range of honours includes peerages, baronetcies, knighthoods and membership of the Privy Council and the orders of chivalry. The latter are:

The Most Noble Order of the Garter (1348)
The Most Ancient and Most Noble Order of the Thistle (1687)
The Most Illustrious Order of St Patrick (1783)
The Most Honourable Order of the Bath (1399)
The Order of Merit (1902)
The Most Exalted Order of the Star of India (1861)
The Most Distinguished Order of St Michael and St George (1818)
The Most Eminent Order of the Indian Empire (1877)
The Royal Victorian Order (1896)
The Royal Victorian Chain (1902)
The Most Excellent Order of the British Empire (1917)
The Order of Companions of Honour (1917)
The Imperial Order of the Crown of India (for ladies) (1878)

No appointments have been made to the Order of St Patrick since 1934 or to the Indian Orders since 1948. The Garter, the Thistle, the Order of Merit and the Companions of

Honour are strictly limited in number and it is not uncommon for the membership to be lower than the full complement. The dates in the list above show when each Order was instituted but some Orders have been revised and enlarged on a number of occasions. Thus the Order of the Bath, remodelled in 1725 and 1815, has been repeatedly enlarged since: the Order of the Star of India and that of the Indian Empire were each augmented eight times. The Order of St Michael and St George has experienced a major transformation. It was founded in 1818 for 'the natives of the Ionian Islands and of the Island of Malta and its dependencies and for such other subjects of His Majesty as may hold high and confidential situations in the Mediterranean'. After the repudiation of the British Protectorate of the Ionian Islands the Order was placed on a new basis by Letters Patent in 1868 and 1877 and extended to cover those who hold, or have held, high office anywhere in the colonies. The statutes of the Order now provide for three grades of membership, Knight Grand Cross (G.C.M.G.), Knight Commander (K.C.M.G.) and Companion (C.M.G.). The Order of the Bath has similar divisions to St Michael and St George, i.e. G.C.B., K.C.B. and C.B. So did the Indian Orders, although at the time of its foundation the Order of the Indian Empire was restricted to Companions only. The Royal Victorian Order has five divisions, Knight Grand Cross, Knight Commander or Dame Commander, Companion, Member (4th Class) and Member (5th Class). The Order of the British Empire is divided in the same way except that 'Officer' replaces 'Member (4th Class)'. The two latter Orders are open equally to men and women.

Appointments to the Orders of the Bath, St Michael and St George, and the British Empire steadily increase. Each Order has limited numbers prescribed by its statutes, but as it is now customary to revise the ceiling figures every five years, the limits are not rigid. The Orders of the Bath and the British Empire are divided into civil and military divisions and maximum complements are fixed for each grade in each division together with a permitted annual total of awards. Maximum complements are further sub-divided between the various Government departments concerned with a particular type of award. Thus the Central African Office is allowed two Knights or Dame Commanders in the civil division of the Order of the British Empire; to permit this the parallel allocation of the Commonwealth Relations Office was cut from 140 to 139 and that of the Colonial Office was reduced from 60 to 59. By way of example the table below shows the permitted membership of the Third Class of the Order of the British Empire—the Commanders.

COMMANDERS OF THE ORDER OF THE BRITISH EMPIRE

Division	Sub-division	Annual Awards		Total Maximum		
Military	Admiralty	14		206		
	War Office	30		459		
	Air Ministry	21		320		
	C.R.O.	40		234		1,248
	Colonial Office	1		234		
	C. African Office			2		
Civil	Prime Minister	210		3,271		
	Foreign Office	18	272			
	C.R.O.	67	763		1,638	4,909
	Colonial Office	47	583			
	C. African Office		20			
	Total	448				6,157

There is no military section of the Order of St Michael and St George, but similar restrictions exist on the membership of its three grades.

No formal controls govern the creation of new peers, baronets, knights bachelor, or membership of the Privy Council. However, in a memorandum to Ramsay MacDonald, King George V expressed the view that creations under Lloyd George had been excessive, and that any one Honours List should not include more than eight baronetcies or twenty-four knighthoods.[1] His wish has been ignored since the figure for knighthoods has been regularly exceeded.

The majority of awards are now made in the regular Honours Lists issued at New Year and on the Monarch's official birthday. Other lists are issued on special occasions,

[1] H. Nicolson, *King George V* (Constable, 1952), p. 389n.

e.g. coronations or jubilees. Shorter lists of political honours appear when a Government resigns or when a Parliament is dissolved. The Cabinet reshuffle in July 1962 produced two new peerages, three Companions of Honour, one Dame and the promotion of Lord Kilmuir from a viscount to an earl. Thus awards may be made at any time; however, except for the Garter and the Thistle, the lists now contain the great majority of appointments. The practice of conferring honours *en masse* on specific occasions started in 1887 under the Conservative Government of the Marquess of Salisbury; a list of honours in commemoration of the Golden Jubilee of Queen Victoria contained the names of 1 earl and 8 other peers, 13 baronets, 33 knights bachelor as well as some minor appointments to the orders of chivalry. Also in 1887 some nominations to the Order of St Michael and St George were made on the Queen's birthday but were not designated officially as a Birthday Honours List. In 1888 the phrases 'New Year Honours' and 'Birthday Honours' appeared for the first time; both lists were short and the Birthday List was again restricted to the same Order. The following year the Birthday List contained a full range of awards and so achieved parity with the New Year List. This pattern was continued when the Liberals returned to office in 1892 and has been followed faithfully ever since. Little contemporary comment appears to have been evoked by the evolution of honours lists, but the Birthday Honours of 1895 earned editorial approval from *The Times* because it contained a large number of literary names due, according to *The Times*, to the personal interests of the Prime Minister, Lord Rosebery.[1]

The modern Honours List is divided into sections: the Prime Minister's List is followed by nominations to the Royal Victorian Order and then by lists from the Foreign Office, Commonwealth Relations Office, Colonial Office, some Dominions and lists of military awards from each of the Services. Dominion lists come from Australia, New Zealand, Nigeria and the Central African Federation. Other Dominions manage without. Canada and South Africa abolished honours

---

[1] *The Times*, May 25, 1895. This list contained the first recognition of the acting profession by bestowing a knighthood on Henry Irving.

on the grounds that they have a corrupting effect.[1] The Prime Minister's List, with which we are principally concerned, contains peerages, appointments to the Privy Council and the Order of Merit, baronetcies, knighthoods, Companions of Honour and nominations to the Orders of the Bath, St Michael and St George, and the British Empire. The civil division of Order of the Bath is dominated by home civil servants, St Michael and St George is for public service overseas, while the Order of the British Empire is widely distributed. The Orders of Merit and the Companions of Honour confer no title on the recipients. The former, restricted to twenty-four persons, is divided into civil and military divisions; the civil awards go to our most distinguished statesmen and to men and women of great eminence in science and the arts. Companions of Honour total up to sixty-five; this award is solely civilian and less exalted than the Order of Merit, although the pattern of distribution is similar except that it includes a rather higher proportion of politicians. Membership of the Privy Council— and the use of the prefix 'Right Honourable'—is automatically accorded to members of the Cabinet; it is also enjoyed by the Lords of Appeal in Ordinary, the Lords Justices of Appeal, the Archbishops of Canterbury and York, the Bishop of London, a few Dominion statesmen of major importance, British Ministers just below Cabinet status, some senior back-bench M.P.s (commonly ex-Junior Ministers) and one or two other leading figures in our public life.

The Prime Minister is assisted in the preparation of Honours Lists by his Secretary for Appointments: from 10 Downing Street go letters to potential recipients which ask if they are willing to accept the proposed award. Nominations reach the Prime Minister through a number of channels. Those who work in, or who have connections with, Government departments have their names put forward through departmental establishment divisions; their lists are co-ordinated and pruned by a committee. The whole of this bi-annual labour is carried on under the aegis of the Ceremonial Officer of the Treasury. Traditionally the Chief Whip—the old-fashioned title was

---

[1] Cf. A. B. Keith, *British Cabinet System* (Stevens & Sons, 1952), p. 430.

Patronage Secretary—has a dominant rôle in relation to nominations for political (and possibly public) services, and he will get suggestions from his party's central office and from M.P.s. Lords Lieutenant may also put forward names, but they no longer do so as a regular practice. Indeed, anyone may write to the Prime Minister and propose himself, or anyone else, for an award. No doubt, the chance of a name being included in the final list will depend upon the influence commanded by its sponsor(s).

A number of general features stand out in the vast growth of the honours system that has taken place since the middle of Victoria's reign. The introduction of new Orders or the expansion of those already in existence has tended to take place under Conservative or Coalition governments.[1] Secondly, and this is partly a related matter, the growth of honours has been stimulated by occasions which evoke patriotic sentiments, i.e. the development of the Indian Empire, jubilees, coronations and wars. Thirdly, there is a tendency for awards to increase. The large number of honours bestowed by Lloyd George between 1917 and 1922 provoked a major political storm[2] and a reaction that drastically curtailed the awards given. But steadily the numbers have crept up again, checked only by the reluctance of the Attlee administration to confer baronetcies and its marked restraint over the grant of political rewards. The table opposite gives an outline of how honours have grown. It is concerned solely with the Prime Minister's List in the Birthday and New Year Honours.

The rate at which new hereditary peerages have been created in this century has fluctuated considerably. Under the Liberal Prime Ministers Campbell-Bannerman and Asquith the average rate of creation was 10 a year; for Lloyd George (1916-22) the annual average was a little under 14; in the remainder of the 1920s the figure fell to about 7 but rose again to 10 in the 1930s. From 1940 to 1957 the average has been roughly 7, with a rather higher figure for the period of the Labour Government due to the need to strengthen the Labour Party in the Upper House and to elevate victorious

---

[1] Cf. the dates mentioned on p. 179 *supra*.
[2] Described in detail in the third section of this chapter.

GROWTH OF HONOURS AND AWARDS
1888-1958

PRIME MINISTER'S LIST

Honours	*1888*	*1898*	*1908*	*1918*	*1928*	*1938*	*1948*	*1958*
Earls	—	1	—	—	—	—	—	—
Viscounts	—	—	—	3	—	3	1	—
Barons	—	4	4*	7	6	7	7	4
Baronets	—	9	11*	34	10	11	—	6
Knights Bachelor	2	15	25*	88	66	70	58	69
Order of the British Empire:								
G.B.E.	—	—	—	25†	3	3	3	2
K.B.E.	—	—	—	122	7	11	13	8
D.B.E.	—	—	—	22	3	3	1	5
C.B.E.	—	—	—	527	36	58	178	202
O.B.E.	—	—	—	1,919	76	131	332	378
M.B.E.	—	—	—	2,445	90	195	551	691

* The New Year List in 1908 contained no peerages, baronetcies or knighthoods.
† Includes 13 Dames G.B.E.

military leaders. Under Prime Minister Macmillan the average has fallen to below 5, possibly due to the introduction of the new class of life peers.[1]

Just as inflation damages the value of currency, so widespread distribution of a particular type of honour damages its prestige. From the table above it can be seen that in 1918 the total of appointments to the Order of the British Empire reached the figure of 5,060. No doubt the exceptional conditions of war-time offered special opportunity and excuse for wholesale allocation. A post-war reaction was inevitable, but was delayed until the fall of Lloyd George in October 1922. The New Year Honours of 1923 (Prime Minister, Bonar Law) contained a mere 77 nominations to this Order; the New Year Honours of 1924 (Prime Minister, MacDonald) included 137 such nominations. The Birthday List of 1924 is of special interest as being the first issued under the aegis of a Labour Government. In previous years Labour spokesmen had frequently urged the abolition of hereditary and political

[1] The issues associated with the introduction of life peerages are treated separately in Chapter Eleven.

honours, so it was no surprise that the list was relatively short. The Prime Minister indicated that he intended it to be still shorter but had had a number of obligations and promises to fulfil. *The Times* welcomed the list. 'After the spate of peerages which has foamed in recent years this modest occasional trickle will serve as a certain relief.'[1]

The general tendency for awards to increase, with a check in the 1920s, can also be seen in relation to the Indian Orders. Again, the figures below are shown from the New Year and Birthday Honours with the exception of 1948; the New Year List 1948 marked the end of the awards of Indian Orders.

INDIAN ORDERS, 1888-1948

Order of the Star of India	1888	1898	1908	1918	1928	1938	1948
G.C.S.I.	1	1	—	2	1	—	5
K.C.S.I.	3	5	5	10	4	3	5
C.S.I.	5	14	10	13	9	9	17
Order of the Indian Empire							
G.C.I.E.	—	2	2	3	1	—	6
K.C.I.E.	6	5	6	14	5	8	14
C.I.E.	10	26	20	66*	48	58	49

* Includes several awards to Army officers on combined civil and military list.

A high percentage of the awards in the Prime Minister's List go to civil servants and those employed in public corporations and other semi-official bodies. Quite complex etiquette governs the pattern of Civil Service awards. All Permanent Secretaries and Deputy Secretaries belong to some Order. So do a majority of Under Secretaries. Thus in the most senior Civil Service posts, appearance in an Honours List is automatically associated with promotion. Among the lower ranks necessarily a lower proportion receive an award. Sometimes these are given near retiring age; sometimes an award to a middle-aged member of the lower ranges of the administrative class is a method both of expressing appreciation for past services and an indication that further promotion is unlikely. There is a fairly well-established code which relates the type

[1] Leading article, June 3, 1924.

of award made to the various stages in the Civil Service hierarchy.[1] Thus:

Civil Service Status	Appropriate Award
Permanent Secretary	K.C.B.
Deputy Secretary	K.B.E.
Under Secretary	C.B.
Assistant Secretary	C.B.E.
Principal ⎫ Chief Executive Officer ⎬	O.B.E.
All lower grades	M.B.E.

Naturally, there are variations and exceptions. Some Permanent Secretaries receive a G.C.B. In the Foreign Office, Colonial Office and Commonwealth Relations Office, and occasionally in other departments, the appropriate grade in the Order of St Michael and St George is used. Members of the various special departmental classes, and the scientific, legal and financial branches of the Civil Service each have an equivalent to the grades set out above which determines the extent of their expectations. Equally, to give a decoration of lower rank than is customary, granted the status of the recipient, would be an insult rather than an honour: a Principal would be shocked to receive an M.B.E.[2]

The automatic character of the honours bestowed on the most senior civil servants does create difficulties. Clearly they are not given in recognition of outstanding services, except in so far as outstanding service has earned promotion. When an honour—or anything else—becomes normal, it ceases to be exceptional. It becomes exceptional not to have the usual honour. For a high civil servant to have the normal award is not a mark of special distinction; not to have it may well make a man feel slighted.

In the past it has been common to argue that honours were used as a bribe, or a subsidiary means of reward, to under-paid

---

[1] This essay is not concerned with military awards but in this sphere the same type of parallels can be found. For example, in the Royal Navy, Admiral=G.C.B. or G.B.E., Vice Admiral=K.C.B. or K.B.E., Rear Admiral =C.B., Captain=C.B.E., Commander=O.B.E., Lt Commander=M.B.E.

[2] Principals who hold the M.B.E. received it before promotion to their present rank.

senior civil servants. The Coleraine Committee, appointed to review the salary scales of top civil servants, has now effected improvements in their remuneration: how far the administrative class is underpaid is a matter for argument. Probably many of them could earn more money in commerce or industry; and no doubt, some could not. The lack of personal expense accounts in the Civil Service renders this type of comparison extremely difficult. Nor can it be clear whether a knighthood confers material benefit as well as psychological balm on a top civil servant: does it add to his potential earning power after retirement or help him to transfer to industry when in his fifties?

Although the present system of automatic honours verges on the absurd, the administrative class as a whole treat the question of honours with due seriousness. The annual ration of awards is widely known and possible contenders for the vacancies keep a wary eye on their distribution. *The Observer* has urged that the number of awards to civil servants be reduced considerably.[1] In principle, this suggestion is excellent. But it must be admitted that the change would have an effect on the morale of the higher Civil Service, especially in the Foreign Office.

Besides public officials, the Honours Lists now include persons drawn from many walks of life. Industry, commerce and, occasionally, trade unionism, are represented. Others who commonly appear are officials of national organizations in touch with Government departments, and those active in voluntary work of all kinds, e.g. local government, philanthropy, welfare work and the Savings movement. A few awards go to scholars, to those prominent in the arts, and to sportsmen; these appointments attract the widest publicity. The distribution of awards is a sitting target for criticism: the grand scale on which awards are granted to civil servants can be contrasted with the paucity of those given to scientists. A number of men who have won international prizes for their contributions to knowledge have yet to find a place in an Honours List. It is invidious to quote names because any one of them may, like George Bernard Shaw, have refused an

[1] In an article entitled 'Toys for the Boys', January 4, 1959.

award.[1] The explanation for their exclusion, however, is not that Prime Ministers are indifferent to the value of scholarship. Some groups in the community are more honours-conscious than others; while there is a regular arrangement for putting forward the names of those who work in, or who are associated with, public service, there is no such system for others. And if no one bothers to suggest the names of scholars —or if scholars themselves are not very interested—naturally they will be overlooked. It can be argued that as Honours Lists become less exclusive they are more democratic and thus in keeping with the contemporary social climate. Yet there are dangers. As the scope of honours widens, various unfortunate distinctions or comparisons suggest themselves. If some sports are recognized, why not others? If motor racing, why not lawn tennis? The examples could be multiplied endlessly. There is also the prospect that some awards could tend to become as automatic as the baronetcy for the Lord Mayor of London. A secretary of an association of local authorities must be, in the long run, a strong candidate for an award. So is a Vice-Chancellor. As more awards are made, so more precedents accumulate and more expectations are aroused. A growing appetite for honours is an unfortunate social phenomenon; yet drastic surgery on the lists may be needed to prevent it.

The honours system developed in the period of imperial expansion and military struggle. It fits far less easily into our more democratic society in the nuclear age. The end of the Patrick and Indian Orders are a reminder of how honours can be washed away in the tide of history. As colonies rapidly obtain independence the need for the Order of St Michael and St George will also diminish. And the phrase 'Order of the British Empire' is itself becoming an anachronism. Yet honours are unlikely to wither rapidly: the British people seem to like their traditions and a little pageantry, even when they verge on the absurd. Honours will do little positive harm —provided always that they are not used by the Government of the day as a political weapon. It is with this possibility that the rest of this chapter is concerned.

[1] Cf. *Honours and Awards*—A *Daily Mirror* Spotlight (1955), pp. 13-14.

II

The Crown is the fountain of honour and all such appointments require the approval of the Monarch. Apart from some exceptions, discussed below, the Queen acts on the advice of her Ministers. The Prime Minister is responsible for the contents of his list and departmental Ministers are responsible for the Foreign Office, Commonwealth Relations and Colonial lists. The Prime Minister may be consulted about the nominations in departmental lists but the tradition is that honours are not discussed in the Cabinet.[1] A Dominion Prime Minister is responsible for the contents of his own list, and a Dominion citizen should not be included in a British list without the approval of the Prime Minister of the Dominion.

The principles of constitutional monarchy allow the Queen to object to the proposals submitted to her; but if a Minister insists, the Queen must give way. Thus George V protested that the public services rendered by Mr Aitken, M.P. (Lord Beaverbrook), were not sufficient to justify the grant of a peerage. The King was then told that Mr Aitken's seat in the Commons was needed to provide a vacancy for a senior Minister; that the peerage had already been promised; that the Ashton-under-Lyme Conservative Association was already warned of the approaching by-election. King George was much annoyed that a promise had been made without prior consultation with him: the peerage was granted but Lloyd George was told that such promises should not be made in future.[2] Three years later, in 1920, the King opposed the award of a peerage to Lord Riddell, owner of the *News of the World*, on the grounds that he had been the guilty party in a divorce case.[3] Again, the protest was unsuccessful. In 1922 when Parliament was discussing the connection between the award of honours and contributions to party funds, the King wrote to Lloyd George to express his misgivings about some recent appointments.[4]

[1] Sir W. I. Jennings, *Cabinet Government*, 3rd edn. (Cambridge University Press, 1959), pp. 235, 237.
[2] Lord Beaverbrook, *Men and Power* (Hutchinson, 1956), pp. 243-4.
[3] *Ibid.*, pp. 245-6.
[4] H. Nicolson, *King George V*, pp. 512-13.

A restricted range of honours is awarded by the personal decision of the Monarch. They are the Orders of the Garter, Thistle and Patrick (now virtually defunct), the Royal Victorian Chain and the Royal Victorian Order which recognizes personal services to the Royal Family. The right to nominate members of the senior Orders of Chivalry, the Garter, Thistle and Patrick, reverted to the Monarch in 1946 in accordance with advice tendered by Labour Prime Minister (now Earl) Attlee.[1] For two centuries the Garter had been a political honour, conferred on the basis of party considerations. As the Labour Party is suspicious of honours, it is possible that the Prime Minister was glad to be relieved of responsibility for choosing recipients. Membership of the Garter is now distributed between the Royal Family, foreign royalty and carefully selected peers including ex-Prime Ministers. Sir Winston Churchill is the only commoner to belong to the Order. The Thistle consists largely of Scottish peers. The Order of Merit has also been in the personal gift of the Monarch. It was founded in 1902, designed as a special distinction for eminent men and women without conferring a knighthood upon them: often it is bestowed on those who have made an outstanding contribution to science or the arts as well as to statesmen and military leaders. Nominations to the Order now appear in the Prime Minister's List. In 1902 it was agreed that the King might have 'unofficial assistance' from the Prime Minister in choosing members of the Order of Merit and the Royal Victorian Order.[2] In addition, the Queen can make any suggestions she chooses about any other sort of award. Only once did George V make a proposal of this kind, and his nomination was not accepted.[3]

Thus the influence of the Monarch on the distribution of honours is limited. So also is that of Parliament. There are a number of barriers which restrain Parliamentary discussion of this topic. In the first place, honours are connected with the Throne; this association creates a sense of inhibition, even

[1] The desire of the King to end the political character of the Garter and the negotiations preceding the reform are described by Sir J. Wheeler-Bennett, *King George VI* (Macmillan, 1958), pp. 755-60.
[2] Sir S. Lee, *King Edward VII* (Macmillan, 1927), p. 99.
[3] Nicolson, pp. 514-15.

although the rôle of the Queen is largely formal. Secondly, criticism of any particular award involves adverse comment about the recipient. Absolute privilege shields Parliamentary debate from the operation of the law of slander, but it is widely accepted that this protection should not be abused. Thirdly, procedural difficulties impede the discussion of honours by M.P.s. Questions cannot be asked in the Commons concerning the use of the Royal Prerogative, and Speaker Lowther ruled in 1907 that he could not allow a question to the Prime Minister about advice given to the Sovereign in connection with the award of an honour.[1] To avoid this rule a question must be asked in general terms: in 1939 Mr Mander (Lib., East Wolverhampton) asked the Prime Minister if he would arrange for future Honours Lists to include not only particulars of public service of recipients but also information as to their donations to party funds over the previous ten years.[2] There is no parallel restriction on the wording of motions, but it is very difficult for a backbencher to obtain sufficient support for a motion to force the Government to find time to debate it. At the time of the honours scandal of 1922, constant pressure and 200 signatures from Members in all parties were needed to force a debate in the Commons. The House of Lords was then notably more active in debating the question; their Lordships had a more flexible timetable of business and they were more directly affected by the number and nature of new peerages created. But there has now been no effective Parliamentary discussion of honours for forty years.[3] Ministers have a free hand, a hand that is too free.

III

A feature of Parliamentary elections in this country down to 1918 was the high number of unopposed returns. In days when

[1] Parl. Deb., 4th Series, Vol. 178, col. 61.
[2] H.C. Deb., Vol. 348, col. 1503.
[3] In June 1959 Mr Wedgwood Benn (Lab., S.E. Bristol) tabled a motion regretting that the Colonial Secretary had recommended the award of an M.B.E. to Mr J. B. T. Cowan, of the Kenya Prison Service. The work of Mr Cowan was discussed in the House, but not the motion. Cf. *The Times*, June 15, 1959, and H.C. Deb., Vol. 607, cols. 278 and 354 *et seq.*

the candidates themselves were normally expected to pay all election expenses, it was not easy for a party to find anyone willing to stand in a constituency where the chances of victory were slim. Many constituencies returned two members to Westminster: here it was common for the opposing factions to agree to take one seat each to avoid the trouble and cost of a contest. This latter form of agreement became more difficult to maintain when political passions ran higher and as the electorate was increased by successive Reform Bills. Elections were expensive because the candidates had to meet the administrative costs of running the election—as well as the costs incurred in trying to obtain support from voters. The Ballot Act and the rise in the number of those eligible to vote both added to the size of the bills that Returning Officers presented to candidates who, successful or unsuccessful, shared equally the cost of the poll in their constituency. The average charge payable by an individual candidate in the election of January 1910 was £245 in a county seat and £122 in a borough seat.[1] Naturally, charges were much lower when a seat was uncontested. Thus it is not surprising that the number of unopposed returns was considerable, especially when the interval between elections was short. The numbers of seats uncontested in 1900, 1906, January 1910 and December 1910, were respectively 243, 114, 75 and 163.[2] The increase of uncontested returns in December 1910 in the midst of the controversy raging between Lords and Commons is surely indicative of shortage of funds. Since 1918 the expenses of Returning Officers have been met from public revenues, but the financial problems of political parties have been aggravated by the further extension of the electorate (from over 8 million in 1915 to 21 million by 1918) and by the need to maintain national party headquarters of growing size in London. In 1918 the total of unopposed returns was as high as 101, but after the disappearance of the Southern Ireland seats it exceeded 50 only in 1931. Since the last war the number has been negligible as the major parties assume that the flag must

[1] J. F. S. Ross, *Elections and Electors* (Eyre & Spottiswoode, 1955), p. 215.
[2] *Ibid.*, p. 214. Irish and university seats were the most frequently uncontested. In January 1910 only ten other seats in Great Britain avoided a poll.

be shown in all areas however unsympathetic.

The strains on party finance were especially acute in the 1880s. The third Reform Act of 1884 increased the electorate by about two million voters and added substantially to the cost of elections, especially in rural constituencies. In 1886 the 'secret service' money was stopped; under Acts of 1782 and 1837 £10,000 p.a. had been paid to the Patronage Secretary for 'secret service' work, and no account was required of how the money was spent. It had been used to meet the administrative expenses of the Government Whip's office and the surplus was diverted to other party purposes, including financial aid to impecunious candidates supporting the ministerial cause. Akers-Douglas, the Tory Chief Whip, took the initiative in ending this abuse.[1] His action may have been stimulated by high principles, but it was also good political tactics, not least because the Liberals needed funds even more than the Conservatives. Another factor was the Corrupt Practices Act, 1883, which although limiting expenditure at constituency level, accentuated the need to disseminate party propaganda on a national basis. Also at this period two General Elections were held unusually close together and the split in the Liberal Party, which created much political uncertainty, made it desirable for all parties to contest as many seats as possible. All this activity cost money. Today the bulk of party finance comes from small subscriptions of the mass membership of large parties; except perhaps in the Conservative Party there are few large payments from individuals. In the nineteenth century and in the earlier part of this century, Conservatives and Liberals got their money from Parliamentary candidates and a relatively small number of subscribers, some of whom donated considerable sums. How were these gifts to be encouraged? Was it an accident that the appearance of regular Honours Lists coincided with the emergence of acute strains in party finance?

According to H. J. Hanham[2] the first clear cases of a sale

[1] Viscount Chilston, *Chief Whip* (Routledge, 1961), pp. 90-1.
[2] 'The Sale of Honours in Late Victorian England' in *Victorian Studies,* Vol. III, pp. 277-89. This article is based largely on researches in the Salisbury papers at Christ Church, Oxford, and the Akers-Douglas papers, i.e. cor-

of honours were those of Stern and Williamson, two undistinguished Liberal backbenchers in the Commons. It appears that these men gave large sums to Party funds in 1891 on the understanding that they would be raised to the peerage at the end of the *subsequent* Parliament, assuming, of course, that the Liberals won the forthcoming election. The Liberals duly won the election of 1892 and the bargain was faithfully carried through in the Resignation Honours of 1895. It is clear that Gladstone knew of this arrangement; indeed Lord Rosebery recommended these peerages only after receiving a personal request from Gladstone to do so. A certain amount of rumour about intrigues of this sort inevitably gets into circulation and in May 1894 it stimulated a short discussion in the Commons about the distribution of titles.[1] Sir W. Lawson, Bt, thought that an official statement should be made giving the reasons for the conferment of honours; this would make the Prime Minister more responsible to the House for his recommendations to the Sovereign. Mr Lambert had heard of a man who had changed his party to get a baronetcy and changed back again to become a peer. There was some criticism of the calibre of recently created peers, including that of M.P.s who had been elevated. As the Prime Minister was in the Upper House, the Chancellor of the Exchequer, Sir William Harcourt, replied to the debate. He agreed that there might be errors of judgment from time to time, but argued that on average justice was done in the bestowal of honours. Existing practice might not be the ideal state of affairs 'but it accommodated the weaknesses of human nature and it was better not to disturb it'.

The Birthday Honours of 1905 again stimulated public discussion. The *Saturday Review*[2] in an article entitled 'The

respondence of the Tory Leader and Chief Whip at this period. In a footnote to his article, Mr Hanham records, 'At the request of the Marquess of Salisbury I have suppressed the details of a number of transactions in which political services were bartered for honours, lest their revelation should prove offensive to the surviving children of those concerned.'

[1] Parl. Deb., 4th Series, Vol. 24, cols. 410-17.
[2] Issue dated December 16, 1905. At the time the Birthday Honours were issued the position of the Conservative Government was steadily weakening. The next election was clearly not far off.

Adulteration of the Peerage' alleged that honours were being bought and sold. Various letters appeared in the correspondence columns of the Press. The Birthday Honours of 1907 led to a question by Mr Lea in the Commons regarding the award of a knighthood to a Sir James Brown Smith. Supplementary questions were ruled out of order by the Speaker. Baulked in the Commons, Mr Lea wrote to *The Times*[1] alleging that honours were being sold in return for donations to funds of the party in power at the time. At elections a candidate unable to meet all his expenses could be aided by party funds: if elected his support for his party could be regarded as secure. Should he rebel by voting according to his conscience the whips could reproach him for violation of what was regarded as a bargain. This letter led to a motion in the Commons by Lord Robert Cecil that its author was guilty of a breach of privilege, but the motion also included a proposal that a Select Committee be appointed to inquire into the allegations. Sir H. Campbell-Bannerman, the Prime Minister, categorically denied that his party had ever brought pressure to bear on a Member through the fact of having given him financial assistance. For the Conservatives, Mr Balfour gave a similar assurance. Lord Cecil's motion was defeated so no inquiry was held. It should be noted that the protestations of party leaders in this debate related to issues of party discipline and not to the sale of titles.

The Bonar Law papers provide conclusive proof that honours were bartered for subscriptions to party funds at this period. When Bonar Law became Leader of the Conservative Opposition in 1911 he received a memorandum from the Party Manager, Arthur Steel-Maitland, on the state of the Party's organization and finances. This document reported that the Party had a 'nest-egg of £300,000' and that 'a year's peerages are hypothecated'. Steel-Maitland went on to hope for an income, by the end of 1913, of £120,000 to £140,000 a year. 'This should be to a large extent, but not wholly, irrespective of future honours.'[2]

[1] July 12, 1907.
[2] R. Blake, *The Unknown Prime Minister* (Eyre & Spottiswoode, 1955), p. 100.

Some members of the House of Lords were gravely disturbed by the knowledge that admission to their august body could be facilitated by cash payments and from 1914 to 1922 Parliamentary discussion of the distribution of honours was concentrated in the Upper House. The first major debate on the subject was held in February 1914. The speech of the Earl of Selborne on this occasion is worthy of some attention. He urged that contributions to party funds should not influence the award of honours; that all Governments, of whatever party, should adhere to this principle; that the Commons be requested to concur with this resolution. He confessed that, in spite of numerous confidences, he could not prove a single case in a court of law, but he believed the evil existed and was growing. It had a harmful effect on the prestige of the Crown and was lowering the standard of public morality. The root of the trouble, the Earl argued, lay in the dependence of the parties on enormous funds controlled by the whips chiefly to defray election expenses. As party machinery became more extensive the whips became obsessed with the idea that money was the essential condition for remaining in office. For them the ends justified the means of its procurement. But, as Lord Selborne inferred, the source of funds would be unknown to party leaders. The whip is very loyal to his chiefs. 'He tells them everything about the party except about the party funds, and his loyalty is shown by telling them as little as possible. The party chiefs are busy men, and they are careful students of the Book of Genesis, and they avoid the tree of knowledge of good and evil.'[1] Other peers supported Lord Selborne, but Lord Ribblesdale, a former whip, asserted that they were tilting at a windmill on which they would make little impression. The Lord Privy Seal, for the Government, denied that the present Prime Minister (Mr Asquith) ever considered political donations when making recommendations for honours. This was, of course, a denial of something that had not been suggested: Lord Selborne had stressed that party leaders were shielded from knowing who paid large sums into party coffers.

After the outbreak of war the matter was dropped until

[1] H.L. Deb., Vol. 15, col. 259.

1917 when the Lords held two major debates on honours.[1] These discussions show interesting developments. The first mention is made of intermediaries—later described as touts—who were concerned in the sale of honours. It was suggested that not all the money paid for honours went to party funds: some went into the pockets of these go-betweens. Lord Loreburn suspected that there might be a chain of persons below the Patronage Secretary who might do things of which the latter would not approve. The second debate in 1917 contained the first mention of actual names. Concrete evidence of individual cases greatly strengthened the critics who previously had relied on generalizations which ministerial apologists could more easily deny. One name mentioned by Lord Selborne was that of a Mr Geoffrey Holman who had been Mayor of Lewes seven times. At the end of his seventh term some of the Mayor's friends felt that he had earned some recognition; they approached the whip at party headquarters who agreed that there was a clear case for an honour. The whip also asked how much Mr Holman could pay to party funds. When this question was put to Mr Holman, he refused to subscribe anything, and the whip subsequently indicated that the matter of an honour would have to lapse. Another case was furnished by Sir George Kekewich, a former Minister and ex-M.P. for Exeter. Sir George was approached by a gentleman, not unconnected with the drink trade, at a time when the Licensing Bill was before Parliament. The gentleman wanted a knighthood so Sir George introduced him to the whip; the latter saw no difficulty if the applicant satisfied two conditions—that he drop his opposition to the Bill and also subscribe £5,000 to the Party. This bargain was accepted and the name duly appeared in an Honours List.

At the end of this debate their Lordships agreed to two principles embodied in the motion under discussion. The first was that reasons should be given for the conferment of an honour: the second was that when proposing names for awards the Prime Minister should make a declaration to the Sovereign that no payment or expectation of payment was linked with the recommendations. These principles were

[1] H.L. Deb., Vol. 26, cols. 172-212 and 835-86.

accepted by the Government without enthusiasm.[1]

The New Year Honours of 1918 were a very long list. It was coolly received by *The Times*[2] which referred to the persistence of 'the old practice of a large periodical output of titles for the rich and the importunate'. In both Houses there was criticism over the lack of publication of reasons for the awards. In the Commons Mr Bonar Law asserted that official reasons for the awards had been issued, but if the Press chose not to publish this information it was not the fault of the Government.[3] Lord Selborne in the Upper House suggested that the Honours List be published in the *London Gazette* where the reasons could appear in full. He also criticized as inadequate some of the reasons that had been given, for example 'Mayor of Bootle' and 'Mayor of Limerick'.[4] Later the same year Lord Selborne suggested that a Committee of the Privy Council be established to help the Prime Minister in preparing recommendations for honours. So many awards were given that the Prime Minister could not be expected to scrutinize diligently all the names submitted to him, so the real initiative fell to private secretaries who were unknown to the constitution. This system left the door open for corruption to creep in.[5] The Government rejected the idea of the committee—but such a body was established four years later.

After the war (May 1919) Brigadier-General Page-Croft tried another line of attack on the connection between honours and political funds. He introduced a motion in the Commons which asked the Government to prepare a Bill to enforce publication of party accounts. Party funds should be audited by a chartered accountant and a list of all substantial subscribers, say of sums over £500, should be made available for

[1] Another speech from this debate is worthy of mention. Viscount Bryce, the distinguished constitutional lawyer, said that there had been many wealthy M.P.s with but a perfunctory interest in politics who were suddenly raised to the peerage, and for this there could be but one explanation. Lord Bryce had been an M.P. himself from 1880 to 1907.

[2] January 1, 1918.

[3] H.C. Deb., Vol. 98, col. 1972.

[4] H.L. Deb., Vol. 29, cols. 513-33. His suggestion about the *London Gazette* was accepted.

[5] H.L. Deb., Vol. 32, col. 6. For other comments at this period on the sale of honours, see H.C. Deb., Vol. 103, col. 913.

public inspection. The Brigadier also urged that the bestowal of honours in return for such contributions be stopped. He was supported *inter alia* by Mr Horatio Bottomley who rejoiced in the fact he was still plain 'Mr' as being evidence that he was still uncorrupted. The Government opposed the motion, which was lost by 112 votes to 50. The ministerial spokesman, Mr Bonar Law, made the customary denial that honours were sold and argued that the auditing of party funds would be ineffective as new organizations would be formed through which funds could be channelled for political purposes.[1]

Feelings in regard to the distribution of honours were undoubtedly exacerbated by the war. The nineteenth-century attitude that it was natural for rich men to get titles had greatly weakened. Instead, public sentiment demanded that men (and women) should be recognized who had served the country during the war with outstanding bravery or ability. In defiance of this view the Honours Lists still contained a high proportion of those distinguished mainly by wealth and/or whose political support was important to the Government. Thus newspaper proprietors were regularly ennobled. As Prime Minister Lloyd George continued to ignore the climate of opinion, the chances of a political explosion about honours remained. A related factor in the situation was the growing strains within the coalition of Conservatives and Lloyd George Liberals. To discuss reasons for this tension would be outside the scope of this book; but influential Conservatives were not made more sympathetic to the coalition by the knowledge that Lloyd George was building a considerable political fund which would be able to finance expenditure at the next election. By the summer of 1922 the next election could not be far away.

The storm broke over the Birthday Honours of 1922. A number of names in the list provoked criticism, and, in particular, that of Sir Joseph Robinson, Bt, who was to be elevated to the peerage. The official statement recorded that his peer-

[1] H.C. Deb., Vol. 116, cols. 1334-80. The idea that the accounts of political parties should be published by law has often been discussed since 1919. It is now usually advocated only by Left-wing opinion. For a discussion in 1949 see H.C. Deb., Vol. 470, cols. 2972-3040.

age was given for 'National and Imperial' services in connection with his chairmanship of the Robinson South African Banking Company Ltd. Now this concern had been liquidated in 1905. Sir Joseph had been created a baronet in 1908, so this latter award presumably covered any services he might have rendered through the bank: clearly he could not have given any services to the nation through the bank since 1908. The official statement was demonstrably absurd. A further source of comment was Sir Joseph's entanglement with the South African courts. In 1906 he had been the chairman of the Randfontein Estates Company and in this capacity he acquired certain mining properties for the company; this operation he performed by first buying the properties himself and then selling them to the company at an enormous profit. When Sir Joseph sold his interest in Randfontein Estates in 1915 these dealings came to light. He was then sued by the company and was ordered by the Appellate Division of the South African Supreme Court to repay a sum exceeding half a million pounds. Why, then, was Sir Joseph deemed suitable for a peerage? A further mystery, which was never cleared up, was from what source did the recommendation come. It was made known that neither the Government of South Africa nor the Secretary of State for the Colonies was responsible.

The House of Lords held two discussions on the Robinson case;[1] during the second it was announced that Sir Joseph had written to the Prime Minister asking to be allowed to decline the peerage offered to him.[2] But this did little to ease the mounting pressure on the Government. In the Commons a motion on the Order Paper asked that a Joint Committee of both Houses be established to review the existing procedure for submitting names for honours to the Sovereign. The motion attracted increasing support, but the Government at

[1] H.L. Deb., Vol. 50, cols. 1126-40 and Vol. 51, cols. 103-36.
[2] Lloyd George's reply to Sir Joseph, accepting his decision to refuse a peerage, was delivered to Robinson by an official of the National Liberal Party at the Savoy Hotel. Sir Joseph misunderstood the message. He reached for his cheque book and asked, 'How much more?' When he realized its meaning, Robinson complained of a breach of faith. It seems that he expected his withdrawal to be declined and the peerage to be conferred after all. This story is taken from F. Owen, *Tempestuous Journey* (Hutchinson, 1954), p. 623n.

first opposed a debate on it, then procrastinated and finally
gave way when the total of signatures to the motion had risen
above 200. Even then, the debate was postponed for a fortnight to allow the Leader of the House to take part.[1]

Meanwhile, King George V sent a strong letter to Lloyd
George:

'Dear Prime Minister,' he wrote, 'I cannot conceal from you
my profound concern at the very disagreeable situation which
has arisen on the question of honours . . . for some time there
have been evident signs of growing public dissatisfaction on
account of the excessive number of honours conferred; the
personality of some of the recipients; and the questionable
circumstances under which the honours in certain circumstances have been granted. . . .

'The case of Sir Joseph Robinson and all that it has evoked
in the debates of the House of Lords and in newspaper reports
of interviews given by him to Press representatives, must be
regarded as little less than an insult to the Crown and to the
House of Lords and may, I fear, work injury to the Prerogative in the public mind at home and even more in South
Africa.'[2]

The King went on to urge the 'establishment of some efficient
and trustworthy procedure to protect the Crown and the
Government' from similar painful incidents. Lloyd George
replied that he shared His Majesty's concern and proposed to
establish a Royal Commission on the subject.

On July 17, 1922, both Houses discussed honours.[3] The

---

[1] H.C. Deb., Vol. 156, cols. 23-4. The Leader, Mr Austen Chamberlain, was
ill at the time.
[2] For the full text of the King's letter, see H. Nicolson, *King George V*, pp.
512-13. Nicolson suppressed the names in the letter but the references to
South Africa makes it clear who was mentioned.
[3] H.C. Deb., Vol. 156, cols. 1745-862 and H.L. Deb., Vol. 51, cols. 475-512.
In the Lords' debate five steps in the rake's progress in the award of honours
were described by Lord Salisbury. They were awards for (i) public services,
(ii) public services plus donations to party funds, (iii) services plus large
donations, (iv) donations plus public services and (v) donations. Salisbury
suggested that the fourth of these stages had already been reached—which
was probably an under-estimate.

Commons debated Mr Locker-Lampson's motion that a joint committee be set up to inquire into the distribution of honours. Sir Samuel Hoare complained that adequate reasons were not given for awards in contravention of the Lords' resolutions of 1917: apart from the Robinson case, there was an instance of a man described in the *London Gazette* as 'author and writer' who had written only a number of popular songs. J. R. Clynes quoted Lord Carson, an eminent K.C. and Conservative ex-Minister, who said that in chambers he had had to advise in cases where a long correspondence showed a regular brokerage in honours. But the noteworthy speeches in the debate are those of the Prime Minister and the Leader of the House, Austen Chamberlain. The Prime Minister, speaking early in the debate, announced the institution of the Royal Commission which had become necessary because of the allegations made. Lloyd George protested that the whole matter had been greatly exaggerated: in spite of the great problems which had faced the Government over the past six years, the lists had been scrutinized with great care. A few mistakes had occurred due to oversight, not corruption. Only four cases had been picked out for censure. (This was misleading. Three of the four cases came from the Birthday List of 1922, when the Prime Minister was not suffering from the strain of running a war. And other names might have been mentioned but for a very proper and decent reticence of the critics.) Continuing, Lloyd George reminded the House that it was traditional for the Patronage Secretary to submit names for political honours. As for party funds, no Prime Minister had the slightest idea who contributed. (It was pointed out immediately that this was quite incompatible with the Government acceptance of the Lords' resolutions of 1917.) The Prime Minister then argued that the system of political honours should be retained. If they were abolished the Party system would collapse(!). The Germans attributed their collapse in 1918 to a lack of politicians to stimulate the spirit of the country(!). And he finished by saying that a Parliamentary committee was not an appropriate body to conduct an inquiry: it must be a Royal Commission because the inquiry would deal with the Royal Prerogative.

Government spokesmen in the various Parliamentary

debates on honours had argued repeatedly that contributions to political funds should not be regarded as a disqualification for an award. The critics had not argued that it should be; their case was that political contributions should not be a (dominant) consideration. On July 17th, Austen Chamberlain put the ministerial view more frankly. Those who served their party on public bodies, in the House or by speaking on public platforms were accepted as being worthy of recognition. Why should a man who conducted a great business which contributed to national prosperity and who said, 'I have not the power of speech, I cannot spare time to sit on public bodies, but I will make my contribution in money,' be not considered equally as a worthy recipient? Thus was Chamberlain's argument. Leaving aside the question of whether political subscriptions should ever be recognized by an honour, there is a clear distinction between a person who contributes regularly because of strong political convictions, and a person, uninterested in politics, who makes a single, large payment in the hope or expectation of a title. The line between these two categories is easy to blur. It is apparent that the practice which Chamberlain defended could easily slip, and had slipped, into a system of bargains with touts taking a percentage.[1]

At the end of Chamberlain's speech Lord Hugh Cecil rose and technically talked the debate out. So it was adjourned, never to be resumed,[2] and no vote was taken on the original proposal to appoint a Select Committee. Given the generally hostile reception to the Prime Minister's speech and the confused state of party loyalties at the time, a vote might have proved an embarrassment to the Government.

The membership of the Royal Commission was announced in August. The chairman was Lord Dunedin and the other members were Lord Denman, the Duke of Devonshire, Mr Arthur Henderson, M.P., Sir Evelyn Cecil, M.P., Sir Samuel Hoare, M.P., and Sir G. Croydon Marks, M.P. All shades of Parliamentary opinion were represented. The terms of refer-

---

[1] Three months later, with the break-up of the coalition, Chamberlain ceased to be Leader of the Conservative Party. It is unlikely that this speech served to strengthen his position as Leader.
[2] H.C. Deb., Vol. 156, col. 2265.

ence were 'To advise on the procedure to be adopted in future to assist the Prime Minister in making recommendations to His Majesty of the names of persons deserving of special honour.' This phraseology was designed to prevent, as far as possible, any searching inquiry into past events: the words 'in future' could be argued to have a limiting effect. Many of Lloyd George's critics did not wish for any investigation into the past. 'Let bygones be bygones' is indicative of a spirit of Parliamentary toleration. Yet it is not easy to legislate for the future if barred from consideration of conditions that have prevailed in the past.

The Commission started its hearings in October. It examined the Prime Minister and ex-Prime Ministers, except Lord Rosebery, who was unable to attend through illness; the various Patronage Secretaries and others responsible for party organization who were still available; and the Earl of Selborne and the Duke of Northumberland, two of the most prominent critics of the existing system. Memoranda were received from Lord Gladstone and Lord Kilbracken, who had been associated with the dispensation of patronage under W. E. Gladstone, and from Government departments responsible for compiling lists of recommendations for honours. A careful study was also made of published correspondence and the various Parliamentary debates.

The Commission's primary concern was with honours given for political services. These they divided into two classes, those given to M.P.s and those given to persons outside the House. Recommendations relating to M.P.s were submitted to the Prime Minister by the Patronage Secretary, the other recommendations came from the Party Organizer who might also be the Patronage Secretary.[1] The Prime Minister also received suggestions from other sources. All the ex-Prime Ministers, Lloyd George himself, and the Patronage Secretaries and Party Organizers in turn denied that they had ever been aware of any bargain that an honour would be contingent on a contribution to party funds. However, the Commission reported that they were convinced that touts had been going

---

[1] This is no longer the case. In more recent years these two positions have not been held by the same man.

about asserting that they were in a position to secure honours for specified payments. To improve existing procedure the Commission proposed that a small committee be set up of not more than three Privy Councillors appointed by the Prime Minister for the period of his government. The names of members would be published. Recommendations for honours should be sent to the proposed committee by the Prime Minister before going to the King. Attached to each name sent to the committee should be (a) a statement of the reasons why the recommendation was made, (b) a statement by the Patronage Secretary or Party Manager that no payment or expectation of payment to party funds was associated with the recommendation, (c) the name and address of the person who the Prime Minister considered had originally suggested the name. Armed with this information the committee would then inquire into whether each individual was a fit and proper person to receive an honour. Should the committee report adversely on any case, and the Prime Minister still persisted in the recommendation, it was proposed that the report of the committee be made available to the Sovereign. Finally the Commission proposed that a short Act be passed to impose penalties on anyone who offered to obtain an honour in return for payment, or who offered payment for an honour. The Commission also opposed the idea that there should be a limit on the number of peerages created in any one year, as this might obstruct the solution of a future clash of opinion between the two Houses by the ennoblement of new peers.

The Report,[1] summarized above, was not unanimous, and included a Note of Dissent by Arthur Henderson. In it he said:

'Though the terms of reference were somewhat restricted, I am of opinion that the Commission might with advantage have made a much more searching inquiry than they have done. I regret that, though the Commission were in possession of the names of persons who are conveniently and appropriately described as "touts", none of them were invited to give evi-

[1] Honours. Royal Commission. Report; 1923 Cmd. 1789, xi. The evidence submitted to the Commission, written and oral, was not published.

dence. Nor was any person who had been approached by "touts" called to give evidence before us, though the names of such persons were also before the Commission. The omission of evidence from those who are alleged to have asserted that they were in a position to secure honours in return for money payments, and from those who have been approached by such persons, has left unexplored one of the gravest abuses concerning the nominations for honours. Had the investigation been pursued more thoroughly, I have no doubt that the evidence forthcoming would have led the Commission to realize the inadequacy of their recommendations.

. . .

'It cannot be doubted that honours have been conferred upon persons whose chief claim to recognition was party service, and it appears to be implied in the evidence of certain witnesses before the Committee, though it was not so baldly stated, that the financial exigencies of political parties were in themselves almost a sufficient reason for the conferment of political honours. This system whereby financial assistance rendered to a party is recognized by the conferment of an honour by the State is, in my judgment, deplorable, and discredits the honours system. It is a means of enabling the temporarily dominant political party to bestow special political power, through membership of the House of Lords, on individuals of their own selection, and it does not secure that the person honoured possesses any distinction except his title.'

Henderson ended by arguing that the abolition of political honours would not 'in any way diminish either the volume or the quality of the services given to the community by its citizens'.

The Commission had worked with commendable speed and their Report was issued in December 1922. But by this time the Coalition Government had broken up and a General Election had returned the Conservatives to office.[1] This change in poli-

---

[1] Lloyd George's Resignation Honours included no fewer than forty-five names. The Marquis of Bute received the Thistle: he was a large and dissident shareholder in Lloyd George's paper, *The Daily Chronicle*. Cf. F. Owen, *Tempestuous Journey* (Hutchinson, 1954), p. 687.

tical fortunes may have affected the reception of the Report in the House of Lords.[1] The Report was generally welcomed but there seemed to be some feeling that its majority conclusions were too radical: Lord Southborough thought that the Prime Minister might be assisted in scrutinizing proposed honours by two members of his Government—not by the committee suggested by the Commission. The peers who had taken a prominent part in earlier debates on honours were notable by their silence. One of them, Lord Salisbury, now occupied the position of Lord President of the Council. Can it be that the gamekeepers were thinking of becoming poachers? However the Government accepted the recommendations of the Commission. The committee was established and still exists—the Political Honours Scrutiny Committee. The Bill suggested by the Commission passed into law in 1925 as the Honours (Prevention of Abuses) Act.[2]

After 1922 the controversy over honours tended to die away, although there were various repercussions for several years. The first related to the position of Lord Farquar as Treasurer of the Conservative Party. In January 1923 he refused to hand over certain funds to the Party on the grounds that they had been collected for the purposes of the Coalition, and that as the Coalition had disintegrated, he had no authority to release them. In March, Lord Farquar was requested to resign; he refused and was subsequently dismissed.[3] In the Liberal Party, where the reunion between Asquith and Lloyd George was always uneasy, the existence of Lloyd George's political fund was a constant source of irritation. Its method of collection, its ownership and use caused much speculation and criticism. At last, Lloyd George issued a statement in December 1927. The fund had been collected by the whips in accordance with the traditional practice of the older parties. Honours Lists were prepared by Chief Whips: the Prime Minister did not know who had subscribed to party coffers. When the

[1] H.L. Deb., Vol. 53, cols. 259-291.
[2] By an odd mischance two standard works on British government record the date of this Act as 1923. This error has survived two editions of A. B. Keith, *The British Cabinet System* and three editions of Sir W. I. Jennings, *Cabinet Government*.
[3] F. Owen, *Tempestuous Journey*, p. 664.

Coalition Liberal Party existed, its whips administered the fund; after this party disappeared as a separate entity, a committee, including three ex-whips, administered it. The size of the fund had grown owing to the success of the *Daily Chronicle* and other papers which had been bought. Lloyd George stated that he himself was only consulted on questions of major policy concerning the fund, which was used for electoral purposes, a bureau dealing with ex-servicemen's problems and for financing various inquiries into economic matters. But it seems clear that Lloyd George had ultimate control over the money and he obtained high legal opinion that he was entitled, if he chose 'to gamble it away at Monte Carlo'.[1] Subsequently, in a letter to the Marquess of Reading, Lloyd George seemed to shift his ground a little by arguing that the fund was not a *party* fund. 'My Fund', he wrote, 'does not represent gifts made to any party. It started through donations made through my Whip to me to be used for such political purposes as I thought desirable. . . .'[2]

The comment of Tom Jones on Lloyd George and honours is needed to complete the picture. 'What did most damage to Lloyd George's prestige was not so much any departure of the principles of his predecessors as the deterioration in the quality of the recipients and the reputation of some of the go-betweens who acted as links between the Chief Whip and persons considered suitable for inclusion in the lists.'[3] These observations have special significance in view of their author's intimate knowledge of proceedings in Downing Street.

Further evidence of trafficking in honours came from two court cases of 1924. The first concerned a Lt-Col G. W. Parkinson[4] who, on the suggestion of a third party, had negotiations with a Mr Harrison, secretary of a charity known as the College of Ambulance. Harrison assured the Colonel that he could obtain a knighthood in return for a donation to the College. After haggling about the amount, the Colonel paid a

[1] T. Jones, *Lloyd George* (Oxford University Press, 1951), p. 203.
[2] Quoted from F. Owen, *Tempestuous Journey*, p. 689. Owen also gives a sketch of the history of the fund down to the death of Lloyd George.
[3] T. Jones, *Lloyd George*, p. 202. Tom Jones had held the position of Deputy Secretary to the Cabinet at this period.
[4] *Parkinson v. College of Ambulance* (1925) 2 K.B.1.

deposit of £3,000. He subsequently went to the Central Conservative Office where he was told he had been fooled. The Colonel then brought an action against the College and its secretary for the return of his £3,000: he succeeded against the secretary but not against the College, and the judge ruled that it would be contrary to public policy to allow Parkinson to recover his money. This decision was, of course, a protection for the touts. If a client paid up, but failed to get the promised honour, there was no prospect of getting money back by legal action. Another point emerges from the Parkinson case: while some touts may have been in touch with the whips, others were merely swindlers.

The second case was the sequestration proceedings of creditors in relation to the will of Sir J. H. Stewart, Bt. In evidence it emerged that Sir John had paid money to the Lloyd George fund and had been rewarded with his baronetcy. Sir John had been on the verge of bankruptcy in December 1922, and £50,000 had been repaid to avoid, it was suggested, the publicity of bankruptcy. For the creditors it was said that the £50,000 represented only about a third of what Sir John had originally paid. Lloyd George issued a statement denying knowledge of the transaction—but he consistently denied knowledge of who contributed to his fund and so the statement is irrelevant when regarded as evidence whether this bargain was made.[1]

Nine years later came the sole prosecution to date under the Act of 1925. J. Maundy Gregory was summoned at Bow Street for pretending to be able to obtain a title in return for payment. The client or victim was Lt-Cmdr Leake who had carefully led Gregory on in order to build up evidence against him. Leake had no desire for a title and was careful to make or promise no payment. At the preliminary hearing Gregory pleaded 'not guilty': subsequently he changed his plea, was convicted and sentenced to three months' imprisonment. From the study of Gregory's life[2] it is clear that he carried on the business of an honours tout for many years. He had a suite of

---

[1] These cases are described in detail by G. Macmillan, *Honours for Sale*, pp. 89-91.
[2] *Ibid.*

offices in Parliament Street with uniformed messengers, he owned a club and published a magazine, *The Whitehall Gazette*, to help to impress his clients and arrange social contacts. It is interesting to speculate why Gregory changed his plea to 'guilty'. Had the case been fought, various facts might have been mentioned in Court which could have been detrimental to Gregory and, no doubt, other people as well. The magistrate might have decided owing to the importance of the case to transfer it to the Central Criminal Court which, under he 1925 Act, had power to impose a heavier penalty than a court of summary jurisdiction. When he first appeared at Bow Street Gregory was known to be in financial difficulties: after his release from prison he went to France where he managed to live in conditions of relative affluence. He died in France under the German occupation. Where did his money in France come from? The conclusion must be that someone was providing a pension to keep him quiet.

Did Gregory have, or had he ever had, authority to negotiate the sale of titles? We cannot be sure. Apparently he was known to influential personages including Ministers, but how far Ministers knew of his activities is another matter. Yet it seems unlikely that Gregory could have stayed in business as a tout for about thirteen years without having some success in obtaining honours. And someone looked after him when he was exposed.

The sole legacy of the events of 1922 is now the Political Honours Scrutiny Committee. It consists of three Privy Councillors who are not ministers and who are not all political supporters of the Government of the day. The committee has a secretary who combines this work with that of Ceremonial Officer at the Treasury, the post concerned with Civil Service awards. How useful has the committee been? No answer can be given to this question for no reports are issued about its work. Nor is it known whether sufficient information is given to members of the committee to enable them to carry out adequate enquiries. Members of the committee are often elderly, and not always in the best of health. Perhaps the feeling exists that there is no longer a great need for the committee to be a vigorous body.

Is it now safe to assume that trade in titles is at an end? Certainly, money cannot buy a seat in the Lords. Certainly, there are no touts in this business. Certainly, under the Attlee Government few political honours were given and then always for obvious services. Any further, the position is not clear beyond doubt. Conservative Honours Lists still contain baronetcies and knighthoods awarded 'for political services' of an unspecified nature. No details are published about the sources of income of the Conservative Party. Since 1948, Party membership, and hence the total of subscribers, have grown appreciably. But the majority of subscriptions to local associations are small in amount. The Party has a Central Board of Finance which is responsible to the chairman of the party organization. According to McKenzie's 'reasonably well-informed speculation'[1] this body is used to approach more wealthy supporters of the party for contributions of at least moderate size which go direct to the central funds of the party. As the chairman of the Party organization is well placed to recommend honours, suspicions may still remain. Nothing as crude as a bargain would ever be made. But is there any correlation between subscription lists of the Conservative Party and the names that appear in Honours Lists 'for political services' or for 'political and public services'? According to some Conservative spokesmen of the past this would be in no way dishonourable or improper. It is possible to find M.P.s in *all* parties who believe that the correlation still exists.

IV

The technique of making awards to stimulate loyalty to the State or to buttress a political policy has been noticed in the previous sections of this chapter. It is most common and successful when the mental climate is conducive to the stimulation of patriotic sentiments—as in war or when the territory of the realm is extending. Thus the two most recent Orders of Chivalry, the Order of the British Empire and the Companions of Honour, were founded in the summer of 1917, one of the most difficult periods of the First World War. Even in 1917-18

[1] R. T. McKenzie, *British Political Parties* (Heinemann, 1955), p. 215

there was some criticism of the Order of the British Empire, partly because of its widespread distribution: within twelve months of its inception 5,950 appointments to the various classes of the order had been made.[1] One M.P. asked in the Commons whether membership of the order could be obtained by application to the Labour Exchange.[2] W. C. Anderson, M.P., was reported by *The Times*[3] as saying that trade union leaders were 'being decorated with honours and one of these days it would be a distinction to have no decoration'. Yet in spite of such cynicism and sarcasm the various types of award had, and still have, a profound effect on recipients. The right to allocate awards becomes, in effect, the possession of a powerful weapon. Since the nature of the power is psychological, the weapon must be used with tact and discretion. When honours become automatic, as with the higher civil service, or too numerous, they must lose something of their appeal. Were it known to be possible to buy them, honours would become a mockery. Were honours used too obviously for party purposes, they would become a source of political controversy. The relative lack of public discussion in recent years about political honours says much for the care with which they have been regulated, especially as the Conservatives utilise honours far more than did the Labour Government 1945-51.

The dangers inherent in Lloyd George's profuse distribution of membership of the Order of the British Empire were widely realized. Subsequently the number of awards was cut drastically. The few appointments to this order in the New Year Lists from 1925 to 1928 inclusive had a common characteristic: all the recipients were women. This exceptional policy may be interpreted as an attempt by Prime Minister Baldwin to conciliate feminist opinion, then still unsatisfied on the franchise issue. The ending of this tactic once the demands of the suffragettes were finally satisfied, and the award of the G.B.E. to Mrs Fawcett, leader and historian of the women's suffrage movement, are both highly suggestive.

[1] H.C. Deb., Vol. 106, col. 2370.
[2] H.C. Deb., Vol. 101, col. 482 (Mr Hogge).
[3] August 27, 1917.

FEMALE APPOINTMENTS—ORDER OF THE
BRITISH EMPIRE

NEW YEAR LISTS 1925-28

	1925	1926	1927	1928
G.B.E.	2	1	—	—
D.B.E.	1	—	1	2
C.B.E.	—	—	7	3
O.B.E.	—	—	2	7
M.B.E.	—	—	—	7
Total	3	1	10	19

Since the Birthday Honours of 1918, reasons for the grant of awards have been officially published. Reasons are now given in a simple and stereotyped form. After a majority of names there appears a statement of the official position—in Government service or in some commercial or voluntary organization—which the individual holds: in such cases it must be presumed that the award is made for services of national value rendered in connection with the position stated. A few names appear with a description of the recipient's occupation, e.g. 'actor', 'painter'. The remainder have phrases attached—'for political and public services', 'for political services', 'for public services', or, more rarely, 'for charitable services'. By a detailed examination of Honours Lists it is possible to see what proportion of awards are given for political, i.e. party, services. The table (pp. 216-17) makes such an analysis of the Birthday List of 1918, in which no reasons were given in relation to the Order of the British Empire, and of the New Year and Birthday Lists for 1928, 1938, 1948 and 1958. What is the difference of meaning between 'political and public services', 'political services' and 'public services'? No official explanation or amplification of these terms is available.[1] It is logical to assume that an award 'for political services' has no

---

[1] In 1936 Mr Thurtle asked the Prime Minister for an explanation of the phrase 'for political services' as used in Honours Lists. Mr Baldwin referred him to the Report of the 1922 Royal Commission. But although the Report describes how political honours are awarded, it does not enlarge on the meaning of the phrase in the context of an Honours List. Indeed it did not appear in the Lists before 1923: previously the phrase had been 'public and local services', 'local' presumably being 'political'. Cf. H.C. Deb., Vol. 308, col. 1408.

connection with any public service and that an award 'for public service' has no taint of reward for party activity. How far 'political and public services' are political, and how far public, can never be assessed.

The year-by-year survey shows the annual total of political awards to be remarkably steady at about 130. One has an impression of loyal Conservative supporters queueing up for a place in the ration made available to their party organizers. It is not a pretty thought. And it is evident from the figures that the proportion of awards for purely political services is tending to increase. Does this imply that the Conservative administration is slipping further along the path of the rake's progress as described by Lord Salisbury? The use of the term 'for political services' is not only more common—it has spread up the hierarchy of honours into knighthoods. Under the Labour Government there were no political knighthoods.[1] In 1948 the three C.B.E.s for political and public services each went to Labour M.P.s who had given many years of work to their party: parallel service by Conservative M.P.s wins a knighthood or even a baronetcy. It is fair to add that just occasionally a Labour backbencher gets a knighthood through the advice of a Conservative Prime Minister, e.g. Sir Tom O'Brien and Sir Frank Benson.

There is an established convention that a Prime Minister or ex-Prime Minister can, if he chooses, obtain an earldom when he retires from the Commons. Similarly, the Speaker will have a viscountcy. Under Conservative Governments it seems that retiring Cabinet Ministers can usually collect a peerage if they wish. Those who have held such senior positions as Leader of the House or Home Secretary receive a viscountcy; those who held lesser positions usually become barons. There is no rigid convention about this: in 1960 Mr George Ward, who held the non-Cabinet post of Secretary of State for Air, was made a viscount. The prospects for Conservative Ministers below Cabinet level are less clear. Normally they do not retire unless they dislike ministerial life, show some measure of ineptitude

---

[1] Except for the conventional awards to the Law Officers. The few knighthoods given to leading trade union officials were not officially classed as political honours.

Honours	1918					1928		
	Total	Public and Parliamentary Services	Public and Local Services	Public and Patriotic Services	Public Services	Total	Political and Public Services	Political Services
Viscounts	2	—	—	—	—			
Barons	3	—	—	—	—	6	2	—
Baronets	14	4	5	2*	3	10	2	—
Knights Bachelor	35	—	10	7*	2	66	24	—
Order of the British Empire:								
G.B.E.	12	—	—	—	—	3	1	—
K.B.E.	55	—	—	—	—	7	3	—
D.B.E.	8	—	—	—	—	3	—	—
C.B.E.	265	—	—	—	—	36	4	1
O.B.E.	1,109	—	—	—	—	76	5	2
M.B.E.	1,376	—	—	—	—	90	1	—

* Including (i) five for 'Active leadership in local patriotic work'; (ii) one for 'Local and patriotic services'.
† 'Public and philanthropic'.

Honours	1959 New Year			Birthday			New Year		196
	Total	Political and Public Services	Political Services	Total	Political and Public Services	Political Services	Total	Political and Public Services	Political Services
Viscounts	0	—	—	0	—	—	1	—	—
Barons	2	—	—	3	2	—	2	—	—
Baronets	2	1	—	3	—	1	5	4	—
Knights Bachelor	29	7	2	30	7	2	31	8	— / 2
Order of the British Empire:									
G.B.E.	1	1	—	1	—	—	1	—	—
K.B.E.	5	1	—	5	1	—	5	1	—
D.B.E.	2	—	—	1	—	—	1	1	—
C.B.E.	94	9	3	92	10	2	91	10	1 / 9
O.B.E.	191	14	3	198	10	7	182	12	5 / 18
M.B.E.	340	19	11	343	21	9	333	21	8 / 33

‖ Life Peers are excluded from this table as they are treated separa
in the following chapter. When an award is made to an ex-membe
the Government, the phrase 'for political and public services' is

1938				1948				1958		
Political and Public Services	Political Services	Public Services	Total	Political and Public Services	Political Services	Public Services	Total	Political and Public Services	Political Services	Public Services
1	—	2‡	1	—	—	—	—	—	—	1
4	—	3	7	2	—	—	4	1	—	1
7	—	1	—	—	—	—	6	2	—	3
30	—	1	58	—	—	3	69	13	3	6
1	—	—	3	—	—	—	2	—	—	1
3	—	—	13	—	—	1	8	1	—	—
1	—	—	1	—	—	—	5	1	—	2
9	—	2	178	3	—	1	202	20	4	6
25	4	4	332	1	—	4‡	378	27	7	13
41	9	1	551	—	—	12§	691	40	21	13

‡...uding one for 'Public and philanthropic'.
§...uding three for 'Public and social'.

		New Year 1961			Birthday 1961			New Year 1962			Birthday 1962	
Political Services	Total	Political and Public Services	Political Services	Total	Political and Public Services	Political Services	Total	Political and Public Services	Political Services	Total	Political and Public Services	Political Services
—	0	—	—	0	—	—	0	—	—	1	—	—
—	1	—	—	2	—	—	4	2	—	1	—	—
—	2	—	—	3	—	—	4	1	—	2	1	—
2	31	5	1	30	8	1	28	4	2	25	6	—
—	1	—	—	2	—	—	1	—	—	0	—	—
—	3	1	—	4	1	—	3	1	—	4	1	—
—	1	—	—	0	—	—	1	—	—	3	—	—
3	88	11	1	86	10	2	89	8	4	89	8	5
6	180	11	6	193	11	6	185	11	6	182	13	4
8	346	12	16	325	8	21	325	13	16	315	9	18

...used—presumably because the reason for the award is obvious.
...cases are also omitted from the totals of political awards shown
...e table.

or disagree with the policy of their senior colleagues. In none of these circumstances would an immediate honour be appropriate. But a Junior Minister who leaves politics for personal reasons after several years of satisfactory service will generally get something; for Commander Noble it was K.C.M.G. It is now rare for a backbench M.P. who has never held any official position to receive an *hereditary* peerage. Another convention is that honours are not bestowed on Ministers or ex-Ministers before they cease to become candidates for ministerial office.[1] A title is the kiss of political death. Thus while many Conservative M.P.s get knighthoods or even baronetcies, Conservative Ministers in the Commons remain plain 'Mr'.

An Honour is almost inevitable for those Conservative backbenchers who stay in Parliament long enough. Each year there are one or two baronetcies and appointments to the Privy Council for them, together with half a dozen knighthoods. But the case of J. H. Mackie illustrates that a knighthood for long service is not quite a certainty; when he died in 1959 Mr Mackie had represented Galloway in the Commons for over twenty-seven years. Mackie's 'crime' may have been that he fought the 1945 Election as an Independent after a dispute with his constituency association, and between 1945 and 1948 he sat in the Commons without receiving the Conservative whip. Knighthoods for Tory M.P.s are thus not as automatic as Civil Service awards. The average requirement is about fifteen years on the backbenches, but some obtain recognition more quickly than others: Sir William Robson Brown, M.P. for Esher, was knighted in 1957 after only seven years in the Commons. It is clear that discrimination is exercised. Probably factors other than Parliamentary service are taken into account.

There can be little doubt that the majority of Tory M.P.s find the idea of a knighthood attractive. It is not surprising that they should. A sense of expectation whets the appetite. At length a sense of justice demands the accolade; 'if others get it,

---

[1] There are minor exceptions to this rule. It does not cover honours awarded personally by the Monarch, e.g. K.G. (Sir Winston Churchill and Sir Anthony Eden) and K.C.V.O. (Sir David Eccles, Minister of Works during the Coronation). The Attorney-General and the Solicitor-General receive knighthoods at the time of their appointment. Occasionally a peerage is created to strengthen the ranks of ministerial spokesmen in the Lords.

why not I?' A knighthood does not decrease the chances of a lucrative company directorship. The sense of vanity still nags, although well hidden: if public men were not a little vain, would they be public men? Also there is the feminine influence —Lady So and So sounds much *nicer* than plain Mrs.

Recommendations for awards to M.P.s are made to the Prime Minister by his Chief Whip. This ability to nominate could give the Conservative Chief Whip a useful additional means of persuasion that his Labour counterpart does not have even when in office. It is tempting to argue that a fairly senior backbencher sickening for a knighthood is as wary of the whip as a newer Member still hoping for a junior ministerial post: however, most Tory M.P.s of a dozen or more years' standing have probably lost the urge to rebel—if ever they had it. Tories certainly stray into the wrong division lobby less often than Labour M.P.s, but this is mainly because they have a more sophisticated control of conscience or less intensity of feeling than their opponents. Nevertheless, the knowledge that your name may be near the top of the list of potential knights might occasionally have an effect. It is also true that Conservative M.P.s have the better attendance records at divisions. At least three reasons can be adduced in explanation: they are younger than Labour M.P.s; more have accommodation easy of access from Westminster after late sittings; they are more accustomed to military discipline. But if it is known —or believed—that the Chief Whip studies division records before making his bi-annual suggestions . . . And if a Conservative M.P. puts forward one or two names for M.B.E.s or O.B.E.s the chances of their adoption may depend on his own reputation in the Whips' office.

The distribution of awards to active Conservatives outside Parliament will help to keep the Party organization in good trim, for it provides a very acceptable means of recognition to those who give exceptional service. Whether the nature of the service is sometimes financial was discussed in the previous section. But there may also be occasions when local officials in the Conservative Party are of particular use to the Party at national level; for example, this could apply if the chairman of a constituency association managed to persuade his own

M.P. to be less critical of some aspects of Party policy. It is not impossible that such service would be known by those who draft subsequent lists of political rewards.

The two preceding paragraphs have suggested various ways in which political awards could be used to strengthen the organization of the party in office inside and outside Parliament. How far is the patronage power, in fact, used in this way? A question of this kind cannot receive a precise answer. In human behaviour the relation between cause and effect is not subject to fine calculation. If X acts in a way pleasing to his party, is he influenced, consciously or sub-consciously, by the vista of some reward? None can tell. The position is further aggravated by the tradition of confidences which dominates our public life. Political gossip of a kind which affects these issues is not publishable, although much of it may be circumstantial and not wholly inaccurate. It follows that it is difficult to demonstrate how far the Honours List is used deliberately to promote the interests of the Conservative Party. Abuses will not become apparent to the point of public outcry unless the patronage power is used blatantly or stupidly.

One indisputable fact is that Conservatives distribute more political awards than Labour. In so doing they continue the custom of past centuries when kings and ministers bestowed gifts on their favourites and supporters. This tradition Labour has never accepted. The difference in attitude towards honours is associated with certain theoretical assumptions of each party. Conservatives believe, in a very real sense, that they are the natural rulers of the country; that they have a duty to serve the Crown and community; that they represent the nation as a whole; that their opponents are but (misguided) members of one section of the community. The Labour Party is more class-conscious; it assumes that each party represents certain sectional interests. While Conservatives will argue, mostly with genuine conviction, that the working man should support their Party to improve his material welfare, Labour spokesmen are never heard to say that it is in the interests of stockbrokers to support them. Their own self-portrait makes it easy for Conservatives to accept as proper that the prestige of the Crown should be associated with rewards for service to their Party. Quite apart from the old Radical suspicion of pomp and pageantry, Labour supporters do not feel that devotion to their Party's cause should end up with a trip to Buckingham Palace.

Political honours are open to abuse. And, as Arthur Henderson argued, their abolition will do no damage to willingness to work for political causes. My view is that rewards for aiding a party could well be brought to an abrupt end. It has been noted that Earl Attlee reduced them to a low figure between 1945 and 1951, but he gave enough to keep the system intact. Once the chain of the past is challenged and broken, it is not easy to re-establish. Had Earl Attlee stopped political awards altogether, and made this an explicit point of policy—would the Conservatives now be able to hand out an annual average of 130 political rewards? A future Labour Prime Minister should re-examine this question before his first Honours List becomes due.

CHAPTER ELEVEN

Life Peerages

⊙

The Life Peerages Act, 1958, did not introduce a brand new conception into British government. On the contrary, the idea was of respectable antiquity. A few life peers were created in the fourteenth and fifteenth centuries. In 1856 the Palmerston Cabinet sought to resuscitate this device to strengthen the legal talent of the House of Lords: Sir James Parke, a judge aged seventy-four with no surviving sons, was granted a barony 'for and during the term of his natural life'. This move aroused strong opposition in the Lords where it was regarded both as an attack on the hereditary basis of the peerage and as a precedent that could be extended to undermine the Conservative majority in the Upper House. The case of Sir James Parke (or Lord Wensleydale) was referred to the Lords' Committee on Privileges which reported that life peerage conferred no right to sit or vote in their Lordships' House: this report was accepted by the Lords with relief. Shortly afterwards Sir James was granted an ordinary hereditary peerage. Twenty years later the Disraeli Conservative Government took up the idea of life peerages as a means of aiding the Lords to carry out their legal duties; the Appellate Jurisdiction Act, 1876, authorized the grant of life baronies to a maximum of four judges eligible to sit in the House of Lords, who would receive salaries and be known by the special title of 'Lords of Appeal in Ordinary'. The maximum of four has been increased on a number of occasions and, since 1947, has stood at nine. Although this exception was made for judges, there can be little doubt about the importance of the Wensleydale decision in blocking a useful means of reform.

The prospect of granting non-judicial life peerages has also been debated for nearly a century.[1] In 1869 Lord John Russell introduced a private member's Bill which sought to authorize a restricted number of life peerages, not more than four a year or a total of twenty-eight at any time. It was argued in favour of the Bill that the House would find advantage from members with a wider variety of experience, and that men from industry and commerce could make a valuable contribution to the work of the Lords. The contrary view, put by Earl Derby, was that the Bill would weaken the Lords by adding to the prerogative of the Crown, which meant adding to the power of Ministers who were dependent on the will of the Commons.[2] The Bill was defeated on the third reading. The life peerage idea was again discussed in both Houses in 1888 when the Prime Minister introduced a measure similar to that of 1869, after a more ambitious project of reform had been withdrawn. One would expect a liberal measure sponsored by a Conservative Prime Minister to be passed: however, the Bill was introduced late in the session, and was dropped as it aroused hostility in the Commons. This incident is of interest because it does show that even in the Victorian age there was support for the view that the Upper House would be strengthened by a modification of the strict principle of heredity. Reform of the Lords was considered by a Select Committee of that House in 1908, and this body also gave its blessing to the idea of a limited number of life peers. It proposed that three-quarters of these peers should have held high office, military, political, diplomatic or in the Civil Service. The maximum number of life peers should be forty, excluding the Lords of Appeal in Ordinary.[3] No action was taken on these recommendations.

From 1909 onwards the House of Lords became an inflammable political issue and the question of composition was overshadowed by disagreements over the proper extent of its powers—a matter outside our present ambit. The Parliament Act, 19 1, which terminated the absolute veto of the Lords

---

[1] Cf. Sydney D. Bailey, *The Future of the House of Lords* (Hansard Society, 1954), pp. 109-20.
[2] Parl. Deb., 3rd Series, Vol. 195, col. 1652-3.
[3] House of Lords. Select Committee. H.L. Report, para. 27; 1908 (H.L. 234), x.

over legislation, contains an unorthodox preamble that expressed the intention of Parliament 'to substitute for the House of Lords as it at present exists a Second Chamber constituted on a popular instead of an hereditary basis'. In pursuance of this intention a conference including representatives of all shades of political opinion was called together in 1917. This conference, presided over by Lord Bryce, carried out the fullest examination yet made by any official body in this country into the problem of constituting a Second Chamber. It considered various methods of providing a popular element in the Second Chamber—nomination by the Crown, acting through Ministers; direct election; election by local authorities; election by a joint committee of both Houses of Parliament; and election by the Commons. The majority of the Bryce Conference favoured the last method, with M.P.s voting in groups based on territorial areas. The conference rejected the idea of nomination by the Crown in a paragraph brief and forthright:

'This plan appeared unlikely to find favour in the country because it did not provide any guarantees for the fitness of persons who might be nominated and because it would be liable to be frequently employed as a reward for political party services.'[1]

Various schemes of reform were discussed by the Lords in 1922, 1927, 1928 and 1933.[2] They included—in varying combinations—ideas ventilated by the Bryce Conference and some of them sought to regain partially the powers lost by the Lords in 1911. But nothing was done. A more limited proposal to admit life peers, based on the Bills of 1869 and 1888, was again brought forward in 1935: the Bill obtained a second reading by 44 votes to 14 and got no further. The post-war period with the Attlee Labour Government saw renewed controversy about the Upper House. While the Bill to reduce

---

[1] *Reform of the Second Chamber*. Conference. Letter from Viscount Bryce to the Prime Minister, para 12; 1918 Cd. 9038, x.
[2] The details are given in Sir W. I. Jennings, *Parliament*, 2nd edn. (Cambridge, 1957), pp. 436-40.

further its delaying power was before the Commons, a small all-party committee of senior politicians was created to see if agreement could be reached on wider aspects of reform. These discussions broke down because of divergent views over the length of the delaying power to be granted to the Second Chamber, and while unanimity was reached on broad principles concerning its composition,[1] these were of limited value since they avoided the central question of how the non-hereditary element in the House should be chosen. Finally, in 1953 Lord Simon introduced another Bill to permit the creation of a maximum of ten life peers a year; the debate on this measure was adjourned and never resumed.

By the mid-'50s the need to acquire fresh faces in the Lords had become acute because of the dwindling numbers on the Opposition benches and the high average age of the peers who still remained. Troubles over similar weakness in Labour representation had occurred before. Both Labour Prime Ministers, Ramsay MacDonald and Attlee, were forced to ennoble some of their supporters to provide a sufficiency of Government spokesmen in the Lords. In 1941 Winston Churchill saw the need to strengthen the voice of Labour in the Upper House and created four Labour peerages—this move led to the troubles of Mr Anthony Wedgwood Benn twenty years later. Thus the problem was perennial. It was aggravated by the unwillingness of leading members of the Labour Party to go to the Lords either because of objection to the concept of hereditary peerage; because they did not wish to saddle their heirs with a title, especially if the latter had political ambitions; or because service in the Lords carries no salary and many Labour men in the Commons cannot easily surrender their Parliamentary pay. Labour resistance to titles is very understandable. Yet by 1957 it was painfully clear that unless recruits were found for the Labour ranks, there would soon be no organized opposition in the Upper House to a Conservative Government. Such a situation would have done irreparable harm to the prestige of the Lords, so the Macmillan

---

[1] E.g. that no party should have a permanent majority, that members should be paid and that women should be eligible. Parliament Bill, 1947. Conference of Party Leaders. Statement, para. 5; 1947-48 Cmd. 7380, xxii.

Cabinet produced the Life Peerages measure which became law in 1958.

The Life Peerages Act is of interest largely because of its omissions. It did nothing about a number of possible reforms connected with the peerage. The powers of the Lords were unchanged; peeresses in their own right were still to be excluded from the Lords, although women life peers would achieve admission; the exclusion of Scottish peers from Parliament, other than their sixteen representatives in the Lords, was unaltered; nothing was done to permit a peer to renounce his peerage in order to remain in the Commons. Also, and this is contrary to most of the reform plans produced since 1869, no limit was placed on the number of life peers that may be nominated, either as a total figure or during any one year. In the second reading debate, Mr R. A. Butler, Leader of the House, gave an indication of the way in which the Bill might be worked. The Prime Minister would make some nominations primarily on political grounds and, in the case of members of an opposition party, the Prime Minister would first consult the leader of that party. The constitutional responsibility for nomination would remain with the Prime Minister. 'It will also be the duty of the Prime Minister, of course, to recommend men and women who, though not actively associated with any political party, are qualified by their eminence in other spheres. . . . In doing so, the Prime Minister of the day will doubtless take soundings in many quarters. . . .'[1]

Conservative opinion accepted the Bill with a few misgivings. The Labour Party opposed it: the Party's attitude seemed to be that the Bill was a Tory trick to make the Lords more respectable. In truth, the Labour Party was and is confused about its policy on the Second Chamber—on whether it is needed at all, and, if it is, on what its powers and composition should be. Mr Gaitskell complained that the Government's attitude to the Opposition was somewhat patronizing and that the Labour Party had not been consulted on whether it felt any need for the Bill.[2] There are, however, eminent

[1] H.C. Deb., Vol. 582, cols. 410-11.
[2] *Ibid.*, cols. 416-17.

Labour leaders on record in favour of life peerages, notably Mr (now Lord) Morrison[1] and Lord Chorley. The latter has commented somewhat acidly that many Labour members who voted against the Bill did so 'no doubt hoping in due course to take up the life peerages against which they knew quite well they were making an ineffectual protest'.[2] As Labour had opposed the Bill, why did it co-operate in making use of the Bill? It must be recalled that Labour does not officially favour unicameralism. It is, therefore, under some obligation to keep the second house in reasonable working order. In 1957 the Labour peers were under strain and the concept of life peerages offered a means to assist them which, from the Labour viewpoint, was unobjectionable in principle although perhaps not in intention. So Mr Gaitskell has used life peerages to give his Party more adequate representation in the Lords but apparently has been unwilling to make more nominations than the bare number required to provide coherent opposition; in January 1959 *The Times* reported that he had refused the Prime Minister's request to make suggestions for inclusion in the second list. So far only three groups of Labour partisans have been chosen, one in 1958 when the Act came into force, another in January 1961, and another in March 1962. The 'elder statesmen' Labour life peerages appear to be treated separately, without formal consultation with the Opposition.

Up to the middle of 1962 the total of life peerages was 43, including 7 women. On analysis they can be divided into 4 categories, although the proper allocation of a few individuals as between these groups is a matter of opinion. Sixteen were middle-aged Labour supporters chosen through Mr Gaitskell; they comprised M.P.s, ex-M.P.s, Parliamentary candidates, leading trade unionists and a leader of the Co-operative Movement. Another 12 were 'qualified by their eminence in other spheres' and were not, at least on the date of selection, active politicians. The third group were a few middle-aged Conservatives, often ex-M.P.s, who were not obvious candidates for the Upper House—this category in-

[1] *Government and Parliament* (Oxford, 1954), pp. 192-3.
[2] *Public Law*, Autumn 1958, p. 217.

cluded three ladies. The remainder consisted of elder statesmen and men who might well have been given an hereditary
peerage had this new alternative not been available. Among
the elder statesmen were three Labour ex-Ministers, Lord
Fisher the ex-Archbishop of Canterbury and Lord Casey from
Australia (a member of Churchill's War Cabinet) who became
the first life peer from outside the United Kingdom. A life
peerage has also been used to provide a refuge in the Upper
House for a Minister defeated at a General Election: J. Nixon
Browne, a Junior Minister at the Scottish Office, was defeated
at the 1959 election but remained in the Government and
became Lord Craigton—Craigton being the name of the
Glasgow constituency which had rejected him.

Initially, life peerages were announced separately from the
bi-annual Honours Lists. However, awards to two 'elder
statesmen', Dr Dalton and Sir Alfred Bossom, were included
in the 1960 New Year Honours. The latter practice was
repeated in 1961, but life peerages are still, in general, kept
apart from the regular lists. Certainly, the Labour Party think
of these awards to their supporters not in terms of honour but
as an invitation to perform a useful public service.

Mr Macmillan's choice of life peers merits criticism from
two angles. The proportion of non-politicians selected is low
and tends to fall still further, and the opportunity to reinforce
the Lords with able men and women from many schools of
experience has not been taken. Supporters of a political party
are not the only people who can make valuable contributions
to debates on public affairs. Over a century ago the Prince
Consort wished to see a sprinkling of literary and scientific
men in the Lords, but the idea was coolly received in political
circles. The possession of landed estate was then thought to
be a pre-requisite for a peerage; that concept has gone, but
perhaps politicians still feel that eminent men from other
walks of life make uncomfortable companions in Parliament.
The other disquieting feature is that, so far, all the political
life peers have been drawn from the two major political
parties, Conservative and Labour. No Liberal has been allowed
to enrich the lists, except Sir Oliver Franks whose nomination
falls squarely into the second of the categories mentioned

above. It is true that the Liberal members in the Commons are a very small band, but it is also the case that their number is a grave under-representation of Liberal feeling among the electors. In these circumstances it would be a gracious step to allow Liberals a share in this new type of Parliamentary representation and so provide a partial remedy for the inequality caused by our electoral system. The omission of Liberals can scarcely have been accidental; presumably Mr Macmillan did not wish to offer this form of encouragement to a second opposition party. Fruits of political patronage go to the strong, not to the weak. The condemnation by the Bryce Conference of the nomination procedure has been at least partly justified by events.

Any attempt to assess what impact life peerages may have on the House of Lords is an impossible task, the more so since it is unrealistic to consider them in isolation. Life peers could play an important rôle in conflicts between the two Houses— but how and when will such conflicts develop? How far will the new arrangements for leave of absence eliminate the 'backwoodsmen' in the Lords?[1] At what pace will life peers be created? How will their numbers compare with those of new hereditary peers? Will salaries be paid to a limited number of peers? Will hereditary peers be permitted to renounce their titles for life and be eligible for election to the Commons? All these questions are central to the future of the House of Lords, so without a crystal ball it is difficult to take the discussion much further. Even so, some implications of the Life Peerages Act are already clear. No longer can there be any pretence that the claim of the Lords to legislative power rests on heredity; this doctrine, of course, has been impossibly weak for years past because so much of the business of the Upper House is carried on by first-generation peers. Thus the Second Chamber is becoming a nominated body rather than a forum of a privileged caste. The speed of this change is uncertain but is likely to be accelerated by the advent of Labour Governments which, presumably, would refrain from in-

[1] P. A. Bromhead, *The House of Lords and Contemporary Politics* (Kegan Paul, 1958), p. 251, thinks that the practical effects may be slight. He is probably right.

augurating any more hereditary titles. And it will now be much easier for a Prime Minister, who may so wish, to alter the atmosphere of debate in the Lords through the distribution of a few dozen life peerages to progressive—and perhaps younger—minds.

So far this new brand of ministerial patronage has produced no exciting results as the Conservatives have remained in control. But would a Labour Prime Minister make more dramatic use of this power? There are grounds for thinking that the answer may be 'No'. A future Labour Government could well feel that it had more urgent problems to face than the reconstruction of the Second Chamber, especially if Conservative Lords were to repeat their 1946 tactics of not opposing major items of Cabinet policy in the period after the General Election. Were basic issues of reform to be shelved, one would expect no action to make the Lords a more vigorous and representative assembly lest any new prestige should hinder more fundamental change at a later date. The Labour view might also be—if Tory dogs are sleeping reasonably quietly, why introduce more mongrels to wake them up?

At present the Life Peerages Act is being used with caution and without imagination. It is on the statute book through the inability of the major political parties to agree on the powers and constitution of the Second Chamber. So no fundamental changes have been made to the House of Lords, and life peers serve to give the House a minor face-lift. The Act lifted perfectly into the British tradition of slow evolution in our political institutions. It also gave the Prime Minister a further type of reward to bestow.

CHAPTER TWELVE

Church Appointments

⊙

I

This aspect of the British Constitution has become known to many through the opening scene of Trollope's novel, *Barchester Towers*. Bishop Grantly of Barchester is dying: his son, Archdeacon Grantly, is at his bedside. The Archdeacon hopes to succeed his father, and his hopes are not without foundation. But as the Bishop lingers on, the Government weakens also. Archdeacon Grantly becomes a helpless, anguished spectator in the race between the end of the Government and the death of his father, for no Prime Minister other than the one in office would be likely to make him Bishop. The news of the Government's resignation comes a few minutes after his father's death; the Archdeacon remained an Archdeacon and the Puritan Proudie is sent to Barchester to symbolize the spirit of reform.

The Church of England, as an Established Church, is in a different position from other religious bodies. It has special privileges but it also suffers special restraints, notably that the doctrine of the Church is subjected to Parliamentary discussion and approval—as was illustrated most forcefully when the Commons rejected the revised Prayer Book in 1927 and 1928. Further, and this is our present concern, many leading appointments in the Church, including all bishops, are made by the State. When a bishopric is vacant, the Crown sends the chapter a *congé d'elire*, or licence to elect, together with a Letter Missive which contains the name of the person to be chosen. Thus the formal election is a farce. If a chapter failed to perform the necessary ritual within twelve days the Crown could nominate by Letters Patent. Further, by a statute of

231

1534, should a chapter fail to elect, or an Archbishop refuse to consecrate, the Crown's nominee, they are liable to the penalties of *praemunire* which involves the forfeiture of the land and goods of the offenders. This savage legislation was introduced to assert the authority of Henry VIII over the Church after his break with the Pope. In our own day, although there is significant controversy within the Church about the method of choosing bishops, no chapter, faced with a royal command, is recalcitrant. At Hereford in 1918 there was a flicker of independence; four out of nineteen prebendaries opposed the election of Dr Henson because of the allegedly unorthodox nature of some of his beliefs which had aroused a storm of controversy in the Press. In 1961, Canon Collins of St Paul's intervened and objected at the formal election of Dr Stopford as Bishop of London.

The royal choice of bishops is made, as Trollope showed, by the Prime Minister. Before 1832, when patronage was exercised without much restraint by public opinion, the sees were often filled by the favourites of the Court and the relatives of Ministers. Queen Victoria had a great interest in Church appointments as can be seen from the volumes of her *Letters*. She seemed to consider that minor appointments should be given to men who had been of assistance to a branch of the royal household. At higher levels, the Queen's influence was used to promote the claims of moderate Churchmen as against 'the Puseyites and Romanizers'. In the later stages of her reign she obtained much advice from Dr Davidson, first as Dean of Winchester and then as Bishop of Winchester. This is not to say that the Queen always had her own way : if the Prime Minister, be he Conservative or Liberal, were resolute, the Queen had to accede. In this century monarchs appear to have taken a much less active rôle in Church patronage and the decisions of Prime Ministers have been unhampered by the Palace.

No man can have had a more lengthy and influential connection with the business of choosing bishops than Dr Davidson. From 1883 onwards he was adviser to the Queen and after her death he became Archbishop of Canterbury, holding that post from 1903 to 1928. As Primate he was consulted by seven Prime Ministers, Balfour, Campbell-Bannerman, Asquith, Lloyd George, Bonar Law, Baldwin and Ramsay MacDonald. The late Dr Bell's biography, *Randall Davidson*, gives what has become a classic account of the relationship between the Archbishop and Downing Street. All seven Prime Ministers realized their responsibilities in relation to Church patronage—though some less strongly than others. 'They all gave careful attention to the Archbishop's recommendations, and never in the many instances of episcopal nominations during twenty-five years, did they make a single appointment which they knew to be fundamentally objectionable to the Archbishop. This does not mean that they always took the Archbishop's advice about fitness for a particular see, but that, if the Archbishop insisted that a particular person was wholly unsuitable for the office of bishop, no Prime Minister ever during these twenty-five years persevered with his name. Some appointments were, of course, less satisfactory than others, and some the Archbishop, left to himself, would not have made.'[1] Dr Bell went on to argue that there was no instance during this period of what 'could fairly be called a mere political job'. Such a phrase does not rule out political influence entirely, especially as political influence often works in a negative fashion. Thus Disraeli had opposed the nomination of High Churchmen in 1880 because he feared it might affect the Tory vote adversely in the coming election. At a late stage in Victoria's reign Lord Salisbury opposed Her Majesty's suggestion that Dr Westcott be translated to London because of the Socialistic tendency of some of his speeches.[2]

When a vacancy arose in the episcopate, Archbishop Davidson would speak or write to the Prime Minister about filling it. He might describe the conditions in the diocese or the type of man he felt to be required at a particular juncture. He might be concerned to keep a balance between differing schools of thought within the Church or to promote an outstanding spokesman of a viewpoint not adequately represented, e.g. the

[1] G. Bell, *Randall Davidson* (Oxford, 1935), Vol. II, p. 1237.
[2] C. Garbett, *Church and State in England* (Hodder & Stoughton, 1950), p. 199.

appointment of the Anglo-Catholic, Dr Frere, to Truro in 1923. The Archbishop would commonly send forward the names of three or more people to be considered. 'He would also make his own inquiries from various sources as to names which might have been independently suggested to the Prime Minister.'[1] Individual Prime Ministers necessarily differed in the way in which they dealt with the Archbishop's representations. Asquith was extremely well-informed about the problems and personalities of the Church: Campbell-Bannerman constantly requested advice but acted on it less frequently: Lloyd George acted independently on all aspects of patronage: MacDonald had to persuade his supporters that Church appointments should not tend to go automatically to Labour sympathizers. Asquith had a great interest in the scholastic quality of the bishops, but Lloyd George had a preference for good preachers.

The biggest storm over the choice of a bishop in this century took place over the elevation of Dr Henson to Hereford in 1918. The High Church party objected to Dr Henson's interpretation of the miraculous events narrated in the New Testament. Dr Gore, Bishop of Oxford, sent a protest to the Archbishop of Canterbury which was published in *The Times*. Others urged the Chapter of Hereford to risk the penalties of *praemunire* and reject Dr Henson. Dr Gore urged that the Archbishop should refuse to consecrate Dr Henson. The Archbishop had a full discussion with Dr Henson about the latter's doctrinal position and refused to intervene; Bishop Henson was duly consecrated and two years later was translated to Durham. This controversial appointment was wholly Lloyd George's doing; the Archbishop's rôle was entirely negative in that he was not prepared to take any step to try and prevent it.[2] Following this incident a group of M.P.s suggested to the Prime Minister that a small unofficial committee be formed of suitable clerical and lay persons with whom he might discuss Church appointments. Lloyd George welcomed this idea rather more than Archbishop Davidson;

[1] G. Bell, p. 1238.
[2] For a full description of this incident, see Bell, Ch. LIII.

such a committee was formed, met a few times and then fell into disuse. Again in 1918, because of the Hereford case, the Convocation of Canterbury discussed the question of Crown nominations. After two years no real conclusion was reached: a proposal that a Standing Committee be established to bring forward suitable names of potential bishops was rejected. Another episcopal controversy centred round Bishop Barnes of Birmingham who had been appointed by Ramsay Mac-Donald in 1924. Bishop Barnes held advanced liberal opinions on theological questions; his views on the doctrine of the Real Presence were widely regarded as heretical. The fact that he had been nominated by a Labour Prime Minister no doubt added to the concern caused by the views of the Bishop and to uneasiness over the constitutional position.

Archbishop Davidson was succeeded by Archbishop Lang. Lang's biography[1] shows that he also was highly influential in episcopal nominations. Thus the moves consequent upon Lang's translation from York to Canterbury were settled rapidly at a conference between Archbishops Davidson and Lang and Prime Minister Baldwin. A war-time record by the Archbishop on the difficulties of dealing with the Prime Minister deserves quotation. On July 23, 1941, Lang lunched with Churchill and discussed the filling of four sees soon to become vacant. The Archbishop noted in his diary, '(1) Of course he [i.e. the Prime Minister] is immensely more pre-occupied with incessant affairs of great importance; (2) He knows nothing whatever about the Church, its life, its needs or its personnel; (3) To his credit he will not let (1) and (2) interfere with his own sense of responsibility: where his hand has a right to be, he will put it in, and he is going to be P.M. all round. The result is much provoking delay and uncertainty as to what motives and how much knowledge may determine his decisions. But he has an admirable Secretary (Anthony Bevir) who knows more, learns more, and takes more pains than any other Secretary I have had to deal with: and he has always given full deference to my recommendations and has always accepted them. And, like other P.M.s, I am sure he

---

[1] J. G. Lockhart, *Cosmo Gordon Lang* (Hodder & Stoughton, 1949).

would never advise any applicant of whom the Archbishop really disapproved."[1]

The reference to Sir Anthony Bevir in the Archbishop's diary is significant. As the Monarch ceased to be concerned personally with Church appointments and as other demands on the attention of the Prime Minister grew, the importance of the work of the Prime Minister's personal assistant in these matters was necessarily enhanced. Dr Garbett, Archbishop of York, wrote that Prime Minister MacDonald was not very interested in bishops, but he was exceedingly well informed about them through efficient briefing by his secretariat.[2] The retirement of Sir Anthony Bevir—his official title was Secretary for Appointments—in 1955 was of sufficient moment to be noticed in the magisterial preface of *Crockford*. Rumour had it that Sir Anthony used to listen to various parsons preaching. He was succeeded by Mr David Stephens, an ex-Treasury official, who was transferred to the staff of the House of Lords in 1961. It must be added that the methods of one Secretary for Appointments are not necessarily those of another.

Information about recent events is obviously difficult to obtain, but certain essentials are clear. In choosing bishops, the Prime Minister exercises independent judgment. He does so without fear of Parliamentary criticism, for questions on ecclesiastical patronage are not allowed. There are two regular channels through which he receives assistance, the Archbishop of Canterbury and his own Secretary for Appointments. The Prime Minister may also consult with anyone he wishes,[3] possibly a Cabinet colleague with special knowledge of Church affairs. The choice of the Prime Minister is limited to those ordained by the Church. Finally, the Archbishop has a veto power which, almost certainly, would be effective at the stage of private consultation; failing that, he could refuse to consecrate a Prime Minister's nominee.

[1] Lockhart, *Cosmo Gordon Lang*, pp. 435-6.
[2] *Church and State in England*, p. 193.
[3] Asquith and Lloyd George discussed Church appointments with Canon Pearce of Westminster. In 1919 Canon Pearce was nominated to the See of Worcester—not on the advice of the Archbishop of Canterbury. G. Bell, *Randall Davidson*, p. 1242f.

Church Appointments

The most important single influence on the Prime Minister is, no doubt, the Archbishop of Canterbury. The Archbishop can submit at least two names in relation to any vacancy; he will be consulted about any name proposed by the Prime Minister. If a Prime Minister is immersed in grave world problems, it would not be surprising if he accepted the Archbishop's guidance more easily and more gratefully. Archbishop Fisher had a reputation more as an administrator than as a scholar: as the same is true of the majority of the present bench of bishops, it is not unreasonable to guess at a connection here. But, in relation to each vacancy, the Prime Minister will also have a report from his Secretary for Appointments on conditions in the diocese concerned and on various opinions within the Church on the nature of its requirements. These, of course, will have implications for the relative suitability of candidates for the see. How the Secretary for Appointments collects his information is a delicious mystery.

Yet the burden of Church business on the Prime Minister is very real. Lord Melbourne's remark, 'Damn it, another bishop dead', is often quoted, and Lord Salisbury complained, 'I declare they die to spite me'.[1] So far this chapter has concentrated on the nomination of bishops but the total of Church appointments in the gift of the Crown is about 970. The Prime Minister is responsible for dealing with 700 of these,[2] including suffragan bishops, deans, Canons of Westminster and St Paul's and a variety of livings. In the case of suffragan bishops the rôle of the Prime Minister is nominal, for he accepts the first of two names submitted to him: the real choice rests with the bishop of the diocese. Other minor appointments may cause more difficulty and give rise to correspondence, including letters from job-seekers.[3] But it is the bishoprics that present

[1] G. Cecil, *The Life of Lord Salisbury* (Hodder & Stoughton, 1931), Vol. III, p. 194.
[2] Sir Ivor Jennings, *Cabinet Government*, 3rd ed. (Cambridge, 1957), p. 453.
[3] One parson wrote a letter to Prime Minister Attlee seeking a benefice on the ground that he had been a supporter of George Lansbury: the files, however, contained his letter to a previous Prime Minister stressing his admiration for Sir Waldron Smithers. This story is in a letter from Earl Attlee to the author.

the major problem and the number of dioceses has increased since Lord Salisbury's day by roughly one half.

What sort of man becomes a bishop? A survey of the background of present bishops is helpful in suggesting criteria for selection. Age on first appointment is between forty and fifty-four, but translations from one diocese to another are made at higher ages. The age range is narrower than it was in the earlier part of this century when the limits were roughly thirty-seven to sixty-two. For a bishop, a university education is *sine qua non*. Above 85 per cent of bishops went to Oxford or Cambridge. In 1955 *Crockford* published a survey of the academic and occupational background of bishops. Twenty had studied theology at the university, 14 classics and 7 history. The record of their academic success is a little untidy for, as far as information was available, 20 took First Class Honours, 10 got Seconds, 2 got Thirds, 1 a Fourth and 4 took courses which did not carry an honours qualification. The previous careers of bishops were: parish priests 25, university teachers 10, theological college teachers 4 and schoolmasters 4. Six university teachers went direct from a university post to a bishopric but, of these, only 4 were theologians. As compared with the earlier part of the century there has been a fall in the numbers of academics and headmasters. The parish priests tend to have had relatively small parochial experience of the normal kind, but to have obtained promotion via administrative posts, e.g. archdeacon or suffragan bishop. The decline in the scholastic quality of the episcopacy is perhaps associated with the growth of an 'administrative class' of clergy. What emerges clearly from this analysis is that bishops are drawn from a narrow social circle: the lad who goes to a theological college from a grammar school and/or a provincial university is unlikely to join the august *élite*. This is emphasized by the extraordinary connection between Repton and Canterbury. Archbishop Fisher succeeded Archbishop Temple as headmaster of Repton and Archbishop Ramsey was one of Fisher's pupils there. The question posed by *Crockford* is apposite. 'Does not the accident of having been brought up in the entourage of some prominent person or in some particular family or social circle, still unduly increase one's chance of becoming a bishop?'

Dissatisfaction with the patronage system is of long-standing among members of the Church of England. Often the issue of patronage is associated with the wider controversy about disestablishment. Those who urge that the Church should have the right to elect its own leaders commonly add also the claim that the Church should be able to determine its forms of worship without Parliamentary supervision. Yet it is possible to keep these questions separate: were the Prime Minister to surrender his rights in relation to ecclesiastical appointments, it is conceivable that other aspects of the Establishment could remain undisturbed. One has the feeling, however, that such a change might lead to others. If the Church were empowered to choose bishops through, for example, some type of electoral college, would bishops still retain twenty-six seats in the House of Lords? If members of one religious association had the right to elect members of the Upper House, would not members of other religious groups feel that they had an equal right to such a privilege? At present the special position of the Church of England in Parliament is not a matter that arouses ire partly because bishops are nominated by the Prime Minister; other denominations would not welcome Parliamentary representation on these terms. The method of choosing bishops is now identical with that of choosing other categories in the Upper House—new hereditary peerages, life peerages and Lords of Appeal in Ordinary; to choose bishops through an electoral college would shatter this identity. Further, it can be argued that the Prime Minister's right of patronage is the price the Anglican Church must pay for the advantages of Establishment, including its seats in Parliament. Were the price no longer paid, the privileges of the Established Church might well become a cause of controversy.

At present the tide of discontent within the Church of England over its constitutional position is flowing strongly. Disestablishment, with all its implications, falls outside the scope of a study of patronage. Here it is of importance to record that twice in recent years, in 1954 and 1960, the Church Assembly has expressed disapproval of the method through which the Crown makes ecclesiastical appointments. In 1954, the Assembly considered two motions on this subject. The first proposed that 'appointments to bishoprics and deaneries be made by the Sovereign on the advice of such ecclesiastical persons as are members of the Privy Council'. As the 'ecclesiastical persons' on the Privy Council are the Archbishops of Canterbury and York and the Bishop of London, this suggestion would exclude the lay element in the Church completely. Further, as the Archbishop of York (Dr Garbett) pointed out, this arrangement might cause great embarrassment to the triumvirate. Should Canterbury become vacant when the Bishop of London was ill, what would the Archbishop of York do if he had a conscientious conviction that he was the right man to fill the vacancy? Faced with these objections, the motion was withdrawn. The following proposal was, however, passed in all three Houses of the Assembly: 'This Assembly, while gratefully acknowledging the care and trouble taken over recent appointments to bishoprics and deaneries, is of opinion that the present procedure for submitting advice to the Sovereign is open to objection and should be modified.' The voting on this resolution is significant. It was carried in the House of Bishops by 10 votes to 8, in the House of Clergy by 113 to 50 and in the House of Laity by 117 to 33. Thus the bishops, the products of the present system, are the least discontented, and the demand for reform is strongest among the laity who have the most objective view of the problem—at least in the sense that personal ambitions are not involved.

No action was taken on the 1954 decision. Six years later the House of Clergy passed, by a large majority, a motion that committees of the House of Clergy and House of Laity be appointed to consider the method of choosing bishops. In 1961, Church opinion was undoubtedly stimulated by the controversy surrounding the choice of the Dean of Guildford and also by the accession of a new Archbishop of Canterbury who was believed to favour change. At the Autumn Church Assembly a commission was appointed to inquire into the whole field of Crown appointments to ecclesiastical office, including bishops, deans and some cathedral canons. It consists of fourteen clergy and laity and the chairman is Lord Howick.

There is a variety of reasons for unrest. Initially a question of principle is involved. The Church of England is a religious association devoted to the worship of God in a particular way and to the propagation of a particular type of Christianity. Yet its leaders are chosen for it, and imposed upon it, by the State. Other religious associations choose their leaders themselves. Why should the Church of England not have a similar right? Is not the appearance of a Church in tutelage harmful to its vigour and reputation? To foreign observers the Church of England may seem a creature of the State with about as much real independence as a Soviet trade union. Such a misconception is serious because of the world-wide responsibilities of the Church, especially in territories newly moving towards political independence. The present system is also open to theological objections. A Christian Church, it is argued, must look for divine assistance in the task of finding its leaders; an electoral college, however constituted, would be guided in its decisions by the Holy Spirit.[1] Alternatively, it is possible to maintain that the power of the Holy Spirit should work through the Prime Minister equally well as through an electoral college. But this is not convincing even to many of those who attach importance to the concept of divine guidance, for the Holy Spirit seems to have been more than a little detached from some Prime Ministers in days past and some episcopal appointments have obviously been governed by very earthy considerations.

A further irritant in the present procedure is that the Prime Minister may not be—indeed, sometimes has not been—a member of the Church of England. He may not be a Christian. He may not conduct his private life in a way acceptable to Church opinion; as divorce is no longer a barrier to a successful political career, this is a distinct possibility. These objections are powerful. Yet, in practice, a Prime Minister who was not a supporter of the Church might well take special pains not to offend it when dealing with Church affairs. An allied argument is that ecclesiastical patronage should not be operated by a

[1] P. Kirk, *One Army Strong?* (Faith Press, 1958), p. 80.

politician heavily burdened with other responsibilities. A Prime Minister with a mass of problems on his mind may fall into the habit of accepting, too easily, advice on Church appointments either from the Archbishop, a private secretary or a personal friend. The increase since 1900 in the number of sees has added to this difficulty. It is also conceivable that political considerations enter into the decisions a Prime Minister makes for the Church: he is after all, a politician, subject to political loyalties. Politics have intervened in Church business in the past; why should this not occur in future? Two reasons suggest that this may be less likely but, even in combination, they are not conclusive. First, the influence of the Church is weaker than it used to be and the political importance of the views of bishops is not great. Second, it can be shown that recent Prime Ministers have nominated bishops with political views opposed to their own; the appointment of Bishop Stockwood to Southwark in 1959 is one example and the elevation of Archbishop Temple to Canterbury in 1942 is another. But the occasional nomination of a man with left-wing sympathies does not prove that political considerations are and always will be ignored. Do parsons who support the Campaign for Nuclear Disarmament reduce their chances of ecclesiastical preferment? Since the last war the Church has failed to give a strong lead on many matters that trouble the Christian conscience. How far is this because its leaders have been drawn from steady men of unsurprising opinions?

There is one further general political consideration. The influence of the State now impinges on many aspects of our national life. It is arguable that a mature vigorous community could well do with less paternal direction. On this view we should look jealously and suspiciously at any activities by the State which fall outside the normal range of its operations. What is, or should be, the normal range of State activities is a wide question, but it is generally accepted that it should not include our spiritual welfare. The province of Caesar should not encroach on the province of God. Thus the State should not be concerned with the appointment of the leaders of the Church.

Finally, there are a variety of objections based not on principle but on an assertion that the present system of choosing bishops and deans does not give satisfactory results. In the Church of England there is never-ending contention between those who belong to opposed schools of thought, e.g. the Anglo-Catholics and the Evangelicals. Each 'party' within the Church is keen that its supporters should attain positions of authority. The Prime Minister has to act as umpire between contending factions and his decisions must from time to time cause displeasure. Thus Mr John Cordle, M.P., has complained that the most able Evangelicals are ignored when new bishops are appointed.[1] The Prime Minister is well apart from the battleground of Church politics and it has often been urged that he can ensure, from his detached position, a fair balance of promotions between the various groups. Mr Cordle denies that such a balance is being kept. Others would deny that it should be kept. The comprehensive character of the Church of England is commonly attributed to the State appointment of bishops. Is such comprehensiveness desirable? May it not be a source of confusion which blurs the impact the Church makes on the world outside? And, as Dr Henson wrote, 'the comprehensiveness of a Church may have its origin in the paralysis of its internal discipline rather than in the charity and tolerance of its members'.[2]

It was noted above that the present patronage system tends to draw new bishops from the charmed circle of Oxford and Cambridge. The influence of the Archbishop of Canterbury was also described. The sum effect is that the Church of England is a peculiar type of despotism in that it has no very clear line of policy except to draw its leaders from a fairly narrow sector of its members. Both cause and effect are debilitating. The debate in the 1954 Assembly of the Church about the present system was revealing. The principal dignitaries who spoke (except Dr Garbett) seemed content with it. Dr Fisher appeared to think that as long as he was consulted—all was well: this opinion, *Crockford* noted, 'suggests that the Primate has a remarkable omniscience of the clergymen of the

---

[1] *The Daily Telegraph*, August 29, 1960. Mr Cordle is the Conservative Member for Bournemouth East and Christchurch.
[2] *The Church of England* (Cambridge, 1939), p. 136.

Church and encourages that very subservience and lack of criticism which we have previously had occasion to deplore'. Or, crudely stated, despotism based on patronage normally leads to boot-licking. Similarly, Dr Henson argued that the advantages of democracy—the stimulation of interest, the diffusion of knowledge and the development of capacities— would apply equally to the government of the Church.[1] If members of a Church have little say in its affairs, they will feel less concern for it and acquiesce unintelligently in the actions of the controlling hierarchy. Erastianism and clericalism both hinder self-government in the Church and the vigour and quality of its religious life.

Thus the present constitutional position of the Church of England is open to a wide variety of criticism. It appears that majority opinion within the Church is in favour of change. Why, then, is there so little positive movement to effect reform? The initial difficulty, noticed above, is the whole question of the position of the Establishment. Can the system of appointments be changed without disestablishment? This might depend on how radically the system was altered. A further complication is that Church opinion is divided on whether disestablishment is desirable, and this is partly because the consequences of disestablishment are not clear. To argue that changes be made in the procedure for choosing bishops is, in effect, to argue that the floodgates be opened which at present dam up the controversies surrounding the Church. Once the floodgates are open, no one can tell how the waters will settle.

Another hindrance to change is that there is no general agreement on how the system of Church appointments should be amended. Some critics, like Dr Garbett, think that the technique of nomination by the Prime Minister should be retained, subject to adjustments to ensure that Church opinion is more fully, or more obviously, consulted. Others would eliminate any patronage by the Prime Minister. Dr Garbett's plan would avoid the wider issues of disestablishment and is of special interest because of the status of its author. The plan

[1] *The Church of England*, p. 136.

had four main points.[1] The penalties of *praemunire* should be abolished. When a vacancy for a bishop arises, the chapter of the diocese might submit three names in confidence to the Prime Minister. The Prime Minister's field of choice would not be limited in any way but his choice should be made known in confidence to the chapter, before any public announcement is made, to give the latter an opportunity to object and the Prime Minister an opportunity to reconsider. Finally, at the consecration of a bishop, the archbishop should have a right to hear objections on grounds of heresy and should be free from all penalties if he then refuses consecration. In sum, Dr Garbett wished to abolish the archaic penalties linked to the present procedure and to ensure that a cathedral chapter has an effective voice in the choice of its bishop. The objection is that the proposed consultation is with the clergy only, and not with the laity; further, the consultation is with a narrow circle of the clergy. The Garbett plan takes no heed of Dr Henson's claim that the Church cannot flourish with full vigour unless it enjoys the responsibility of democratic self-government. However, the Anglican Church is essentially an episcopal church, and there is unlikely to be unanimity on the problem of how far democratic election of leaders is consistent with episcopal organization.

Those who favour Dr Henson's views will feel that bishops should be selected by some form of electoral college, perhaps on the lines of those used in Wales.[2] Yet this is not a simple

---

[1] C. Garbett, *Church and State in England* (Hodder & Stoughton, 1950), pp. 200-3.
[2] Welsh bishops are chosen by an Electoral College consisting of the Archbishop and bishops of the Church of Wales, 6 clerical and 6 lay electors from the vacant diocese, and 3 clerical and 3 lay electors from the other Welsh dioceses, making normally a total of some 47 persons. Voting is by ballot and a candidate requires the support of two-thirds of those present and voting to secure election. If the electoral college is unable to make a choice after meeting for three consecutive days, the choice is transferred to the Archbishop of Canterbury. The election of the Archbishop of Wales is conducted on similar lines, except that for this purpose each diocese has 7 electors, its bishop and 3 clerical and 3 lay representatives. The Archbishop is chosen from the existing Welsh bishops, and after election he remains the bishop of his diocese, thus the office is not anchored geographically to any one see; further, the election of an Archbishop cannot take place until any

solution. Even if the principle of an electoral college were accepted, it would not be easy to obtain agreement on the details of its constitution—e.g. on the balance between clerical and lay electors or whether a simple majority should be adequate to secure election. And the principle itself is open to attack by those who argue that an electoral college would become a focus for lobbying of an unpleasant kind: opposing groups would put forward rival candidates and the stresses and controversies of the Church would be aggravated. In some measure, this must be true. A democratic institution cannot avoid argument. If the Church wishes to avoid argument, it had better avoid change.

The present method of selecting bishops and deans is almost impossible to defend. But it has an important merit—it works tolerably well. Criticisms are directed far more to the nature of the system than to the appointments that are made. Prime Ministers are careful to sound Church opinion and take pains not to cause offence; the choices made are never eccentric and rarely exciting. So long as the present machinery goes on smoothly and silently the advocates of reform are deprived of any sense of urgency; but if a future Prime Minister arouses Church hostility the whole atmosphere would be speedily transformed. The trouble over the Deanery of Guildford in 1961 was a fair warning. Like many other aspects of British government, the system of Church appointments is anomalous: it has worked only because the influential people concerned agreed that the system be made to work. The creation of the Howick Commission suggests that this agreement is breaking down.

vacancies in the bishoprics have been filled. As is the case with bishops, if the electoral college cannot produce a two-thirds majority in three days, the election goes to Canterbury.

CHAPTER THIRTEEN

The Influence of Patronage

⊙

Addressing the Liberal Assembly at Torquay in September 1958, the Party Leader, Mr Grimond, asserted 'The first thing we want is to bust open the patronage and privilege by which both Tories and Socialists manipulate our politics and maintain their rigid out-of-date party structure. . . . Far too many prizes in the law, the Church, commerce and social life go to those whom the ruling clique find agreeable.' As the Liberals have suffered almost complete exclusion from the patronage system for the last forty years, it is not surprising that their voices be raised in complaint. Speeches at political conferences frequently exaggerate and are frequently forgotten in a day, but the impact of Mr Grimond's speech was aided by the intervention of Lord Attlee, the Labour ex-Prime Minister, who demanded an apology for the suggestion that he had been influenced by political considerations when making appointments. This stimulated a public exchange of letters that lasted a fortnight. The Liberal Leader refused to apologize on the ground that he was raising a point of principle 'and did not intend my remarks as a personal reference to yourself'.[1] His case would, however, have been more powerful had he attacked on a wider front including honours and life peers. Also, from Mr Grimond's point of view, the wrong target put himself in the line of fire; least of all recent Prime Ministers can Earl Attlee be said to have used patronage for party advantage.

[1] *The Times* in a magisterial leader (October 21, 1958), suggested that Earl Attlee had had the better of the correspondence. 'If appointments have not been bad why change the system? If the charge is that they have been, an ex-Prime Minister has a right to demand substantiation or withdrawal.' *The Times* went on to urge that more attention should be given to the issue of accountability for patronage appointments, especially in relation to administrative posts.

Ministerial patronage is operated so smoothly that there are no easy targets for criticism. Obvious excesses are avoided and the reforms of earlier years have eliminated the major dangers. Venality is held at bay and the spending of public money is untainted by corrupt practices. Nor can patronage determine the political complexion of our Government, for this is controlled by free elections based on universal suffrage. The distribution of ministerial favours can affect the polls only if the electorate is restricted in number and the ballot is not secret. Thus the impact of 'influence' on elections was killed by the nineteenth century Reform Bills and, to a lesser extent, by the Ballot Act. Probity in the spending of public money was helped first by the spread of commercial financial morality into affairs of state, a process aided by Parliamentary agitation against waste, and by the pervasive influence of the nonconformist conscience. Then the establishment of the Civil Service Commission produced a body of public officials increasingly independent of ministerial favours, and who resist automatically claims for special treatment as part of their professional ethic. The comprehensive audit system, which has operated since 1866, provides a further safeguard. An earlier check on corruption, the Parliamentary disqualification of Crown contractors, was withdrawn in 1957 as it had become anomalous and indefensible. This law had been framed in an age when trade was carried on mainly by individuals acting singly or in partnership, and not by large companies: in consequence an M.P. with financial interests in a large firm holding valuable state contracts could sit in the Commons undisturbed while another M.P. who supplied a small quantity of goods to a Government department might be disqualified. There never has been anything to prevent an ex-Minister joining the board of a company which had, and has, important dealings with his former department. In theory, at least, this opens a door for possible abuses; it would be no bad thing if a convention developed which inhibited such relationships. But where a number of political parties compete for office, any scandal involving improper use of official powers for personal gain can throw discredit on the Government. In this country public insistence on the need for ministerial integrity is overwhelming; Mr Belcher's association with the attempted malefactions of Sydney Stanley cost him the penalty of immediate dismissal from political life.

All this is not to deny that patronage leaves a substantial mark on the development of public policy. The Prime Minister selects the personnel of his Government and, as Members of Parliament are keen to secure political advancement, this patronage must strengthen the influence of Ministers over the opinions of their own party supporters. In particular, the right to make appointments exalts the status of party leaders, in office or in opposition, over that of their immediate subordinates. The Australian Labour Party restricts the powers of its Leader by insisting that the members of a Labour Cabinet shall be elected by its Parliamentary group or 'caucus'. The Leader, the Prime Minister, is left with the task of allocating portfolios to the Ministers that have been chosen for him. As Labour in Australia has an unenviable record of strife and fission, it is unlikely that their example will be copied elsewhere. The unique authority of a Prime Minister is inevitable: it is, perhaps, less dangerous if squarely recognized. There are, moreover, important countervailing forces to check that of patronage. Members of the Commons normally hold political opinions of some intensity and are not easily swayed on matters of principle, especially as constituents will demand justification if their representative modifies his views. So in normal circumstances the Prime Minister, even should he so wish, cannot persuade Opposition M.P.s to join the Government: in 1951 Mr Clement Davies refused an invitation from Sir Winston Churchill to join his administration. The differences between a Prime Minister and his followers will normally be less deep and less publicised (at least in the Conservative Party) so the possible influence of patronage over them is far greater. Even so, the number of jobs a Prime Minister may distribute is limited and this must restrict the total of aspirants. Further, for Conservative politicians at least, the financial rewards of office are not attractive and do not add to any inclination to political subservience.

In a democratic state the ultimate safeguard against misuse of the appointing power must be public feeling. This will be particularly effective where significant opinion is specialised and concentrated. It was argued above that the views of the Bar had a healthy influence on judicial appointments and, to a lesser extent, the same may be true of Church appointments. In the ultimate analysis, political opinion has a similar effect on the choice of Ministers, but the last ten years have shown conclusively that a Prime Minister has a high degree of freedom. He can control the size and shape of his cabinet; he can surround himself with old cronies; he can appoint to the highest positions men of but moderate public stature. In the broad field of administrative posts the safeguard of opinion is still weaker. Here the range of possible candidates is almost unlimited: judgment must depend upon results and—except with top jobs in nationalized industries—the results may escape general attention. But the worst case of all is where the public are automatically barred from participation in a controversy because of the needs of security. Critical military and scientific choices are made in secret and only a select few will even understand the nature of the issues. If the Prime Minister has a favourite adviser on these matters, e.g. Lord Cherwell, the position of the latter is well-nigh unassailable.[1]

Various institutional devices have been suggested to check the abuses of patronage. One method, advocated many years ago by Viscount Bryce,[2] would be to decentralize administration and so reduce the range of business for which Ministers are responsible. Any such movement, however, is contrary to the spirit of our age which demands both an increasing range of social services and increasing uniformity in their operation. Another possibility is a 'watch-dog' committee on the lines of the Political Honours Scrutiny Committee: it is manifest that a Government will not agree to establish a body of this kind until the need for it is proved beyond doubt. More commonly, representative committees are formed to suggest names to the patron, as in the case of Justices of the Peace and some members of tribunals. But the central safeguard, noted by Bentham,[3] is to concentrate the power to make appoint-

---

[1] Cf. C. P. Snow, *Science and Government* (Oxford, 1961), pp. 63-6.
[2] *Modern Democracies* (Macmillan, 1921), Vol. II, p. 376.
[3] Cf. Bowring edn. (Tait, 1843), Vol. V, p. 345.

ments in the hands of Ministers responsible to Parliament. The constitutional position is thus highly unsatisfactory in the cases of the Church and with the award of honours where the interjection of the royal prerogative provides a partial shield for the Prime Minister.

Granted that the link of responsibility to an elected assembly is maintained, the technique of patronage is not undemocratic; on the contrary, it is more democratic than allocating the power to make appointments to individuals or institutions answerable to no one but themselves. The scheme of appointing trustees to choose members of the old London Passenger Transport Board was a retrograde step. The Ministry of Health has been right to resist any demand that local authorities or the medical profession should nominate members of Regional Hospital Boards. If a Minister is responsible—financially and otherwise—for a service he must retain control over the selection of those who are given a share in its direction. Were the Boards to be nominated by separate bodies they might tend to assume a degree of independence which ignored their financial subordination to the monies voted annually by Parliament and members of the Boards might be tempted to think of themselves as the delegates of particular local or professional interests. Appointment by the Minister helps to stress that an individual has been chosen in a personal capacity, that he should act in accordance with his own views and not submit to partisan instructions from associates.

The most insidious danger of patronage is that those chosen for high positions win favour because, in thought and action, they conform to patterns that the patron thinks are desirable. Besides adequate ability and experience, it becomes essential that prospective nominees should possess this undefinable 'acceptability'. They tend to have typical British tastes, values and loyalties. The concept of 'acceptability' is also linked with personality and social background. It is important to have a reputation of sound character, of steady disposition, to be not prone to violent outbreaks of emotion and, above all, to be of a reasonable and responsible nature. (Divorce is a barrier of decreasing importance.) These qualities are not to be discovered through examinations or even interviews, but rather through intimate acquaintance with the individual or through the evidence of trusted intermediaries who have such personal knowledge. Social conformity at high levels does have advantages. If all men in senior positions fit easily and naturally into London's Clubland, this is an important aid to the smooth and easy functioning of public bodies: civil servants meet in the Reform Club and Conservative Ministers at the Carlton. But the demand for 'acceptability' can prevent full use being made of the talents of those who are even moderately eccentric. It is also responsible for keeping a high proportion of senior posts in the hands of a limited social *élite*, commonly public schoolboys, trained in the habits that make men 'acceptable' and who are more likely to be known by those who make, or who advise on, the appointments. This is notably true in the case of the Church.

Even the patron with prejudices of the most admirable kind cannot be expected to secure the best man for a job. He will not know all the possible candidates; those he does know he will not know equally well; the information received about those unknown will be of varying quality. Thus patronage can well produce inefficiency. This could produce most serious consequences where the holder of a patronage appointment, e.g. a bishop or judge, is virtually irremovable. And where change is possible the patron may be unwilling to admit publicly that he has made a mistake: Cabinet Ministers, unless they are promoted, usually hold office at least for a year. The result was well described by Bentham. 'As to patronage, under the generally established system, taken as it is, so far from affording a security against unfitness, it operates as a security for unfitness.'[1]

It was shown in Chapter Three that the creation of a capable and impartial Civil Service demands a complete absence of political favouritism in the recruitment and promotion of its personnel. This condition is exceptionally hard to achieve in states that have newly gained their independence. The Ministers, fresh in office, find that the ability to dispense jobs can cement their hold on power. Even more dangerously, it can strengthen the movement towards a one-party state:

[1] Bentham, Vol. V, p. 570.

where civil servants are chosen for political reasons they have an equal interest with Ministers in keeping the Opposition at bay. Further, Ministers of new states would not welcome, or perhaps tolerate, advice to the degree to which civil servants proffer it in more advanced or stable societies. This is not an unmitigated evil; in the ferment of independence, politics seems to be a more attractive career than administration and it attracts the more able men. These factors together are likely to inhibit the growth of a highly qualified and able class of senior administrators. As Ministers feel that their authority is secure, as their volume of work grows, as material and educational standards rise, then the pressures which helped to produce the Civil Service Commission in this country should begin to apply. Yet the extinction of patronage involves the creation of impersonal techniques for the highly personal task of choosing men. This can be done only in a cultured, sophisticated community. And the smaller the community, the more difficult it will be to secure the impersonal approach.

A Government may also strengthen its position by the distribution of honours and titles. Such a policy is most effective in societies, notably monarchies, which love a little pomp and show. Here honours will win most respect and be most prized. In Siam, before the democratic revolution of 1932, all public officials, except the most humble, received a title; in ascending order of dignity these were *Khun, Luang, Phra, Phya* and *Chao Phya.* When it was inconvenient, because of the state of the exchequer, to give an official the salary rise he might reasonably expect, the matter would be settled satisfactorily by bestowing on him the title immediately higher than his present rank.[1] It may seem unkind to compare the British Civil Service with the Siamese example. Yet the parallel is apt. Our highest civil servants receive honours automatically, the honours are carefully graded and it is not fanciful to suggest that they act as partial compensation for salary levels lower than these men could obtain in other employment.

Turning to local affairs, it is notable that patronage appoint-

[1] W. D. Reeve, *Public Administration in Siam* (Royal Institute of International Affairs, 1951), p. 32.

ments, Lords Lieutenant and Justices of the Peace, played a dominant rôle in the evolution of British local government before the emergence of democratic institutions. Then, with the spread of elected authorities in the nineteenth century, their significance declined. In recent years the growth of local business conducted by Central Government departments has redeveloped the flow of patronage. Hospital boards and the members of local tribunals and advisory committees are all appointed by Ministers: hospital boards appoint the hospital management committees. These arrangements give Government departments a substantial amount of valuable assistance, which is often unpaid. They help to bring local opinion into the local administration of national services, especially for functions which have been taken away from elected councils in the interests of efficiency or uniformity. It has been shown also that the nominated bodies, although creatures of ministerial selection, have a representative flavour which may do something to restrain local units of the Civil Service from becoming a self-sufficient bureaucracy.

Why are so many people prepared to devote time and effort to public responsibilities that bring no tangible reward? Often these duties are the result of, or an extension of, activities connected with various voluntary organizations concerned with politics, freemasonry, trade, employment or charity. In such cases the individual is impelled towards public service by the same motive that led to active participation in the work of the voluntary organization. This can range from pure altruism to selfishness and self-conceit. On many local committees, of course, one finds pensioners, housewives who are no longer youthful, and people of independent means. For them committee work can become a hobby to fill in hours that might otherwise be empty. An invitation to join a public body, however minor, is also flattering; it is a mark of recognition of personal qualities or past services. There is also a strong trace in our society of the old patrician sentiment that one should serve one's country if asked to do so. Membership of a public body will also enhance status in the local community and helps to achieve admission to the cadre of people who provide social leadership in the area. In every town and

county a survey of local councils, school governors, hospital
authorities, magistrates' benches, and advisory committees
would show the same names cropping up time and time again.
This is the local Establishment, ill-defined, undefinable but
nevertheless real.

This local élite is largely self-recruited. The advisory committees that propose names of new J.P.s consist of leading
members of the local Bench. Where membership of a tribunal
panel or a committee is on a representative basis, any vacancies
tend to be filled through suggestions from the organizations
that had sponsored the previous member. Successful candidates
in local elections are often nominated through the support and
goodwill of existing councillors. It is true that the electorate
may, from time to time, infuse not only fresh but different
blood into a local authority, especially when there is a change
of mood, as in the case of the current Liberal revival. Thus the
local élite is not static; especially where it has a high average
age, death and failing health will increase the turnover. The
major qualification to join is the desire to do so, combined
with the ability and inclination to spend time on the affairs
of voluntary organizations, including political parties. A minimum of education is required and some financial costs may be
incurred, although in industrial areas these may be very small.
In this way local communities throw up their own leaders:
patronage appointments do not create leadership, but they do
provide status, official recognition and sometimes authority.
The distribution of the Order of the British Empire is thought
by some to add a touch of dignity. The local élite, generally
speaking, is tolerant and open-minded about the question of
its own composition, perhaps because of a sense of substantial
security or, in some places, because of its heterogeneity. Any
desire for exclusiveness is kept under cover. Barriers based on
class, religion, sex or colour are rarely specific. Yet the choice
of a negro magistrate is a rare event that wins national head-
lines. In nineteenth-century Wales there was a low proportion
of nonconformist J.P.s, not due, however, solely to successive
Lord Chancellors, but rather because of the prejudices of
Anglican magistrates in office. Patronage merely reflects local
influential opinion and, owing to the way the system works,

cannot be judged the ultimate cause of any social exclusiveness there may be.

In general, patronage is unable to resist the rising tide of social mobility. The social status of the individual depends less and less on that of his parents; it depends on his own job, or in the case of a woman, on the job of her husband. Social status is then linked through occupation with education. There is a recognized ladder from primary school to university; the level of education attained and, therefore, the nature of one's employment, depends increasingly on individual ability and effort. It is easier to move up the social scale than in the past; to some extent, it is easier to become downgraded. The middle class family has various means available to save children with limited qualities from falling too far. Educational opportunity can be bought outside the State system and private schools, or some of them, retain a snob value. Daughters can be helped to find husbands in the appropriate social category. Private influence still obtains many posts for young men in industry and commerce—posts of higher status than could have been attained by their own educational qualifications. Yet as the size of economic units become larger and as the need for technical competence becomes acute, the scope for this kind of private patronage is declining. Public patronage has disintegrated in the Civil Service and in local government with the rise of professional standards and examination requirements. In these conditions, patronage has but limited influence on the overall status pattern of the society.

The situation is quite different with the more restricted number of posts of national importance. Patronage matters at the top. It is, indeed, the ideal weapon with which to preserve an entrenched minority. Public school domination of the Cabinet and the bench of bishops can scarcely reflect the social distribution of ability in politics and the Church. The first woman County Court judge, Mrs Elisabeth Lane, was not appointed until 1962. And, as already argued, patronage has major political consequences. It strengthens the authority of the Prime Minister over his party. It secures that posts of major administrative importance go to 'acceptable' men with conformist incliniations. Advisory bodies are chosen from highly responsible persons who, it is hoped, will not cause undue difficulties for Government departments.

All this can limit the scope for initiative and imagination in our national affairs. But patronage also helps to make things run smoothly. It can still be defended in eighteenth-century terms as a valuable social cement, although it is now rather an administrative cement. It also, as again the eighteenth century will remind us, opens the door to substantial abuse. At present the abuses are not grave due to adequate ethical standards in the conduct of public business. Perhaps the greatest danger for the future is the possibility that one party will exercise uninterrupted power for too long a period. Temptations would grow as security bred carelessness. It has been shown that the Conservatives are increasing their use of the honours system for Party use. The distribution of paid offices to M.P.s has also increased substantially in the 1960s, although a few jobs have gone to 'acceptable' Opposition Members. These are tendencies that demand close attention.

Yet the lack of public discussion about public patronage in recent years is almost total. Church appointments provide the major exception. Also, in 1958, there was the Grimond-Attlee correspondence noted at the start of this chapter. These exchanges showed some of the difficulties of assailing the patronage system. If the critic argues that bad appointments have been made, he is asked to be specific. He may be reluctant to cite individuals for various reasons. In any case, a single appointment that turns out badly proves little; mistakes are made under any system of selection. The three valid grounds for criticism are—a series of bad choices that show the patron to be lacking in judgment, that insufficient care has been taken to collect information about possible candidates, or that nominations are affected by political or social prejudices. The first type of charge is difficult to substantiate unless blatant errors occur: if a few slightly unfortunate appointments are made to, e.g. Area Gas Boards, who is to know? Nor is detailed information available about selection procedures, so lack of care is impossible to prove save where the person nominated is found to have been concerned in criminal activities. The mere fact that a particular choice is unpopular does not necessarily demonstrate an absence of forethought, for the patron may have calculated the probable consequences. With Church appointments, however, the regular policy of Prime Ministers is to try to give general satisfaction to interests most closely affected, so the development of a row over a nomination is *prima facie* evidence that a mistake has been made. The third type of criticism, that choices are prejudiced, is the most fundamental because it involves an analysis of the impact of the patronage system as a whole. Thus I have concentrated on this approach.

It is also possible to object to patronage in principle. This leads back to the distinction made in the opening chapter between appointments barren of political considerations, made solely to advance the quality of a service, and appointments which are influenced at least in part by political considerations. In the former category there is no case for change unless the patronage can be shown to produce bad results. Today there is general satisfaction with senior Civil Service promotions and judicial appointments, and no change is likely. The wide scope of administrative posts filled by patronage offers more targets for criticism, but no alternative selection procedure is preferable. The case of the Church is quite different; there are basic objections to the retention of appointing powers by the Prime Minister and it should not be impossible to devise a means of selection wholly within the Church. For other types of patronage discussed in this book the political element looms larger and, while a Second Chamber could be elected, over the rest of the field it is not possible to substitute other means of choice. Here one can suggest but two safeguards. First, an alert public opinion ready to protest against abuses. Second, some patronage might be eliminated, e.g. unpaid whips, P.P.S.s for Junior Ministers and political honours.

Above all, unfettered patronage is a menace to democracy. It has been seen how changes were forced in the appointment of civil servants and J.P.s and in the distribution of honours. The pressures involved varied with the circumstances of each case. Yet all the time a sound democratic instinct was at work which insisted that those in positions of influence, nationally or locally, should not have free licence to allocate favours to their friends and supporters.

APPENDIX

House of Commons Disqualification Act, 1957
(with amendments in force on January 1, 1962)

FIRST SCHEDULE
OFFICES DISQUALIFYING FOR MEMBERSHIP

PART I

Judicial Offices

Judge of the High Court of Justice or Court of Appeal

Judge of the Court of Session

Judge of the High Court of Justice or Court of Appeal in Northern Ireland

Commissioner exercising jurisdiction under Section 70 of the Supreme Court of Judicature (Consolidation) Act, 1925, or Section 1 of the Criminal Justice Administration Act, 1956

Judge of the Courts-Martial Appeal Court

Vice-Chancellor of the County Palatine of Lancaster

Chancellor of the County Palatine of Durham

Chairman of the Scottish Land Court

Recorder of London

Recorder of Liverpool

Recorder of Manchester

Common Serjeant

Assistant or Additional Judge of the Mayor's and City of London Court

Judge of a County Court in England and Wales, Temporary Judge of such a Court or Deputy Judge of such a Court appointed by the Lord Chancellor or the Chancellor of the Duchy of Lancaster or acting with the approval of the Lord Chancellor under paragraph (b) of the proviso to subsection (1) of Section 11 of the County Courts Act, 1934

Sheriff, Salaried Sheriff Substitute or Interim Sheriff Substitute appointed under the Sheriff Courts (Scotland) Act, 1907

County Court Judge or Temporary County Court Judge in Northern Ireland within the meaning of the Government of Ireland Act, 1920, or the deputy of such a Judge

Presiding Judge of the Liverpool Court of Passage

Judge of the Salford Hundred Court of Record

Chairman or paid Deputy Chairman of London Quarter Sessions

Chairman or paid Deputy Chairman of a court of quarter sessions
for the county in Lancashire

Stipendiary Magistrate within the meaning of the Justices of the
Peace Act, 1949

Stipendiary Magistrate in Scotland

Resident Magistrate appointed under the Summary Jurisdiction
and Criminal Justice Act (Northern Ireland), 1935

Official Referee to the Supreme Court

Industrial Injuries Commissioner or Deputy Industrial Injuries
Commissioner

National Insurance Commissioner or Deputy National Insurance
Commissioner

National Insurance Commissioner for Northern Ireland or Deputy
National Insurance Commissioner for Northern Ireland

Umpire or Deputy Umpire appointed for the purposes of the Old
Age Pensions Act (Northern Ireland), 1936

Umpire or Deputy Umpire appointed for the purposes of Section
43 of the National Service Act, 1948

Adjudicator appointed for the purposes of Part II of the National
Insurance Act, 1959, and any corresponding judicial office under
any Act of Parliament of Northern Ireland passed for purposes
similar to that Act.

PART II

*Commissions, Tribunals and other Bodies of which
all Members are Disqualified*

The Agricultural Land Commission and the Welsh Agricultural
Land Sub-Commission

The Air Transport Licensing Board

The Appellate Tribunal constituted under the provisions of the
National Service Act, 1948, relating to conscientious objectors

An Area Electricity Board in England and Wales

An Area Gas Board

An Area Railway Authority constituted under the British Transport Commission (Organization) Scheme Order, 1954

The British European Airways Corporation

The British Film Fund Agency

The British Overseas Airways Corporation

The British Transport Commission

The Central Electricity Generating Board

The Civil Service Arbitration Tribunal
A Colonial Currency Board
The Colonial Development Corporation
The Commission for the New Towns
The Commonwealth Telecommunications Board
The Council on Tribunals
The Covent Garden Market Authority
The Crofters Commission
The Crown Agents for Oversea Governments and Administrations
The Crown Estate Commissioners
The Development Commission established under the Development
and Road Improvement Funds Act, 1909
A Development Corporation within the meaning of the New
Towns Act, 1946
A Development Council established under the Industrial Organiza-
tion and Development Act, 1947
The Electricity Board for Northern Ireland
The Electricity Council
An Executive constituted under Section 5 of the Transport Act,
1947
The Foreign Compensation Commission
The Forestry Commission
The Gas Council
The General Board of Control for Scotland
The Great Northern Railway Board constituted under the Great
Northern Railway Act (Northern Ireland), 1953
The Herring Industry Board
The Horticultural Marketing Council
An Independent Schools Tribunal constituted under the Sixth
Schedule to the Education Act, 1944, or under the Fifth
Schedule to the Education (Scotland) Act, 1946
The Independent Television Authority
An Industrial Court, including a court established in Northern
Ireland
The Industrial Estates Management Corporations constituted by
the Local Employment Act, 1960
The Industrial Injuries Advisory Council
The Iron and Steel Board
The Iron and Steel Holding and Realization Agency
The Lands Tribunal
The Lands Tribunal for Scotland
The Leather Industries Export Corporation

The Local Government Commission for England
The Local Government Commission for Wales
A Medical Appeal Tribunal constituted for the purposes of the National Insurance (Industrial Injuries) Act, 1946, or the National Insurance (Industrial Injuries) Act (Northern Ireland), 1946, including any panel constituted for the purposes of any such Tribunal
A Medical Board or Pneumoconiosis Medical Board constituted for the purposes of the National Insurance (Industrial Injuries) Act, 1946, or the National Insurance (Industrial Injuries) Act (Northern Ireland), 1946, including any panel constituted for the purposes of any such Board
A Medical Practices Committee constituted under Section 34 of the National Health Service Act, 1946, or Section 35 of the National Health Service (Scotland) Act, 1947
A Mental Health Review Tribunal constituted under the Mental Health Act, 1959
The Monopolies Commission
The National Assistance Board
The National Assistance Board for Northern Ireland
A National Broadcasting Council
The National Coal Board
The National Dock Labour Board
The National Film Finance Corporation
The National Insurance Advisory Committee
The National Research Development Corporation
The North of Scotland Hydro-Electric Board
A Panel of Chairmen of Reinstatement Committees constituted under Section 41 of the National Service Act, 1948
The Panel of Official Arbitrators constituted for the purposes of the Acquisition of Land (Assessment of Compensation) Act, 1919
The Panel of Referees constituted for the purposes of Section 5 of the Family Allowances Act, 1945
The Panel of Referees constituted under Section 34 of the Finance (1909-10) Act, 1910
A Pensions Appeal Tribunal
The Performing Right Tribunal
The Pig Industry Development Authority
The Red Deer Commission
The Research Council within the meaning of the Department of Scientific and Industrial Research Act, 1956

The Restrictive Practices Court

The Scottish Committee of the Council on Tribunals

The Scottish Land Court

The Sites Commission constituted under the Industries Development Act (Northern Ireland), 1945

The South of Scotland Electricity Board

The Sugar Board

The Tithe Redemption Commission

The Traffic Commissioners for any area (including the Commissioner for the Metropolitan Traffic Area)

The Transport Tribunal

The Tribunal established under Part II of the Wireless Telegraphy Act, 1949

The Ulster Transport Authority

The United Kingdom Atomic Energy Authority

The University Grants Committee

The War Damage Commission

The War Office Teachers' Selection Board

The War Works Commission

The White Fish Authority constituted under Section 1 of the Sea Fish Industry Act, 1951, and the Committee constituted under Section 2 of that Act.

PART III

Other Disqualifying Offices

Accountant of Court appointed under Section 25 of the Administration of Justice (Scotland) Act, 1933

Accountant appointed by the Secretary of State under Section 73 of the Education (Scotland) Act, 1946

Agent in Great Britain of the Government of Northern Ireland

Ambassador representing Her Majesty's Government in the United Kingdom

Assessor of Public Undertakings (Scotland)

Attorney-General of the Duchy of Lancaster

Auditor of the Civil List

Auditor of the Court of Session

Boundary Commissioner or Assistant Boundary Commissioner appointed under Part I or Part II of the First Schedule to the House of Commons (Redistribution of Seats) Act, 1949

Chairman or Deputy Chairman of an Administrative Board constituted for the purposes of any scheme made under the Workmen's Compensation (Supplementation) Act, 1951, or the Industrial Diseases (Benefit) Acts, 1951 and 1954

Chairman or member of a panel of deputy chairmen of an Agricultural Land Tribunal

Chairman or Reserve Chairman of an Appeal Tribunal constituted under the Fifth Schedule to the National Assistance Act, 1948, or the Fourth Schedule to the National Assistance Act (Northern Ireland), 1948

Chairman of the Cinematograph Films Council

Chairman or Director-General of the British Council

Chairman or Vice-Chairman of the Dental Estimates Board or member of that Board appointed at an annual salary

Chairman or Reserve Chairman of a Local Tribunal or Local Appeal Tribunal constituted for the purposes of the National Insurance Act, 1946, for the National Insurance Act (Northern Ireland), 1946, the National Insurance (Industrial Injuries) Act, 1946, or the National Insurance (Industrial Injuries) Act (Northern Ireland), 1946

Chairman or Deputy Chairman of a Local Tribunal constituted under the provisions of the National Service Act, 1948, relating to conscientious objectors

Chairman or Reserve Chairman of a Military Service (Hardship) Committee constituted under the Third Schedule to the National Service Act, 1948

Chairman of the Mining Qualifications Board

Chairman of the National Institute for Research in Nuclear Science

Chairman or Deputy Chairman of the National Parks Commission

Member appointed by the Secretary of State of the Horserace Betting Levy Board

Chairman of the Scottish Dental Estimates Board or member of that Board appointed at an annual salary

Chairman of the Technical Personnel Committee appointed by the Minister of Labour

Clerk of Assize

Clerk of the Crown and Peace in Northern Ireland

Clerk or other officer or servant of a Metropolitan Magistrate's Court appointed under Section 5 of the Metropolitan Police Courts Act, 1839

Clerk of the Peace in Scotland

Clerk or Assistant Clerk of Petty Sessions in Northern Ireland

The Commissioner appointed by Her Majesty's Government in

the United Kingdom under Article 3 of the Agreement con-
firmed by the Nauru Island Agreement Act, 1920

Commissioner or Assistant Commissioner of Police of the Metropolis

Commissioner of the City of London Police

Comptroller and Auditor-General

Comptroller and Auditor-General for Northern Ireland

Constable, Lieutenant or Major of the Tower of London

Correspondent appointed by the Commissioners of Customs and
Excise

Counsel to the Secretary of State under the Private Legislation
Procedure (Scotland) Act, 1936

Crown Solicitor in Northern Ireland

Delegate for Her Majesty's Government in the United Kingdom
to the Central Rhine Commission

Director of the British Sugar Corporation Limited appointed by
the Ministers as defined by Section 17 of the Sugar Act, 1956

Director of Cable and Wireless Limited

Director of the Commonwealth Institute

Director nominated by the Secretary of State of any company in
respect of which an undertaking to make advances has been
given by the Secretary of State under Section 2 of the Highlands
and Islands Shipping Services Act, 1960, and is for the time
being in force

Director appointed at a salary of the National Institute of House-
workers Limited

Director appointed at a salary of Remploy Limited

Distributor of Stamps appointed by the Commissioners of Inland
Revenue for the Stock Exchange at Manchester or Glasgow

Election Commissioner

Examiner or member of a board of interviewers appointed by the
Civil Service Commissioners

Examiner for entrance examination to, or member of a board
of interviewers for entrance to, the Civil Service of Northern
Ireland

General Manager or Secretary of the Scottish Special Housing
Association

Chairman, Deputy Chairman or member of the Council of Management of the Scottish Special Housing Association, appointed
at a salary

Governor of the British Broadcasting Corporation

Governor, Deputy Governor or Director of the Bank of England

Governor, Lieutenant Governor and Secretary, or Captain of Invalids at Chelsea Hospital

Governor, Medical Officer or other officer or member of the staff at a prison to which the Prison Act (Northern Ireland), 1953, applies

High Commissioner representing Her Majesty's Government in the United Kingdom

Industrial Assurance Commissioner appointed under the Industrial Assurance Act (Northern Ireland), 1924

Judge Advocate of the Fleet

Judge Advocate General, Vice Judge Advocate General, Assistant Judge Advocate General or Deputy Judge Advocate

Lecturer or teacher appointed by or on behalf of the Ministry of Education for Northern Ireland under Section 59 of the Education Act (Northern Ireland), 1947, in any training college or school run in connection with such a college

Legal Adviser to the Ministry of Home Affairs for Northern Ireland

Local government officers, the following:

  Clerk or deputy clerk of the council of a county in England and Wales or of the council of an urban or rural district in England and Wales or Northern Ireland;

  County clerk or depute county clerk of a county in Scotland;

  Secretary or deputy secretary of the council of a county in Northern Ireland;

  Clerk or depute clerk of a district council in Scotland;

  Town clerk or deputy town clerk of the City of London, of a metropolitan borough, of a borough in England and Wales outside London or of a county borough or borough in Northern Ireland;

  Town clerk or depute town clerk of a burgh in Scotland

Lyon Clerk

Lyon King of Arms

Member of an Agricultural Marketing Board appointed by the Minister under Section 1 of the Agricultural Marketing Act, 1949

Member of an Agricultural Marketing Board appointed by the Minister of Agriculture for Northern Ireland under Section 2 of the Agricultural Marketing Act (Northern Ireland), 1933

Member appointed by the Minister of Agriculture, Fisheries and Food of the Agricultural Wages Board for England and Wales or of an agricultural wages committee established under the

266

Agricultural Wages Act, 1948, or Chairman of such a committee

Member appointed by the Secretary of State of the Scottish Agricultural Wages Board or of an agricultural wages committee established under the Agricultural Wages (Scotland) Act, 1949, or Chairman of such a committee

Member appointed by the Minister of Agriculture for Northern Ireland of the Agricultural Wages Board for Northern Ireland

Member of a Wages Council or Central Co-ordinating Committee appointed under para. 1(a) of the Second Schedule to the Wages Councils Act, 1959, Chairman of a Committee appointed under para. 1(1) (a) of the Third Schedule to that Act, or Member of a Commission of Inquiry appointed under para. 1(a) of the Fourth Schedule to that Act

Member of a Wages Council or Central Co-ordinating Committee appointed under para. 1(a) of the First Schedule to the Wages Councils Act (Northern Ireland), 1945, or Member of a Commission of Inquiry appointed under para. 1(a) of the Second Schedule to that Act

Member of a panel of valuers appointed at an annual salary under Section 4 of the Inland Revenue Regulation Act, 1890

Minister of Northern Ireland or other officer in the Executive of Northern Ireland

Officer of the Board of Referees appointed for the purposes of Section 287 of the Income Tax Act, 1952

Officer or servant employed under the Commissioner of Police of the Metropolis or the Receiver for the Metropolitan Police District

Officer or servant of the Crown Estate Commissioners

Officer or other member of the County Court Service within the meaning of the County Offices and Courts Acts (Northern Ireland), 1925 and 1933

Officer, clerk or servant appointed or employed by the Admiralty under Section 20 of the Greenwich Hospital Act, 1865

Officer of the Supreme Court within the meaning of Sections 115 to 120 of the Supreme Court of Judicature (Consolidation) Act, 1925

Officer of or attached to the Supreme Court of Northern Ireland to whom Section 76 of the Supreme Court of Judicature (Ireland) Act, 1877, applies

Official Arbitrator appointed under subsection (2) of Section 1 of the Administrative Provisions Act (Northern Ireland), 1928

Principal Clerk of Justiciary appointed under Section 25 of the Administration of Justice (Scotland) Act, 1933

Procurator fiscal or procurator fiscal depute appointed under the Sheriff Courts and Legal Officers (Scotland) Act, 1927

Public Works Loan Commissioner

Receiver for the Metropolitan Police District

Referee appointed under Section 1 of the Safeguarding of Industries Act, 1921, or member of the Panel constituted under Section 10 of the Finance Act, 1926

Registrar of any district of the Court of Chancery of the County Palatine of Lancaster

Registrar or Assistant Registrar appointed under Section 16 or Section 25 of the County Courts Act, 1934

Registrar or Assistant Registrar of Friendly Societies

Registrar of the Privy Council

Registrar of Restrictive Trading Agreements

Secretary of the First Scottish National Housing Company or the Second Scottish National Housing Company

Sheriff clerk or sheriff clerk depute

Solicitor in Scotland to any department of Her Majesty's Government in the United Kingdom

Solicitor for the Scottish Hospital Service

Speaker of the Senate or House of Commons of Northern Ireland

Standing Counsel to any department of Her Majesty's Government in the United Kingdom

Standing Counsel to the Speaker of the Senate or House of Commons of Northern Ireland

Substitution Officer of the Royal Air Force

Superintendent registrar, registrar or registrar of marriages appointed under the Births, Deaths and Marriages Registration Act (Northern Ireland), 1956, otherwise than at a salary and any salaried officer so appointed

Technical Adviser to the Commissioners of Customs and Excise

Temporary Commissioner appointed under para. 2 of the Second Schedule to the Tithe Act, 1936

Under-Sheriff appointed under Section 1 of the Sheriffs (Ireland) Act, 1920

PART IV

Offices Disqualifying for Particular Constituencies

Office	Constituency
Her Majesty's Commissioner of Lieutenancy in the City of London	The Cities of London and Westminster
Her Majesty's Lieutenant for a county in Great Britain	Any constituency comprising the whole or part of the area for which he is appointed
Governor of the Isle of Wight	The Isle of Wight
High Sheriff of a county in England and Wales	Any constituency comprising the whole or part of the area for which he is appointed
Recorder of a municipal borough having a separate court of quarter sessions	Any constituency comprising the whole or part of the city or borough for which he is appointed
Chairman or deputy chairman appointed under the Administration of Justice (Miscellaneous Provisions) Act, 1938, of a court of quarter sessions	Any constituency comprising the whole or part of the area for which the court has jurisdiction
Member of a County Agricultural Executive Committee, Sub-Committee or District Committee constituted under the Agriculture Act, 1947	Any constituency comprising the whole or part of the area for which the Executive Committee acts
Member of an Agricultural Executive Committee or Sub-Committee constituted under the Agriculture (Scotland) Act, 1948	Any constituency comprising the whole or part of the area for which the Executive Committee acts

SECOND SCHEDULE

MINISTERIAL OFFICES

PART I

Prime Minister and First Lord of the Treasury
Lord President of the Council
Lord Privy Seal
Chancellor of the Duchy of Lancaster
Paymaster-General

Secretary of State
Chancellor of the Exchequer
First Lord of the Admiralty
Minister of Agriculture, Fisheries and Food
Minister of Aviation
Minister of Defence
Minister of Education
Minister of Health
Minister of Housing and Local Government
Minister of Labour
Minister of Pensions and National Insurance
Postmaster-General
Minister of Power
President of the Board of Trade
Minister of Transport
Minister of Works

Minister of State

PART II

Attorney-General
Lord Advocate
Solicitor-General
Solicitor-General for Scotland

Secretary for Technical Co-operation
Parliamentary Secretary to the Treasury
Financial Secretary to the Treasury
Economic Secretary to the Treasury
Parliamentary Under Secretary of State

270

Appendix

Parliamentary and Financial Secretary to the Admiralty
Civil Lord of the Admiralty
Parliamentary Secretary to the Ministry of Agriculture, Fisheries and Food
Parliamentary Secretary to the Ministry of Aviation
Parliamentary Secretary to the Ministry of Defence
Parliamentary Secretary to the Ministry of Education
Parliamentary Secretary to the Ministry of Health
Parliamentary Secretary to the Ministry of Housing and Local Government
Parliamentary Secretary to the Ministry of Labour
Parliamentary Secretary to the Ministry of Pensions and National Insurance
Assistant Postmaster-General
Parliamentary Secretary to the Ministry of Power
Parliamentary Secretary to the Ministry of Science
Parliamentary Secretary to the Board of Trade
Secretary for Overseas Trade
Parliamentary Secretary to the Ministry of Transport
Financial Secretary of the War Office
Parliamentary Secretary to the Ministry of Works

Junior Lord of the Treasury
Treasurer of Her Majesty's Household
Comptroller of Her Majesty's Household
Vice-Chamberlain of Her Majesty's Household

The Third Schedule, which contains modifications of these lists in relation to the Parliament of Northern Ireland, is not reproduced.

INDEX

Index

S

Index

Index

Index